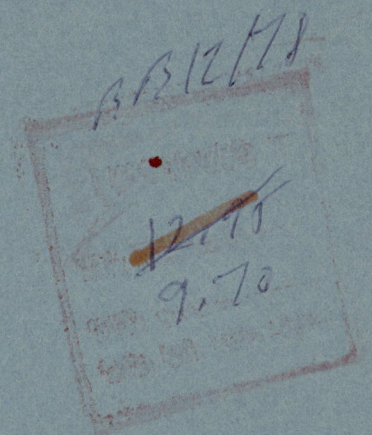

©1976 by Wadsworth Publishing Company, Inc., Belmont, California 94002. All rights reserved. No part of this book may be reproduced, stored in a retrieval system, or transcribed, in any form or by any means, electronic, mechanical, photocopying, recording, or otherwise, without the prior written permission of the publisher.

1 2 3 4 5 6 7 8 9 10 / 80 79 78 77 76

Library of Congress Catalog Card Number: 75-46322

International Standard Book Number: 0-8396-0062-3

Printed in the United States of America

The Psychology of Human Learning and Instruction in Education

Charles K. West
The University of Illinois, Urbana

Stephen F. Foster
The University of British Columbia

A Charles A. Jones Publication

Wadsworth Publishing Company, Inc.
Belmont, California

To:
- 2 Anns
- 1 Andrea
- 1 Bruce
- 1 Kenyon
  and
- 1 Susan

Contents

Preface	xi
Chapter 1 Introduction to Learning and Instruction	3
The Importance of Learning	4
What Is Learning?	6
Motives for Change	7
Planning for Instruction	9
Stage 1: Establishing Instructional Objectives	10
Stage 2: Assessing Students' Entering Capabilities and Inclinations with Respect to Goals and Assessing Resistance to Change	12
Stage 3: Selecting and Organizing Appropriate Learning Experiences for Students	12
Stage 4: Guiding the Learning Process in the Classroom	13
Stage 5: Evaluating the Outcomes	14
Conclusion	15
Discussion Questions	15
Recommended Readings	16
References	16
Chapter 2 Major Concepts from Theories of Learning	19
Concepts Associated with Theories of Learning	21
Classical Conditioning—Pavlov	21
Early American Behaviorism—Watson	25
Contiguous Conditioning Theory, Learning by Doing—Guthrie and Estes	25
Learning Theory of Behavior—Hull	27
Reinforcement Psychology—Thorndike and Skinner	28
Purposive Behaviorism—Tolman	32
Gestalt Theory	33
Field Theory—Lewin	33
Modern Social Learning Theory—Bandura	34
A Brief Synopsis of Learning Theory	35
Concepts Associated with Theories of Instruction	36
Toward a Theory of Instruction—Bruner	36
The Psychology of Meaningful Verbal Learning—Ausubel	38
Conceptual Systems Change—Hunt	41
The Conditions of Learning—Gagné	42
A Brief Synopsis of Instructional Theory	45
An Overview of Educational Implications of Learning and Instructional Theory	46

Contents

Conclusion	47
Discussion Questions	48
Recommended Readings	49
References	50

Chapter 3 The Frame of Reference: A Cognitive Relativistic View of General Behavior and Learning — 55

Relativism	56
The Frame of Reference and Its Relationship to Cognitive Behavior	58
The Individual's Frame of Reference	59
A Summary of Some Central Ideas in the Frame of Reference Theory	60
Six Components of the Frame of Reference	61
Concepts	61
Structures	63
Affect	68
Values	71
Needs	74
Interests	75
A Summary of the Frame of Reference Model	77
Educational Implications	80
Discussion Questions	82
Recommended Readings	83
References	83

Chapter 4 Motivation, Reinforcement, and Imitation — 91

Motivation	92
Motivation and the Frame of Reference	94
Needs	95
The Transient and Specific Nature of Motivation	97
Motivation and Instruction	98
Reinforcement	99
Imitation	104
Conclusion	106
An Overview of Practical Applications	106
Discussion Questions	107
Recommended Readings	108
References	108

Chapter 5 Retention and Transfer in Human Learning — 113

Retention	114
Theories of Forgetting	115
Some Modern Views of Memory	117
Memory Process	119
Functions of Memory	119
Configurational Forms	120
Representational Forms	120
Memory and the Frame of Reference	123

Contents

Memory and the Characteristics of the Material Recalled	123
Memory and Attention	124
Transfer of Learning	126
Formal Discipline Theory	126
Generalization Theory	127
Identical Elements	127
Similarity	127
Learning to Learn	128
Degrees or Kinds of Transfer	129
Conditions of Original Learning Facilitative of Positive Transfer and Retention	130
Verbalization	130
Practice	130
Degree of Original Learning	130
Summary	131
Discussion Questions	132
Recommended Readings	132
References	133
Chapter 6 Thinking, Problem Solving, and Creativity	139
Thinking	141
Five Approaches to Thinking	142
Associationism	142
Logical Analysis	143
Gestalt Psychology	144
Computer Simulation	145
Cognitive-Structural Analysis	146
Piaget and the Development of Human Thought	146
Basic Concepts	147
Piaget's Method	148
The Periods of Cognitive Development Summarized	149
The Sensorimotor Period	149
The Period of Preoperational and Intuitive Thought	151
The Concrete Operations Period	152
Formal Operations Period	153
Piaget and Instruction	154
Summary of Major Dimensions of Cognitive Development	154
Thought and the Nature of Stimuli	155
Human Thought and the Frame of Reference	157
Guiding the Problem Solver	158
Teaching Concepts	160
Creativity	161
The Measurement of Creativity	162
Learning to Be Creative	163
Characteristics of Creative Personality	165
Conclusion	166
Discussion Questions	166
Recommended Readings	167
References	168

Chapter 7 Educational Approaches to Individual Differences — 175
Mastery Learning — 176
  J. B. Carroll's Model of School Learning — 177
  Formative Evaluation — 179
  Criticisms of the Mastery Learning Model — 180
  Strategies for Mastery — 180
  Summary and Evaluation of Mastery Learning — 183
Programmed Instruction — 185
  Description of Instructional Program — 185
  Basis for Programmed Instruction in Psychological Theory and Research — 186
  Summary and Evaluation of Programmed Instruction — 188
Open Education — 189
  Research on Open Education — 192
A Concluding Note about the Three Approaches to Individual Differences — 194
Discussion Questions — 195
Recommended Readings — 196
References — 197

Chapter 8 Attitude Learning in the Schools — 201
Attitude-Definitions—Distinctions — 202
Ways in Which Students Learn School Attitudes — 205
  School Attitude Learning—Conditioning Paradigm — 205
  School Attitude Learning—Operant Conditioning — 207
  School Attitude Learning—Concept Formation — 208
  School Attitude Learning—Social Learning Theory — 210
Other Theories of Attitude Change — 211
  Consistency Theories — 211
  Achievement and Attitudes — 212
  Should Schools Teach Attitudes? — 212
Moral Attitudes and Values — 214
  The Cognitive Development Theory — 215
  Social Learning Theory — 216
  Recommendations for Teachers' Education — 217
The Teachers' Attitudes Toward Pupils—Teacher Expectancy — 217
Self-Regarding Attitudes — 219
Educational Attitudinal Objectives — 221
Discussion Questions — 224
Recommended Readings — 225
References — 226

Chapter 9 Measurement and Evaluation of Learning — 232
Measurement and Evaluation of Student Achievement—Some Issues and Points-of-View — 233
  Errors of Measurement—Reliability — 235
  Errors of Measurement—Validity — 237
  Correlation — 240
  Formative and Summative Evaluation of Learning — 241

Instructional Objectives and the Evaluation of Learning ... 243
   The Behavioral Objectives Controversy ... 244
   Item Analysis ... 247
The Measurement and Evaluation of Pupil Attitudes ... 248
   Semantic Differential Scales ... 250
   The Libert Technique ... 252
   Sociometry ... 253
Summary ... 254
Discussion Questions ... 254
Recommended Readings ... 255
References ... 256

Chapter 10 Teacher-Influences Learning Variables and Implications for Teaching ... 259

Stage 1: Establishing Goals and Objectives ... 261
   Suggestions for Stage 1 ... 262
Stage 2: Assessing Pupil-Entering Behaviors and Resistance to Change ... 262
Stage 3: Selecting and Organizing Learning Experiences ... 265
   Suggestions Regarding Motivation ... 265
   Suggestions Regarding Retention ... 265
   Suggestions Regarding Transfer ... 266
Stage 4: Guiding the Learning Process in the Classroom ... 267
   Suggestions Concerning Concept Formation and Problem Solving ... 268
   Suggestions to Teachers Concerning Pupil Creativity ... 269
   Suggestions to Teachers Concerning Individual Differences ... 270
   Suggestions to Teachers Concerning Pupil Attitudes ... 272
   Suggestions Concerning Values ... 273
Stage 5: Evaluating Pupil Outcomes ... 274
   Comments and Suggestions to Teachers on Measurement and Evaluation ... 274
Summary ... 276
Discussion Questions ... 277
References and Recommended Readings ... 277

Author Index ... 279

Subject Index ... 285

Preface

This book is intended to be used as a text in educational psychology courses which focus on learning as applied to teaching. Basic concepts are presented clearly and concisely so that little prerequisite psychology is necessary. On the other hand, the text's discussions will challenge most students and some background study in psychology may be helpful to the student reader.

That human behavior is not entirely external stimulus bound; that the person is both cause and causing; and that the human being continuously projects, exerts self on the world, shapes the world, and is in turn shaped by it—this is the central theme of this book. One facet of this theme is that *being* human *is* processing. The human being is not just a part of a process or an accumulation of processes, the human is processing. These points are elaborated in the following pages. Many of the findings of experimental psychology support this position. Of course, this approach does not preclude the possibility of influencing human behavior through the application of the concepts and principles of educational psychology. Rather, it involves a broader conception of human functioning than is typically included in contemporary behaviorism.

While the book reflects a dynamic and relativistic position, the psychological literature and research which is included illustrates the applicability of principles, ideas, and findings from many key theoretical stances in modern human psychology. In this sense this work is eclectic. The following chapters organize theory together with both laboratory and field research concerning applied human learning around a model of the "processing person."

The science of educational psychology may aid the educator in two general ways, through *understanding* functions and *influencing* functions. Much of what is known about human behavior in the educational setting helps the educator to understand why the teacher and students are behaving the way they are. Other knowledge in this science helps the educator to influence directly the educational atmosphere. Knowledge of both kinds is relevant for the educator.

The authors wish to express their special appreciation to several of their colleagues and students who gave helpful, often crucial, reactions and advice on the content and structure of this volume, especially Professors Thomas H. Anderson, James Jay Rubovits, Ray H. Simpson, Kenneth E. Sinclair, and Merlin C. Wittrock. A particular thanks also goes to Henry R. Angelino, Donald E. Hendrickson, Stewart Jones, and William C. Lynch, Jr., for their kind and helpful suggestions in reviewing the manuscript. To their families who put up with a variety of idiosyncractic behaviors on the part of the authors during the production of this work, especial gratitude must be expressed.

Charles K. West
Stephen F. Foster

Acknowledgements

Appreciation is expressed to these authors and publishers for granting permission to use the following published material.

Anderson, T. H. & Essex, Diane, *Report to the National Science Foundation on Programs and Plans. An Experiment in Engineering Education*, N.S.F. Grant # GY 9300. List of problems frequently encountered in the classroom (see pp. 14-142).

Ausubel, David, *Educational Psychology—A Cognitive View*. (New York: Holt, Rinehart and Winston, Inc., 1968) paraphrasing of pp. 37-41 (see p. 38).

Gagné, Robert M., *The Conditions of Learning* (2nd ed.). Copyright © 1965, 1970 by Holt, Rinehart and Winston, Inc., New York. P. 304, "Nine Components of Instruction" and Table 3, p. 334, "Summary of Essential Conditions Appropriate for Each Type of Learning" (see p. 44 and p. 45).

Hunt, D. E., *Matching Models in Education*. The Ontario Institute for Studies in Education, Monograph Series #101, 1971. Adaptation of Table 4, p. 30 (see p. 42).

Krathwohl, D. R., Bloom, B. S. and Masia, B. B. *Taxonomy of Educational Objectives, Handbook II—Affective Domain*. Copyright © 1964 by David McKay Co., Inc. New York. Abstraction and summarization of pps. 176-185 (see pp. 221-222).

Oldridge, O. A., *A study of instructional innovation involving beginning teachers' attempting to nongrade an open-area elementary school*. (Report No. 9), Vancouver, B.C. Educational Research Institute of B.C., 1971 (see p. 191).

A Note to the Reader

This book is intended to provide you, the student, with a rationale of psychological theory and research for decisions you make in applying your teaching skills to helping people (yourself and others) to learn.

In the authors' opinion, early chapters of book in educational psychology, and especially in human learning, are exceedingly important to the student. One reason for this importance is because of the introduction of new terminology. Although many serious students of education lament that technical words have confusing meanings and obscure relations to one another, we have tried to facilitate the learning of new terminology by including a glossary of terms at the end of the book. The learning of these technical terms is essential if you wish to consult the sources referenced herein, read many professional and scholarly journals, or communicate with specialists in educational psychology. The terms provide you with the language to deal with many of the substantive and, hopefully, exciting and relevant issues which are dealt with in later chapters.

There is also a cry for relevance to educators in terms of day-to-day activities with students. While we have tried to weave relevant examples and suggestions throughout the text, chapter 10 summarizes the practical applications. However, in order to understand these applications, you will need a command of the basic terminology and an understanding of how the concepts which are indexed by those technical terms relate to one another and to real learning experiences.

Since we are trying to "practice what we preach" in this book, the initial paragraph at the beginning of each chapter, called the "Practical Organizer," attempts to establish a practical predisposition or "set" in the reader. We want you to engage our material in terms of your frame of reference, which includes in most readers a need for practical applications. We have established an applied set for each chapter, except for chapter 10, which as mentioned before, is a summary of all practical applications.

And since our own theory of learning and behavior, which is discussed in chapter 3, emphasizes the role of structure in behavior and learning we are including an "Advance Organizer" for each chapter which follows the practical set and the chapter title.

Practical Organizer for Chapter 1

The psychology of learning can provide the educator a very useful perspective about instruction. Most issues the educator faces and most educational decisions will involve some assumptions about how people learn. The more sound these assumptions are, the more effective the decisions will become. Every educational issue should be weighed against our knowledge of how humans learn.

The effective educator must be keenly aware that except for physical and biological attributes most human characteristics are shaped, modified, or developed as a result of environmental factors through learning. The educator, in structuring experiences for students, is in the business of making humans—making young people more fully human day by day and hour by hour. Thus, it may be that knowledge of how people learn is the single most practical and relevant knowledge which the educator can attain.

After an introduction to human learning we will present a breakdown of the instructional process in five stages. Instruction is such a complex process that to always look at the whole is confusing and impractical. There is great practical value in breaking down instruction into component parts and analyzing each part as we have done. These five stages become organizers for the entire text for we allude to one or more of the stages during discussion of major topics.

Introduction to Learning and Instruction

1

In this chapter we wish to introduce you to the psychology of learning and instruction. Several basic ideas in the chapter include: (1) learning is of central importance in human behavior, (2) learning may be defined in a variety of ways, (3) resistance to learning may be expected and at least partially overcome, and (4) instruction may be organized into a logical series of stages or phases.

Introduction to Learning and Instruction

In the most basic sense, this book is about you—that very personal you. It is about how you learn and how you came to be the unique individual you are. Every sensitive person reflects on these "hows" periodically. These human questions—the "hows"—have been responded to by psychologists for nearly a century and by Western philosophers since the ancient Greek culture.

From a variety of contexts—philosophical as well as psychological—support emerges for the belief that to be human is to be processing; the human is both caused and causing in that the human is impacted by the environment while the human impacts the environment. The responses one makes create and modify one's internal and external world. Like the environment, the person is not inviolable.

In other words, a person's behavior is not influenced solely by the factors in the environment which are occurring at the time of the action. Behavior is also influenced by the person's own characteristics arising in genetic endowments and prior learnings and their interactions.

These beliefs about the dynamic nature of humanity contrast with the belief that humans are passive, that behavior is caused by external environment. These beliefs also contrast with some subjectivistic beliefs which place strong emphasis on the idea that humans are inviolable beings--that humans are not greatly influenced by environmental stimuli.

The Importance of Learning

It is difficult to imagine a waking situation in which there is no possibility of a human learning. The kicking behavior of a fetus *in utero* may be conditioned, accidentally or experimentally, according to the paradigm of classical conditioning. The child of four months kicking and twisting in his crib may be learning rapidly about self and world. A child of two years playing with blocks or running about with an acquaintance learns a great deal. The learnings which occur may be as spontaneous, varied, and unplanned as the activities in which a child is engaged. Nevertheless, learning occurs—new skills are developed and old ones are changed.

The environment of child play seems to be very different from the structured situation in which formal classroom learning occurs. However, some similar conditions of learning are in evidence in both situations. Generally speaking, *there are sequences in which the learning of various skills takes place,* for example, where a first skill

4

The Importance of Learning

is necessary for the performance of a second, more advanced, or more complex skill. One skill may need to be learned prior to another skill. Another common condition is that learning *takes place within the context of some kind of activity*. A third common condition is that frequently *several different learnings may accrue within the same activity*. For example, the child at play may be refining language and psychomotor skills as well as learning to get along in groups. Likewise, the student who is doing class work in math may be learning to multiply fractions while learning certain study and work habits or skills and simultaneously be learning attitudes toward such contextual objects as school, math, and self as a student.

The roles which learning plays in human development are greater than most of us realize. Psychologists are just beginning to become aware of the tremendous plasticity of the human (Hunt, 1969) even in the early years of development, and the role that learning plays in this plasticity. Almost every human behavior is influenced by learning in some way. For example, while the infant must grow and thus develop muscle group strengths prior to walking, the infant must acquire many aspects of the behaviors associated with walking, such as coordination. These are developed and learned through experiences of crawling and pulling up on furniture. Another area of human behavior affected by learning involves basic needs. One does not learn to have basic needs, but we do learn the *manner* of expression and satisfaction of these needs. These learned aspects of needs may be as important in understanding the behavior of the person as the basic need itself (Malinowski, 1944). According to Maslow (1954), if the basic needs are satisfied, secondary or learned needs take over as important determinants of behavior. Examples of the basic needs are hunger, thirst, and sex. Examples of the secondary needs are social approval and self-actualization. Thus, even basic human needs are affected by learning.

Another area impacted by learning which may be considered is neurophysiological structures. Bennett et al. (1964) have conducted a line of inquiry which indicates that learning which accrues from a highly stimulating environment during the years of growth and maturation may change the living organism sometimes in surprising ways. The investigators, using a split litter of rats, provided one group with an extremely stimulating environment during the maturation period. The other group experienced a deprived and stark environment. At the end of the period, the investigators observed not only larger brains in the stimulated group, as well as increased learning ability, but also different chemical constituents in the area of the brain. It would seem that early stimulation and resultant learning can change the biological structures!

5

What is Learning?

At least one learning psychologist, after attempting to develop a comprehensive definition of learning, has said that the experiments done in learning define the process of learning (Hilgard, 1951). Unfortunately, this does not leave the beginning student with a very clear understanding of the term. There is no single definition which readily encapsulates learning, but we can discuss aspects of this crucial psychological process. Central to learning is the idea of *relatively permanent change in behavior*.

Not all changes in behavior may be due to learning. Only those which emerge from experience or practice are generally considered to have been learned. However, growth, fatigue, and illness may result in behavior changes but these changes cannot be said to be learned even though experience produced them.

The question arises as to when must the response or behavior occur in order for it to be attributed to learning. It may be said that *learning is relatively permanent changes in the ability, tendency, or capacity to respond.* If that is true, learning occurs prior to behavioral change. Of course, an organism cannot respond unless it has the capacity to make that response. Frequently teachers wish to teach behavior which is not readily observable—such as efficient problem solving. One can only observe the products of thinking, or the results of problem solving, and not these processes themselves. In this instance, the teacher wishes the student to acquire ability or capacity to behave in certain ways rather than specific overt responses. Of course, it may be maintained that problem solving consists of distinct response patterns or sequences—it is only that these responses are covert rather than overt. In all instances, when a student is learning something, he is not only changing a behavior but also is changing the capacity or potential to respond in future situations.

Up to this point we have discussed two definitions of learning—one pertaining to change in behavior and a second pertaining to change in capacity to behave. A third definition has been offered by neurophysiologically oriented psychologists—that of *change in neurophysiological structure*. It seems obvious that some alteration occurs within the organism during the change in capacity to respond. Hebb (1949) began a line of speculation about the functions of the central nervous system. This line of speculation and investigation has resulted in a neurophysiological definition of learning. The following definition is offered by Bugelski (1956):

> Learning is the process of the formation of relatively permanent neural circuits through the simultaneous activity of the elements of the circuits-to-be; such activity is of the nature of change in cell structures through growth in such a manner as to facilitate the arousal of the entire circuit when a component element is aroused or activated [p. 120].

For the purposes of this book, learning can be defined in all three ways—behavior changes, changes in capacity to behave, and changes in the nervous system. However, emphasis will be placed upon the first two ways in most of the discussions which follow because they seem more central to the concerns of educators.

Motives for Change

We have seen that basic to learning is change in behavior. Some underlying motives for this change have been discussed by various psychologists. White (1959) has offered the *need for competence* to account for much of behavior and change in behavior. By competence, White means the ability of coping with the environment in ways which enable the person to grow and maintain selfhood. Humans, White maintains, must learn almost all the ways of dealing with the environment. Competence is demanded if the person is to survive and flourish. Because the human's environment changes, behavior must frequently change in order for competence to be maintained. The demands for competence seem to be especially important in the lives of growing children. Combs and Snygg in *Individual Behavior* (1959) proffer two primary tendencies in humans which are related to the competence motive: (1) maintaining the present state of organization and (2) increasing the state of organization, that is—making it more efficient. Being organized means that a person is capable of establishing and ordering relationships with the environment, to include other people, so that the person is able to deal with the environment in an efficient, orderly fashion. Combs and Snygg believe that there is only one need—that of *adequacy*. Thus, the needs for competence and adequacy can be seen as summarizing the relationship between a person and the physical and social environments.

Many psychologists have discussed the roles of needs and drives. Some have felt that the origins of all behavior lie in the basic physiological needs such as food, water, oxygen, and sex; and that behaviors not obviously related to these are nonetheless indirectly connected. For example, any social need would be explained as being derived from experiences associated with meeting the basic needs. From this point of view, the child comes to love the mother because she is associated with food and warmth. Other psychologists feel that other needs are as significant in determining behavior as the primary or basic needs, especially when the basic needs have been more or less satisfied. Maslow (1954) has described a hierarchical order of needs in which he includes physiological as the most primary need and self-actualization—the realization of potentiality—as a less basic need. He also believes that humans have the inherent need to know and to

7

understand, and that these represent the highest levels of human motivation.

Of course, the history of psychology is rife with descriptions of motives underlying behavior. The pleasure principle has a hoary history in philosophy prior to its inclusion in psychology. In 1920 in a book entitled *Beyond the Pleasure Principle,* Freud postulated two underlying motives—the eros, or life wish, and thanatos, the death wish. Freud's followers have since established numerous variations on this theme.

A modern variation on the pleasure principle is exemplified by neobehaviorism or reinforcement psychology. The basic assumption is that the behaver does what is reinforced and avoids doing what is not. The organism learns to perform responses which result in reinforcement while nonreinforced responses usually drop out of the behavioral repertoire. These reinforcers are generally, though not always, related to some basic physiological need. Certain exceptions will be discussed later. Skinner, however, defines a reinforcer as whatever increases the probability of a response occurring again and, in this somewhat tautological fashion, sidesteps some of the philosophically related issues which confound other theorists. Skinner's reinforcers are initially related to the basic needs of living organisms.

During recent years, psychologists have begun to posit a need for external stimulation. This line of investigation offers yet another prime motive. Research has indicated the necessity of continuous and variable external stimulation for proper cognitive functioning (Zubek, 1969). Some psychologists have referred to this as the *need for stimulation* and others have spoken of it as the *curiosity drive.*

Lilly (1956) and Shurley (1960) submerged subjects with breathing apparatus in vats of water at body temperature. The water temperature tended to cut off senses in the skin area. The experimental chamber was dark to cut off visual sensation. Very little sound reached the subjects except the lapping of the water against the sides of the vat. Subjects reported unsuccessful attempts to concentrate on one aspect of their environment. Very quickly their thoughts became circular. They reported inability to concentrate or attend to any specific internal stimulus, for any extended period. Yet subjects continued to attempt to create internal stimulation. Soon subjects began to lose contact with reality, to fantasize, and to hallucinate.

In an earlier study (Bexton, Heron, & Scott, 1954), subjects were placed alone in a soundproof room. Their eyes were covered and their hands and arms covered with soft cloth. They reclined on a soft couch. Subjects became bored, unable to think systematically, restless, unable to concentrate for very long, and began to daydream; they reported periods during which they were not able to think of anything at all. Subjects rarely participated in the experiment longer than two to three days even though they were paid twenty dollars for a twenty-four-hour day. Subjects also hallucinated. When tested they performed poorly on intelligence tests. The research of Platt (1962) supports the apparent necessity for more or less continuous external stimulation which varies in intensity.

It would appear that humans do indeed need continuing external stimulation. There is also evidence that stimulation occurring immediately after a response acts as a reinforcer. Animals will perform a variety of responses just to receive the stimulation. This line of investigation has been conducted in the study of the "curiosity drive" or the "exploratory drive." Rats (Montgomery & Segall, 1955) and monkeys (Butler & Harlow, 1954) learned to choose alternatives when the only reward was the opportunity to explore different maze pathways in the case of rats, and the opportunity to look out a window or hear the sounds of other monkeys in the case of enclosed monkeys.

We have seen that some students of psychology take a simplistic view of motives for behavior. Inherent in most conceptions of motive is a tendency to change behavior, or to be adequate or competent, as one's environment changes. In conflict with this tendency there is also resistance to change—the tendency to utilize previous modes of behavior in new situations and to "project" one's self onto the environment. Allport (1961) has characterized this tendency for behaviors to persist long after the original need for them has diminished as the "functional autonomy of motives." The tendency to utilize previous behavioral modes will be discussed in chapter 3 in terms of the influence of the frame of reference on human cognition and in chapter 5 in connection with explanations of memory and forgetting.

By the frame of reference, we primarily mean the previous learnings and the predispositions of persons to behave in certain patterns. The frame of reference consists of the person's concepts, structures (how concepts are organized), affects, needs, values, and interests. These six components of the frame of reference direct behavior and may result in behavior change as well as resistance to change.

Planning for Instruction

We have seen that, however learning may be defined, some type of change is involved—whether it is a behavioral change, a change in capacity, or a change in neural structure. We have also noted that two coordinate tendencies appear to exist in humans: a tendency to change as the context of behavior shifts or the requirements of the environment shift, and a tendency to resist change, that is to use old responses or previous modes of behavior. The teacher's primary instructional task is facilitating change in directions which are consistent with personal and educational goals.

In promoting change the teacher must counter the tendency on the part of the learner to resist change. The stages listed in figure 1 are recommended in planning and conducting instruction. These stages are similar to those listed by Loree (1970).

Stage 1: Establishing Instructional Objectives

Objectives may be both global and specific. The teacher may or may not be involved in setting the more global objectives of instruction. Certainly the teacher plays some part in setting objectives, if only the specific ones. The society at large provides the context in setting global objectives of instruction, although school personnel are held responsible for whatever objectives are apparent. Problems do exist in that confusion and conflict arise about society's mandate to education with respect to global objectives. Whatever the stated global objectives are, they must not be sought in school atmospheres which are sexist, impersonal, irrelevant, bureaucratic, racist, restrictive, inhumane, and undemocratic. Such contexts are inimical to much of what educators and the public wish to accomplish in formal education. Specific instructional objectives need to be assessed in relation to the global educational objectives of the public.

One school of thought which has emerged out of behaviorism and task analysis is the notion that the specific objectives of instruction must be stated in behavioral terms—in terms of the overt, observable responses of the students. There are at least two advantages with this approach. First, it may aid evaluation. Once the teacher knows exactly what behaviors are to be changed, the teacher simply evaluates the student's performance of that behavior. Second, stating behavioral objectives forces the teacher to examine the content of instruction in terms of student responses, rather than in other terms (e.g., teacher behaviors) which may be inconsistent with the desired learning outcomes. This examination may amount to actual restructuring and redefining the content—and this may increase the teacher's understanding of the content.

There are also at least two disadvantages with this approach. First, it accents the product rather than the process, since the behavioral product will be easier to define in observable terms than the process. It is easier to speak of the student's "being able to give the sum of two and two" or "being able to solve a problem involving the principles of the lever" than it is to attend to the problem-solving processes involved. The teacher really may wish to shape the processes involved such as thinking, perceiving, reasoning—all of which are impossible to observe directly and difficult to state precisely. Behavioral objectives tend to become trivial. Second, the behavioral objectives

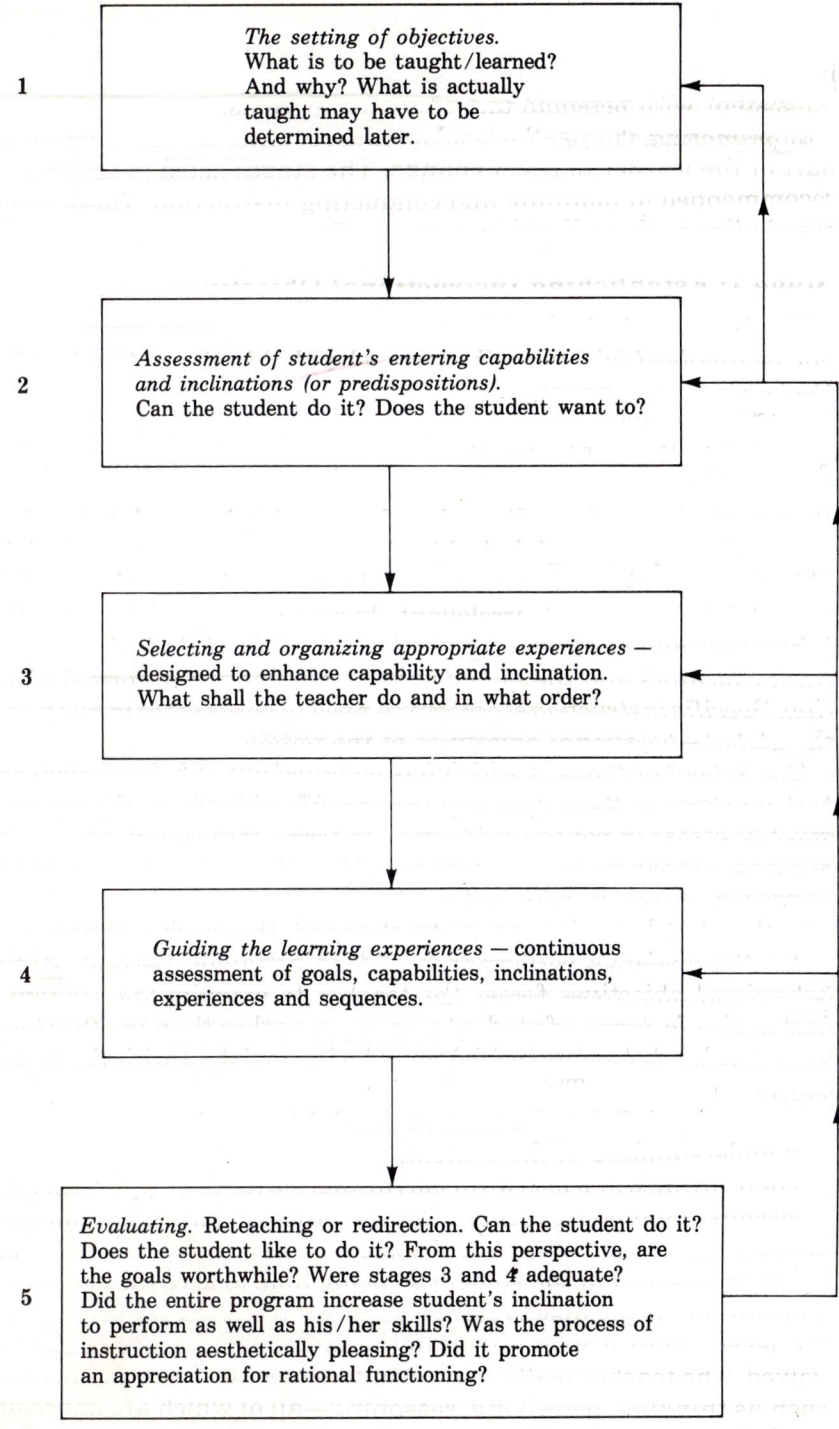

Figure 1. Five stages of instruction showing sequence and feedback loops. Includes examples of questions a teacher might ask at each stage.

approach tends to avoid the affective-feeling aspects of behavior accompanying instruction and learning. These affective aspects of learning and behavior are just as important as the cognitive-intellectual aspects of learning. At any rate, to emphasize only the observable response is to ignore the many concerns arising within the person that should be considered during the course of instruction. Especially when instruction involves social interaction, all important factors cannot be attended to sufficiently. *What* occurs during human interaction may only be ascertained in retrospect by inferring process from an examination of products. This is so because it is never possible to specify in advance everything that could occur during instruction. This brief discussion is developed further in "The Behavioral Objectives Controversy" in chapter 9.

Stage 2: Assessing Students' Entering Capabilities and Inclinations with Respect to Goals and Assessing Resistance to Change

This second stage of planning for instruction involves the students' entering competence and predispositions. Both considerations are of crucial importance to the conduct of instruction. Any deficiency in either area will interfere with the attainment of instructional goals. Entering competence may be easier to determine with available normed achievement tests on some occasions, or with teacher-made tests in others. In most cases, informal assessment by observation or interview is what occurs. The students' predispositions (including affect, interests, needs, and values) may not always be so readily determined. Any lack of competence on the part of a student, or any prerequisite knowledge lacking, should be identified and remediated. That is, if the student does not know some prerequisite skill, that skill must be learned before the teacher can teach toward the established goal. Formidable resistance must also be identified. Perhaps the students' attitudes about the material or goal will have to be changed prior to working toward the objective. The teacher may encounter resistance from any of the six aspects of the frame of reference—concepts, structures, affects, values, interests, and needs—which are discussed further in chapter 3 and in considerable detail in subsequent chapters.

Stage 3: Selecting and Organizing Appropriate Learning Experiences for Students

Normally, there are many options open to the teacher in the selection of experiences to achieve a certain outcome. Some experiences would undoubtedly achieve the outcome better than others. All too fre-

Planning for Instruction

quently experiences are chosen which consist of passive roles for the students. The most desirable are those which achieve the goals with a maximum of student involvement and interest. Many disciplinary problems arise in the classroom, for example, as a result of forcing the students into passive roles or into positions which directly conflict with their social status or academic inclinations. Perhaps experiences which influence as many aspects of the frame of reference as possible and still attain the objective would be most appropriate.

Another guide in choosing the learning experiences may be the potential incidental learnings of the various options. Incidental learnings are those which take place as side effects of working toward the objectives. For example, the main goal of instruction may involve learning concepts about some age or period of Latin American history. Discussion skills or writing skills may be learned at the same time.

Learning experiences which promote long-term retention and transfer require careful decision making on the part of the teacher, as it is often much easier to assign trivial tasks to students than to devise, modify, or select activities relevant to their interests and potential uses.

After the experiences have been selected and devised, the instructional problem becomes one of organizing the learning experience. Such concerns as materials needed and the sequence of presentations are considered. Time should be allowed to follow routes of emerging student interest and inclinations which may not have been planned. Too rigid instructional structuring may be detrimental to developing the kind of instructional serendipity which originates in such inclinations. Practice in transfer and applications should be planned. Student participation in the structure of the course as well as in the formulation of objectives for formal learning experiences has the dual motivational advantages of early direct involvement of pupils and the increased likelihood of their interests being included in the instructional activity.

Stage 4: Guiding the Learning Process in the Classroom

The fourth stage involves guiding the learning while assessing the six aspects of the frame of reference which induce either cooperation or resistance. The teacher carries out the organization of the instruction while attempting to evaluate not only what is being learned in terms of *concepts* and *structures*, but also accompanying *affects, needs, interests,* and *values*. During the instruction, students may exhibit resistance to change due to any one or combination of these six aspects of the frame of reference. Barriers must be anticipated and plans made for surmounting them where possible.

Introduction to Learning and Instruction

It is generally accepted that humans learn through imitation, reinforcement, and response guidance. These three concepts should guide the development of techniques utilized by teachers to promote pupil learning. A distinction between formal and incidental learning and the recognition that imitation functions for both is important. The teacher must be careful to observe the actual impact of what is thought to be reinforcing. All too frequently teacher praise, for example, is seen by the teacher to be positively reinforcing when, in fact, it can be regarded very differently by pupils (see Thompson & Hunnicut, 1944). Acceptance by the teacher may result in peer disapproval and thus have the opposite effect of that intended by the teacher. Especially as students grow older, peer approval may be expected to become as reinforcing as teacher approval (Brittain, 1963). Thus the teacher may wish to explore approaches which may result in peer approval for the desired behaviors.

The teacher should be cautious in following plans that do not allow time for responding to inclinations which emerge during the process of instruction. Much may be gained from allowing time for these routes to be carefully traced. Otherwise the teacher may be concentrating so heavily on the teacher's own processes that desirable processes will not be initiated in the students. This point touches on an advantage of stating specific instructional objectives in terms of student outcomes rather than in terms of teacher behavior.

Stage 5: Evaluating the Outcomes

The final stage of instructional planning involves evaluating the outcomes. Reteaching may be desirable. Generally, techniques of evaluating primarily involve testing for short-term memory of the concepts and structures taught. It may be that one instructional technique may produce better short-term retention than another. On the other hand, for long-term memory, a second approach may be superior. More attention should be paid to long-term retention and the transfer of what is learned. The other four aspects of the frame of reference—affects, interests, needs and values—should also be evaluated. The teacher should attempt to determine whether students' interests have changed and whether or not students feel more positively toward aspects of the subject matter than they did prior to the instruction. All too frequently formal instruction serves to drive the student away from the content. Formal instruction should not result in a learned dislike for the areas of knowledge offered in schools.

In chapter 9, the important distinction between summative and formative evaluation is further explained as are some of the classical and contemporary issues in educational measurement and evaluation which relate to this stage of planning for instruction.

Conclusion

We have seen that learning involves change. There appears to be an underlying human tendency to change as the environment changes (to become more competent or adequate). Knowledge of the consequences of one's own behavior is one means of knowing how adequate one's behavior is. The pleasure-pain principle is one approach to explain this feedback, since pain to oneself generally may be interpreted as a result of an inadequate response.

Somewhat in opposition to this tendency to change is the human tendency to utilize responses which have worked in the past, and to receive new stimuli in terms of what has happened to oneself in the past.

The teacher's primary role includes the induction, retention, and transfer of relatively novel pupil responses. The teacher should expect both cooperation and resistance during that induction. These two factors of cooperation and resistance will vary in time and context, both between students and within the same student.

Discussion Questions

1. What relationships do you see between psychology and philosophy?
2. Of what value is the scientific study of learning and motivation to educators?
3. Which of the three definitions of learning do you think has the most potential usefulness for educators?
4. Mankind seems to contain tendencies for change and for the resistance to change. How can these apparently opposing forces be reconciled?
5. Do you agree with the proposition that the five stages of planning for instruction are just so much common sense? What value could there be in the enumeration of them here?
6. What would you like to know about learning and motivation that was either not mentioned in this chapter or only touched on briefly?
7. Enumerate some learning experiences and teaching methods which have more aesthetic appeal than others. Which do you prefer aesthetically? Why?
8. Think of your responses to your best teachers, to the best books you have read, and to films seen. Think of the worst of such experiences. Do you think that for any subject matter there must be one best teaching method for all teachers and students?

Recommended Readings

Carpenter, F. *The Skinner primer: Behind freedom and dignity.* New York: The Free Press, 1974. Carpenter criticizes Skinner's controversial book and extends the discussion of freedom and dignity.

Chein, I. *The science of behavior and the image of man.* New York: Basic Books, 1972. A humanistic response to the behaviorist's conception of man.

Field, F. L. *Freedom and control in education and society.* New York: Thomas Y. Crowell, 1970. A good general discussion of freedom and control.

Frick, W. B. *Humanistic psychology: Interviews with Maslow, Murphy, and Rogers.* Columbus, Ohio: Charles E. Merrill, 1971. Overviews of three humanistic psychological theories.

Gronlund, N. E. *Stating behavioral objectives for classroom instruction.* London: Collier-Macmillan, 1970. An eclectic approach to the topic. Very well written for teachers. (Paperback)

Mager, R. F. *Developing attitude toward learning.* Palo Alto, Calif.: Fearon, 1968. Like the above reference but oriented toward a behavioral conception of attitudes. (Paperback)

Mager, R. F. *Preparing instructional objectives.* Palo Alto, Calif.: Fearon, 1962. A behaviorist approach to the topic which is very clearly written as a self-instructional branched program. (Paperback)

Maslow, A. H. *Toward a psychology of being.* (2nd ed.) Princeton: Van Nostrand, 1968. A concise statement of an important humanistic theory. (Paperback)

Skinner, B. F. *Beyond freedom and dignity.* New York: Alfred A. Knopf, 1971. Skinner's discussion of the controversial implications of his work.

References

Allport, G. W. *Pattern and growth in personality.* New York: Holt, Rinehart & Winston, 1961.

Bennett, E. L., Diamond, M. C., Krech, D., & Rosenzweig, M. R. Chemical and anatomical plasticity of the brain. *Science,* 1964, *146,* 610-19.

Bexton, W. H., Heron, W., & Scott, T. H. Effects of decreased variation in the sensory environment. *Canadian Journal of Psychology,* 1954, *8,* 70-76.

Brittain, C. V. Adolescent choices and parent-peer cross pressures. *American Sociological Review,* 1963, (3), *28,* 385-91.

References

Bugelski, B. R. *The psychology of learning.* New York: Holt, Rinehart & Winston, 1956.

Butler, R. A., & Harlow, H. F. Persistence of visual exploration in monkeys. *Journal of Comparative and Physiological Psychology,* 1954, *47,* 258-63.

Combs, A. W., & Snygg, D. *Individual behavior.* (Rev. ed.) New York: Harper & Row, 1959.

Hebb, D. O. *Organization of behavior.* New York: Wiley, 1949.

Hilgard, E. R., & Stevens, S. S. (Eds.) *Handbook of experimental psychology.* New York: Wiley, 1951.

Hunt, J. McV. Has compensatory education failed? Has it been attempted? *Harvard Educational Review,* 1969, *39,* 278-300.

Lilly, J. C. Mental effects of reduction of ordinary levels of physical stimuli on intact, healthy persons. *Psychiatric Research Reports,* 1956, *5,* 1-28.

Loree, M. R. *Psychology of education.* (2nd ed.) New York: Ronald Press, 1970.

Malinowski, B. *A scientific view of culture.* Chapel Hill, N. C.: University of North Carolina Press, 1944.

Maslow, A. H. *Motivation and personality.* New York: Harper & Row, 1954.

Montgomery, K. C., & Segall, M. Discrimination learning based upon the exploratory drive. *Journal of Comparative and Physiological Psychology,* 1955, *48,* 225-28.

Platt, J. R. *The excitement of science.* Boston: Houghton Mifflin, 1962.

Shurley, J. Profound experimental sensory isolation. *American Journal of Psychiatry,* 1960, *117,* 539-45.

Thompson, G. G., & Hunnicutt, C. W. The effects of repeated praise or blame on the work achievements of "introverts" and "extroverts." *Journal of Educational Psychology,* 1944, *35,* 257-66.

White, R. W. Motivation reconsidered: The concept of competence. *Psychological Review,* 1959, *66,* 297-333.

Zubek, J. P. (Ed.) *Sensory deprivation: Fifteen years of research.* New York: Appleton-Century-Crofts, 1969.

Practical Organizer for Chapter 2

Every educator has some strong beliefs about how people learn and how people should be taught. These beliefs are a result of ordinary experience and, perhaps, more academic kinds of learning. In view of the importance of learning and instruction, these beliefs should be as accurate and comprehensive as possible. These beliefs should include positions on the need for stimulus and response control on the part of the teacher, on the necessity of the learner's cognitive organization of material, and on the helpfulness of reinforcement, to mention only a few.

A knowledge of the concepts from learning and instructional theory should provide some consonance and/or contrasts to beliefs developed through nonacademic experience. The concepts which we discuss in this chapter should serve the educator by providing relatively new and practical ways of looking at human learning and instruction. That is to say, these concepts should help the educator to perceive new aspects of learning and instruction and to note interaction between students and the teacher and between students and the instructional climate. The concepts also may suggest new ways of promoting learning. Nothing is more practical than provisional explanations—theories—which suggest new instructional perceptions and actions!

Major Concepts From Theories Of Learning And Instruction 2

This chapter will introduce you to a wide variety of concepts in learning and instructional theory. Think of these interrelated concepts as provisional explanations for how behavior is changed and how instruction best occurs.

"Theory!! What I want are facts!!" is the perennial cry of the student of learning. This is a rational appeal, but the problem is that many of our facts are generated from theories. One may construct a theory from a set of facts or a set of facts from a theory. In other words facts may, and frequently do, depend heavily on theories and hypotheses. Knowledge in the sciences proceeds in both directions.* Knowing a theory may enable you, the teacher, to perceive many classroom events and make them understandable in new ways.

Generally, a theory is a broad set of statements which encompasses as many consistent empirical findings about related phenomena as possible. Theory is an attempt to explain parsimoniously the phenomena, to make them understandable. Further, the theory should make prediction of the phenomena possible. Scientists do not speak of theories as true or false. The criteria used in judging a theory are its adequacy to account for available evidence, its usefulness in generating investigation, and its efficiency in predicting future occurrences of the phenomena in question.

During the first half of this century psychologists developed a number of theories in attempts to explain and predict behavior. Most of these theories can be said to be "obsolete" in the sense that they have failed to be sufficiently comprehensive to account for the wide variety of human and animal behavior that can be observed. Typically, instead of trying to build comprehensive theories, psychologists today construct models or miniature theories in attempts to account for given domains of behavior. The main purpose of studying the psychological theories presented in this chapter is not to choose one and become an adherent of it against all others, but to gain a knowledge of the key concepts and an understanding of how they may be applied in classroom instruction. As such, these theories are likewise neither true nor false but may be judged according to the criteria noted above.

As you will discover in this chapter, various explanations of how learning occurs exist in psychology today. It would seem important that teachers be aware of these explanations of learning even when teacher control of the conditions which produce certain kinds of learning is considerably less than full. Teachers should be curious about how students have learned and will learn. Some of the concepts or generalizations from various learning theorists are not amenable

---

*In fact (?!), what a fact is and its status and function depend on your theory of knowledge!

to teacher control. In chapter 10, variables over which teachers can exert varying degrees of control are enumerated. The theory and research behind these "principles of learning" as well as some implications for education are discussed in intervening chapters.

In this chapter we are presenting brief overviews of theories by discussing the major concepts associated with them. Our purpose is to introduce some key psychological concepts from research and theoretical work in learning and instruction. You will have occasion to employ these concepts in understanding the material in chapter 3 and in the remainder of the text. We have not attempted to present a complete discussion of any theory.

A teacher may wish to use the key concepts in this chapter to develop a personal, broad, and more or less coherent set of beliefs and commitments—call this a personal theory if you wish—about learning and behavior. These beliefs should guide the teacher as periodic reviews of what is taught and how it is taught are conducted. These beliefs should also provide some guidance as the teacher considers and experiments with instructional innovations. The key concepts should provide not only a psychological validity to educational practices but also a consistency.

It is anticipated that readers, students, and instructors will wish to further develop, selectively, some of the ideas presented here. For more detailed discussions of these theories the reader is referred to the primary sources referenced in the introduction of each theory and to texts on learning theory, such as those of Hilgard and Bower (1966) and Hill (1971). Suggested additional readings and discussions in subsequent chapters will contain details of the educational implications of these ideas.

Concepts Associated with Theories of Learning

Classical Conditioning—Pavlov

Many psychologists think that very discrete, small response units are learned through classical conditioning in natural settings. These smaller units, it is contended, must be learned at some point in the sequence of learning whether the learner begins with small units of behavior or larger units of behavior. Gagné (1970), as you will note toward the end of this chapter, presents Pavlovian conditioning as the most simple type of learning, but as being basic to all other types of learning.

Early in the history of learning, psychology specialists were intrigued by several questions. One of these questions was the role of contiguity, or closeness between stimuli, in its role in the association of one stimulus with another stimulus. Another kind of contiguity is the association of certain responses with certain stimuli or of a

Major Concepts from Theories of Learning and Instruction

specific response to a specific stimulus. Another important question was the role of *repetition* in association; that is, whether or not repetition was necessary and the role it played in association. Ivan P. Pavlov (1927) was one of the earliest to investigate thoroughly these two questions. Pavlov was a physiologist who, in the process of studying digestion in dogs, discovered some of the variables in the questions of contiguity and repetition. He investigated how animals begin to associate certain responses with certain stimuli. Starting from the observation that his experimental dogs would salivate in anticipation of being fed at the very sound of the person coming with the food, he developed the paradigm of conditioning which is now termed *classical* or *respondent conditioning.*

Pavlov typically would restrain a dog in a harness which kept him standing rigid in a given direction. He performed a minor operation on the oral cavity of the dog in order to observe whether or not the dog was salivating and if it were, to what degree. He had originally done this to study the digestive process, but upon noticing that the salivation response could occur to cues associated with the food as well as the food itself, he became interested in studying that phenomenon.

Pavlovian researchers isolate a certain response, usually one which occurs naturally, and then begin to study conditions which produce it. Exemplifying this methodology is Pavlov's work in conditioning the dog to salivate at the sound of a bell. In this case the original *unconditioned response* (UCR) is that of salivation. The *unconditioned stimulus* (UCS) which produced this response is the food introduced into the dog's mouth. That is to say, when food is introduced into the mouth of the dog, the dog will reliably salivate. At this point, Pavlov would ring a bell, introduce the food into the dog's mouth, and then would get the response of salivation. The sequence is bell, food, salivation. The bell in this case is the *conditioned stimulus* (CS). Note the repetition of events—first is the conditioned stimulus, then the unconditioned stimulus, and then the unconditioned response. After this sequence is repeated a number of times, the dog is conditioned to salivate at the sound of the bell.

Eventually, the unconditioned response begins to occur sooner in the sequence. For example, the bell is sounded at second one, food is presented at second three, and the response occurs at second seven. (The actual times in some experiments is much briefer than this illustration.) The fifth time around in this repetitious sequence the response comes at the fourth second and then after more repetitions it comes at three and a half seconds, at three seconds, at two and a half, and then at two seconds. Soon the dog is salivating before the food is presented (see figure 2). At this point the dog is conditioned to salivate at the sound of the bell. What has happened here in summary is that upon repeated trials the unconditioned response keeps occurring

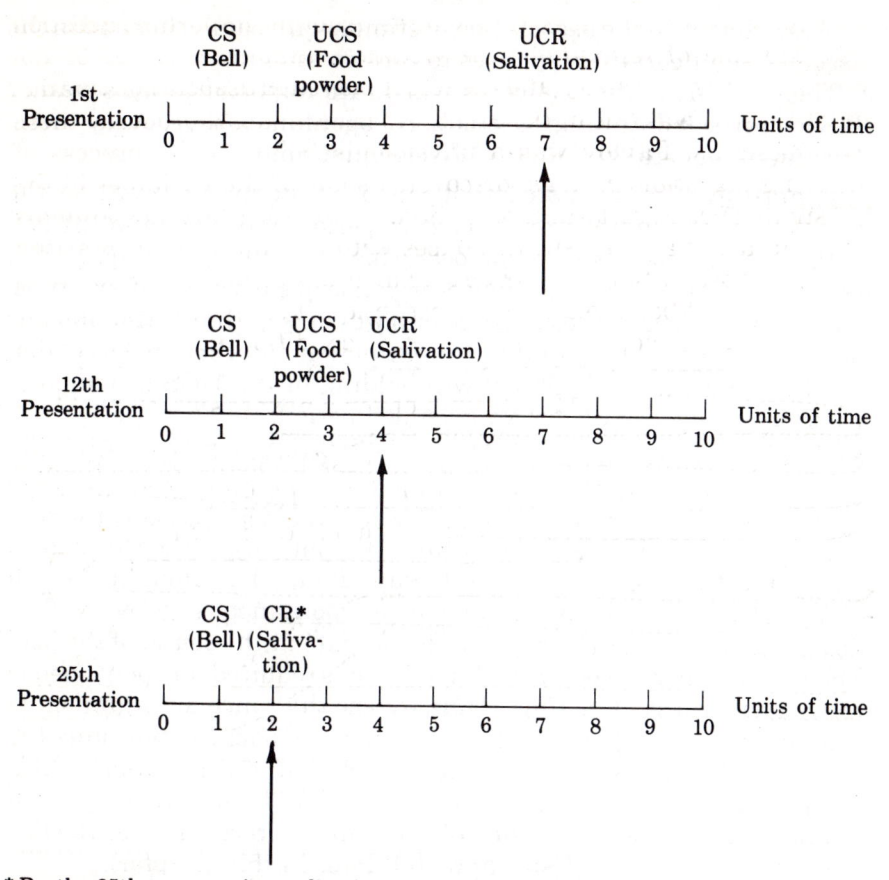

Concepts Associated with Theories of Learning

```
              CS      UCS         UCR
            (Bell)   (Food     (Salivation)
                    powder)
1st
Presentation └──┴──┴──┴──┴──┴──┴──┴──┴──┴──┘  Units of time
             0   1   2   3   4   5   6   7   8   9  10
                                         ↑
```

```
             CS     UCS   UCR
           (Bell)  (Food (Salivation)
                   powder)
12th
Presentation └──┴──┴──┴──┴──┴──┴──┴──┴──┴──┘  Units of time
             0   1   2   3   4   5   6   7   8   9  10
                           ↑
```

```
             CS    CR*
           (Bell) (Saliva-
                   tion)
25th
Presentation └──┴──┴──┴──┴──┴──┴──┴──┴──┴──┘  Units of time
             0   1   2   3   4   5   6   7   8   9  10
                     ↑
```

* By the 25th presentation, salivation occurs prior to the
introduction of the food powder into the dog's mouth (at time 3).
The response has been conditioned. Presence of the UCS is
no longer necessary for the response to occur.

Figure 2. Pavlovian (classical) conditioning—illustration of how the response (salivation) becomes conditioned to the stimulus (bell) after repeated pairings (first to 25th presentations)

earlier in the sequence of events until it occurs before the presentation of the unconditioned stimulus.

It should be noted that while the conditioned response is alike in type to the unconditioned response, there is some difference in the amount or strength of the conditioned response. As an illustration, the amount of salivation in the conditioned response is less than the amount of salivation of the unconditioned response. Note that Pavlov found contiguity and repetition to be important in the conditioning process, that is, in the association of stimuli with each other and in the association of certain responses to certain stimuli.

There are five other concepts which are important in discussing Pavlovian conditioning: extinction, spontaneous recovery, reinforcement, generalization, and discrimination.

Extinction. Pavlov noted that when he stopped presenting the unconditioned stimulus for a lengthy period and just rang the bell with the response of salivation occurring, continuing to ring the bell no longer elicited the conditioned response of salivation after a time. At the point when the response ceases we can say that extinction has occurred. All that is required for extinction to occur in Pavlovian conditioning is the continued withholding of the UCS in temporal contiguity with the CS for an extended period.

Spontaneous Recovery. This second concept is an interesting one. Pavlov noted that not presenting the food for an extended period of time would result in extinction. The dog would no longer salivate at the sound of the bell. At a later time he would begin the experiment again and the dog would begin to salivate at the sound of the bell alone. This phenomenon is known as spontaneous recovery. The dog seems to recover the capacity to salivate at the sound of the bell. The principle involved here is that all that is required for spontaneous recovery is a period of time. Thus we see that once an organism is conditioned it is very difficult to cause permanent extinction since the conditioned response may recur after a period of time. This is difficult to explain theoretically and it remained for later psychologists to develop plausible explanations of spontaneous recovery (see the discussion of the work of Estes and Hull later in this chapter).

Reinforcement. We have to make some distinctions between reinforcement in classical conditioning and the way the word is used in operant (Skinnerian) conditioning, to be discussed later. Reinforcement in the Pavlovian sense is simply the presentation of the unconditioned stimulus with the conditioned stimulus. In our example, reinforcement would be ringing the bell and presenting the food. The reinforcing stimulus is the one which controls or directs responding in this sense.

Generalization. Pavlov noted that there was a general tendency for the animal to produce the conditioned response to other stimuli similar to the original conditioned stimulus. For example, if he conditioned with a bell of a certain tone, he found that a bell of a slightly different tone would also elicit the conditioned response of salivation. The amount of generalization would decrease as the stimulus became decreasingly like the original conditioned response.

Discrimination. This fifth concept contrasts with generalization. If the experimenter desires to produce discrimination, the subject can

Concepts Associated with Theories of Learning

be conditioned to discriminate one stimulus from another. It would be necessary to ring the bell of a certain tone and reinforce this presentation, that is, the experimenter would ring the bell of tone A and provide food (condition the response), but when the bell of tone B is rung, no reinforcement is provided. If the experimenter does this repeatedly, the animal will learn to make the discrimination. That is, the animal will perform the conditioned response to the sound of the bell of tone A but not to the sound of the bell of tone B. Examples of classical conditioning in education, particularly in terms of attitude learning, are discussed in chapter 8.

Early American Behaviorism—Watson

John B. Watson popularized the conditioning process of Pavlov in America. Watson used young human subjects in order to study the learning of emotional responses in children. One of his most famous conditioning experiments was carried out with a male child named Albert (Watson and Raynor, 1920). He conditioned in Albert the response of fear of furry objects. Watson placed a small furry white rat in the presence of little Albert. Originally this did not produce a fear response. Then he began the experiment by showing Albert the animal, then making a loud noise which frightened him. Finally Albert showed fear and would withdraw when the animal was produced alone. In effect, he conditioned Albert to be frightened of white rats in particular and furry animals in general (through generalization). One instance of generalization occurred when Albert also exhibited withdrawal or fear responses in the presence of rabbits and even cotton or wool balls.

Watson has been called "the father of American behaviorism." In the following sections several learning theories are discussed which fall generally into the category of behaviorism. We will also mention a school of psychology which is in apparent conflict with the behavioristic position—Gestalt-field theories. The behaviorists believed that the sole and proper task of psychology was the study of that which is overtly observable and measurable. They defined psychology as the study of physical or observable stimuli and responses. There was a strong tendency not to infer any internal processes, and behaviorists did not trust introspection (reporting on one's own sensations), which was the primary research tool of earlier psychologists. They also distrusted speculation about internal mediating processes as being too speculative or inferential.

Contiguous Conditioning Theory, Learning by Doing— Guthrie and Estes

Guthrie's Theory. E. R. Guthrie has made a seemingly simple but profound contribution to modern psychology of learning in his analysis of the contiguity of stimulus and response. Guthrie disregarded both practice and reinforcement as essential for learning. The essential requirement for learning is for behavior to occur for any reason in a setting. Subsequently when a similar setting (set of *stimuli*) occurs, there is a likelihood for the same behavior (*movements*) to accompany it. "In any situation one learns to do what he does and nothing else" is a nontechnical way of saying Guthrie's principle. He said the same thing formally: "A combination of stimuli which has been accompanied by a movement will on its recurrence tend to be followed by that movement" [1952, p. 23].

If many movements occur in a situation, the entire chain of responses may be learned, each response becoming the stimulus for the next response. Or the last response in a sequence may be learned to the situation with the preceding ones dropping out of behavioral repertoire if they are not strong stimuli. This has been called the principle of *postremity*. In an extreme analysis of this effect, responses may be said to be learned in the reverse order of their occurrence. Reinforcement is not necessary for learning according to Guthrie, only the contiguous occurrence of stimuli and responses is necessary. One reason that reinforcement may appear to cause learning is that it serves to "punctuate" experiences or chains of responses, thus designating the last response in any sequence of behavior. That is as far as Guthrie would be willing to go in ascribing a place to reward or reinforcement.

Likewise the notion of practice was disallowed as affecting learning. To practice a response is to perform it, not to acquire it. Response acquisition constitutes learning and may be accomplished in one trial. Subsequent performance has to do with retention. Of studies purporting to show behavior improvement with practice, Guthrie would argue that a new movement or responses may be acquired at each trial, and these combine to make it appear that learning was gradual rather than all or none.

Estes' Theory. One contemporary outgrowth of Guthrie's contiguity theory of learning has been advanced by W. K. Estes (1950, 1955) as *stimulus sampling theory*. This approach assumes that learners perceive different aspects of the learning situation on different occasions so that different responses may be learned to different "samples" of stimuli. According to this interpretation, increases in responding to a stimulus as a function of practice may merely be that the response becomes associated with different elements of the stimulus on each trial. That is, the contiguity on any trial is between the response and those aspects of the stimulus that the learner attends to. On subsequent trials the response may be conditioned to other aspects of the stimulus and, through the phenom-

Concepts Associated with Theories of Learning

enon of *stimulus compounding,* learning appears to gradually improve with practice, whereas one-trial learning can be said to be actually taking place.

Estes' theory presents a challenging explanation of the *spontaneous recovery* concept discussed in connection with Pavlov's work. Extinction may mean that a new competing response has been learned to the stimulus; however, elements of the original stimulus may remain unconditioned to the new response if not sampled during the newer learning. Subsequently, the learner may perceive such elements and emit the "extinguished" response.

These controversies between one-trial vs. multitrial learning and between contiguity vs. reinforcement still exist; see, for example, Rock (1957), Underwood and Keppel (1962), Estes (1964), and Nuttin and Greenwald (1968).

Although lacking in both formal elegance and extensive research support, Guthrie's theory has the advantage of both practicality and parsimony, and extensions of it as proposed by Estes stand as a modern expression of Watson's early behaviorism and even of Pavlovian "classical" conditioning.

Learning Theory of Behavior—Hull

Clark Hull's theory (1952) offers several concepts worthy of study. Among these are: primary reinforcement, secondary reinforcement, intervening variables, and habit-family hierarchy.

Primary Reinforcement. Hull's basic principle of learning was that no learning occurs unless some drive is reduced. Behavior which leads to drive reduction is learned. A primary reinforcement diminishes some physiological need.

Secondary Reinforcement. A secondary reinforcer is a stimulus that is present when a primary reinforcer reduces a drive and comes to assume some of its power to satisfy the need. This may be considered an example of association by contiguity as in classical conditioning. For example, the presence of the mother may become a secondary reinforcer to a child. After experiences with the mother feeding the child, that child will find the presence of the mother reinforcing.

Intervening Variables. Intervening variables are constructs hypothesized by Hull to mediate between behavior (dependent variables) and its causes (independent variables). As such, Hull can be considered to be a forerunner of modern mediation theory which attempts to account for observed behavior in terms of implicit stimulus producing responses. Mediation is thus related to the concept of habit-family hierarchies in that the hierarchy may be thought of as consisting of a variety of learned potential responses which can mediate overt behavior.

Habit-Family Hierarchy. The concept of habit-family hierarchy essentially refers to organisms having acquired a variety of different responses which could be made in any specific stimulus situation. When given a cookie, a two-year-old boy can make a number of responses and these can be thought of as arranged in a hierarchy in terms of his tendency to perform them. He can (1) eat it, (2) say "thank you," (3) share it, (4) carry it around, (5) toss it, or a variety of other things. The most dominant response may be to eat it. The parent may wish the child to say "thank you" or share the cookie. Training the child, in this instance, primarily consists of rearranging the order of occurrence of these responses (which the child is already capable of making). The position of any potential response in a person's habit-family hierarchy, that is, the likelihood of occurrence of a response in a situation, would depend upon *habit strength* based upon prior learning and drive which constitutes motivation to respond. In contrast to Estes' stimulus sampling explanation of the phenomenon of spontaneous recovery of responses thought to have been extinguished, Hull's position would be that all learned responses retain some position in a person's habit-family hierarchy. In any situation, then, a response which once has entered a person's behavioral repertoire has some probability of occurrence, even if very low. Once the response is made, for any reason, that fact alone increases its likelihood of occurring again. Hull termed the likelihood or probability of a response *habit strength*.

Reinforcement Psychology—Thorndike and Skinner

Thorndike's Theory. E. L. Thorndike's work has been of tremendous influence in American education and educational psychology. Thorndike (1911, 1949) developed his "provisional laws of learning," the most important of which are: the *law of effect* and the *law of exercise*. The *law of effect* states that responses which are closely followed by satisfaction will become connected with the situation. Conversely, responses followed by discomfort will have their connection to the situation weakened. The law of effect had to be modified several times to account for findings which questioned this reciprocity of response contingent upon reward and punishment. The *law of exercise* states that repetition increases the connection between responses and the situation. By "situation" Thorndike means the present environmental stimuli. Thorndike revised the law of exercise several times during his lifetime to the extent that it was practically dropped as a law of learning.

Concepts Associated with Theories of Learning

One of Thorndike's typical experiments involved placing a cat in a box. The box had a door with a latch which could be pulled by the cat to open the door. Food was placed outside the door in full view of the cat. Thorndike observed initial "trial and error" behaviors which finally resulted in tripping the latch. The animal's behavior initially appeared to be random movements, but after several trials the animal learned to open the box. Thorndike concluded that repeated trial and error produced learning. Later in this chapter the "trial and error" explanation will be contrasted with the Gestalt theory interpretation of problem solving by insight. Thorndike's "trial and error" learning explanation influenced the work of B. F. Skinner who advanced the concept of shaping by successive approximations as a replacement for trial and error.

Skinner's Theory. The reader may note several points of agreement between the works of Thorndike and B. F. Skinner. Skinner believes that Pavlovian conditioning is adequate to explain a type of behavior which he terms "respondent." Respondent behavior is behavior which occurs after and as a result of stimuli. Skinner discusses a second type of behavior which his experiments explain. He terms this "operant" behavior—responses which serve to operate on stimuli, on the environment.

Skinner (1953) developed the method of conditioning through what has been termed operant or instrumental conditioning. His most famous experimental apparatus consisted of a box-like construction which included a lever which could be pressed by an animal and a mechanism which delivered bits of food or water (reinforcement) to the animal through a delivery tube. Pushing the lever resulted in the reinforcer being dropped into the experimental chamber. There are several concepts in operant conditioning with which the reader should be familiar: (1) positive and negative reinforcement, (2) shaping, (3) successive approximation, (4) extinction, (5) chaining, and (6) schedules of reinforcement.

First, though, reinforcement will be introduced. Skinner defined the reinforcer as any event which increases the probability of a response occurring again. For an event to function as a reinforcer, it must occur contingent upon a response being performed. Note that while Thorndike spoke of "connection" Skinner speaks of "probability" of occurrence. In operant conditioning the reinforcement must immediately follow the response during the initial training procedure. The chain of events is (1) the organism makes a response to some stimulus in a setting and (2) reinforcement is presented. A rat, for example, presses the lever and a bit of food is delivered through the tube. This results in increasing the probability that the response of pressing the lever will continue.

Major Concepts from Theories of Learning and Instruction

- *Positive and negative reinforcers* are both associated with an increase in the behavior being reinforced. In the case of a positive reinforcer, its presentation increases the future likelihood of that response occurring in a similar situation. Negative reinforcement involves the termination of aversive events. If a response is followed by the removing of a negative reinforcer (aversive stimulation), that response will be reinforced. That is, the presentation of a positive reinforcer has the same effects as the termination of a negative reinforcer—learning of whatever was done immediately before. Thus, if food is presented to a hungry animal when it performs a certain response, it will learn to perform that response in that situation. If doing something results in the turning off of a painful electric shock, the subject will learn to do that thing in similar situations in order to avoid the aversive stimuli. Note that the termination of aversive stimulation is reinforcing to the response which led to that termination.

    Positive and negative reinforcers may themselves be conditioned as in secondary reinforcement discussed before. A stimulus which occurs in the presence of a positive reinforcer may acquire positive reinforcing power. Words of praise or reproof appear to acquire their reinforcing powers in this way. Because every person has a different learning history, the same events (e.g., words of praise) acquire different reinforcing properties for different individuals.

- *Shaping* is a concept referring to the process of getting the behavior of an organism closer and closer to that desired by the experimenter. The subject receives reinforcement for responses which more closely approximate the desired end result.

- *Successive approximation* is a concept that describes the technique of shaping behavior. By applying the reinforcement at just the right time (manually in some experiments, automatically in others), the experimenter is able to shape the response which he is trying to condition. For example, if a rat is placed in the experimental apparatus and it stays at the end of the chamber away from the lever which it is to press, the rat's responses can be shaped to press the lever through the process of successive approximation. Suppose the rat is facing the wall opposite the lever. The experimenter waits until the rat turns in the direction of the lever and then reinforces that movement. Thereafter, every time the rat makes a move toward the lever that response is reinforced until the rat is near the lever. Finally, when the rat presses the lever and as soon as it does, the experimenter applies reinforcement according to any one of a number of schedules. Schedules of reinforcement will be discussed later. Skinner and others have demonstrated the shaping of behavior by successive approximations in a variety of organisms from rats and pigeons to man.

Concepts Associated with Theories of Learning

- *Extinction,* the next concept, occurs in operant conditioning much as it does in classical conditioning. That is to say, behavior diminishes in the absence of reinforcement. The principle of learning derived from Skinner is that a reinforced response usually stays within the organism's repertoire of responses and a nonreinforced response generally drops out of the behavioral repertoire. Extinction occurs with a continued period of nonreinforcement.
- *Chaining* of responses is a concept resulting from attempts by Skinner to explain more complex behaviors such as those involving the use of language. Originally suggested by Watson, chaining simply means a series of stimulus response connections wherein one response produces the stimulus for the next. Much of human learning may be approached from a standpoint of response chaining according to operant conditioning advocates.

The techniques of reinforcement have been studied by Skinner and his students (see Ferster & Skinner, 1957) to the extent that they have identified the following four basic *schedules of reinforcement:*

1. *Fixed Ratio Schedule*—continuous reinforcement is an example of the fixed ratio schedule. Ratio refers to the number of responses. In this schedule the subjects would be rewarded after emitting a given number of responses, say after every fifth response. Continuous reinforcement is usually used when the experimenter is initially conditioning a response of an animal. Continuous reinforcement means reinforcing every correct response. The advantage of this schedule of reinforcement is that the organism is more rapidly conditioned than with the other schedules.
2. *Variable ratio schedule*—the organism may be rewarded on the third, seventh, and fifteenth response, or according to any varied sequence. This schedule is associated with the highest sustained effort/work output.
3. *Fixed interval schedule*—the subject is rewarded after every fixed period of time, say every fifth second, as long as it continues to respond.
4. *Variable interval schedule*—the animal is rewarded at variable times, for example, on the third, seventh, and fifteenth second.

One advantage of the continuous schedule (a fixed ratio schedule where every response is reinforced) is that conditioning the response occurs rather quickly. The disadvantage is that extinction occurs more rapidly when the reinforcement is stopped. The advantage of the variable schedules is that even though conditioning takes longer, the

31

conditioned response is more resistant to extinction. The subject becomes accustomed to receiving reinforcement sometimes but not always. If properly "motivated" (e.g., by food deprivation) the animal will continue to respond even when reinforcing events are few and far between.

Skinner's work has been important in many ways, but its primary impact in formal instruction has been in placing greater stress on reinforcement and in establishing a framework for programmed instruction. These applications are discussed in greater detail in chapters 4 and 7 and are summarized in chapter 10.

Purposive Behaviorism—Tolman

E. C. Tolman developed a theory which can be considered to be a link between behaviorism and Gestalt-field theories, combining some of the advantages of each.

Like Guthrie, Tolman(1959) rejected reinforcement as a concept affecting learning. In drawing the distinction between learning (the acquisition of behavior) and performance (the subsequent doing of things already learned), Tolman held that learning consisted of pairing or associating stimuli. The concepts of *significate* (similar to an unconditioned stimulus) and *sign* (similar to a conditioned stimulus) were used in describing stimulus events. A response originally made to a significate, when the significate is paired with a sign, becomes attached to that sign. In a later encounter with the sign, it is as if the sign leads the subject to expect the significate (food, as in the Pavlovian example). The concept of *expectancies* forms the basis for subjects to develop cognitive structures or maps (mental pictures of objects) of their environment. Behavior, then, is purposive or oriented toward the achievement of specific goals. Subjects follow (respond to) signs with the expectancies of attaining the goals. Along the way, new sign-significate relationships are learned.

For Tolman, learning may take place quite independently of any concurrent performance. This is known as *latent learning*. Likewise for Tolman, motivation is a factor which affects performance but not learning (acquisition). Another factor which according to Tolman affects performance is confirmation of expectancy. This is close to an idea of reinforcement in that correct responses result in confirmation and are more likely to reoccur whereas incorrect responses lead to disconfirmation thereby decreasing the likelihood of future performance. The major emphasis in this viewpoint is to account for the learner's purposes as well as stimulus-response contiguities in understanding behavior.

Concepts Associated with Theories of Learning

Gestalt Theory

One reason for differences between Gestalt psychology and behaviorism is that behaviorism's major tenets have emerged from experiments in the area of learning, and Gestalt theory primarily emerged from perception studies. "Gestalt" is a German word meaning shape or form. It refers to a learner's activity in organizing his private world. The three major Gestalt psychologists were Max Wertheimer, Wolfgang Köhler, and Kurt Koffka. For a more detailed discussion of Gestalt psychology see Wertheimer (1959).

Köhler's studies with apes (1925) epitomize Gestalt views on learning. An ape was placed in a cage with two sticks which could be fitted together. A banana was placed outside the cage which could only be reached by the two sticks fitted together. After a time of fruitless trying with one then the other stick, the ape would pause, then join the sticks together and immediately reach and get the banana. The ape appeared to Köhler to have attained a sudden *insight* to the problem. Insight was considered to be a cognitive restructuring of the perceptual field. Thus the learner appears to reorganize mentally his environment in order to achieve its aims.

Köhler's conclusions have been criticized from the stance that the ape may have already learned solutions to such problems by trial and error. Critics maintain that Köhler was ignorant of the experiential background of his subjects. Apes are known to develop such techniques in the wild to obtain food, thus the animal simply may be using a response previously learned. Replication studies with apes reared in captivity have failed to obtain Köhler's results (Birch, 1945). It is suggested that a background of specific learnings is necessary to perform what appears to be "insightful" behavior.

Field Theory—Lewin

Another important theoretical view is field theory which emerged from studies in physics and mathematics, particularly a branch of mathematics known as topology. Sharing the Gestaltists' views on the undesirability of trying to understand behavior by fragmenting it into irreducible bits, Lewin (1936) posited that behavior is a function of the person and his environment: $B = f(P,E)$. This view is an antecedent of the authors' general model of human behavior discussed in chapter 3 of this text.

Life-Space. A key concept of field theory is life-space, the psychological world in which each person lives. Life-space includes a person's perceptions of all other persons, cultural influences, physical objects, concepts, and various stimuli with which the individual has current psychological contact. The person's past history is largely irrelevant except when residues (memories, habits, etc.) remain in the current situation. As such the theory is ahistorical and seeks causes for behavior in the here and now. These causes are not in objective reality—out there—but in the subjective perceptions each individual has of his situation. A contemporary example of this idea is the "private world" concept of Wilson, Robeck, and Michael (1974).

Differentiation. Another concept of field theory is differentiation. As a consequence of experience with his/her environment, a person becomes progressively more differentiated or sophisticated. Meanwhile perceptions of the environment gain structure. One's life-space develops from a relatively unknown, unexplored region to one which is better understood (mapped, in Tolman's terminology) and organized.

Motivation. Motivation in Lewin's system involves *vectors,* which are directional forces, and *valences,* strengths of attraction or repulsion of goal objects in a life-space. *Barriers* in one's life-space frustrate attempts to attain desired goals and results in reactions such as fantasy (the development of imaginary life-space), dedifferentiation (the shifting to simpler cognitive structure and goals), or aggressive behavior. As is the case with most of the major theoretical systems of psychology, field theory is no longer a focus of large-scale research activities. Lewin's views, however, have had major impact on such areas as social and child psychology. Also, field theory is clearly in the intellectual heritage of current formulations in educational psychology such as the relativistic view the authors present in chapter 3 of this text.

Modern Social Learning Theory—Bandura

Albert Bandura and his associates (1963, 1965) have developed a theory of social learning based upon the principles of *imitation* and *modeling.* Whereas Guthrie can be credited with promoting the notion of one-trial learning mentioned before and thus, rejecting repeated practice as promoting learning, Bandura presents the case for *no-trial learning*—learning by observation. This is like Tolman's concept of latent learning in that mental representations and rehearsals of environmental events are presumed to occur.

In social learning theory, a child watches a person *(the model)* perform some act and if given an opportunity to do so, is more likely to behave in the same or in a similar fashion *(imitation).* A classic study reported by Bandura (1965) involves groups of children, some of whom observe an adult model aggressively assault a toy clown and some who do not. When later placed alone in a room with the toy clown, the children who had observed the aggressive model were

Concepts Associated with Theories of Learning

much more likely to assault it than the groups who had not witnessed the attack. This occurred even when neither the model nor the child were given any clear reinforcement for the act. Reinforcement of the model or child did seem to encourage higher levels of performance of behavior, which were already learned but did not facilitate new learning.

Obviously, characteristics of both observer and model influence the degree of imitation which may result in social learning. Observers who are attentive to what the model does, who have the capability to perform the modeled act, and who admire the model are more likely to engage in social learning than those who do not have these characteristics. The model must be a person of some status—a significant other—to the observer-learner in order to garner the attention necessary for imitation of behavior. These ideas are expanded in chapter 4 in connection with motivation and in chapter 8 concerning attitude learning.

A Brief Synopsis of Learning Theory

The preceding brief introduction to some of the major concepts in learning theory is an attempt to provide an overview of learning. The following points should help you to organize many of these concepts and think of them in an educational context.

1. Learning theory emphasizes the need for careful analysis of the stimuli in the learning situation. What stimuli constitute the learning situation? What stimuli are likely to aid the person to make the desired responses?
2. Of equal importance is the emphasis on the responses of the learner. A careful analysis of responses to be required in a learning situation may facilitate learning. This emphasis is supportive of a behavioral objective point of view to which the authors alluded in chapter 1.
3. Tolman's work and Gestalt psychology show how personal structuring and organizing is involved in learning. Teachers must provide ample opportunity and stimulation for that organizing on the part of pupils.
4. There is a definite need for some form of reinforcement in most learning situations. Either the learner or the environment (to include the teacher) should provide that reinforcement. Reinforcement will be discussed in greater detail in chapter 4.
5. The necessity of action for all kinds of learning is open to question. Action followed by reinforcement seems to be necessary for operant learning, but is not necessary in imitative learning.
6. Successive approximation emphasizes a relative point of view about the accuracy of performance. Responses which show

progress toward the desired response should be reinforced. Approximately correct responses are very desirable in the early stages of learning.

Concepts Associated with Theories of Instruction

In actual practice there are no theories of instruction. Yet a few psychologists have set forth systems which begin to approximate instructional models. Hopefully, at some future time instructional theories can be developed which would guide teachers through the five stages of formal instruction as presented in chapter 1. In this section we turn from learning theory to discuss systems by Jerome S. Bruner, David P. Ausubel, David E. Hunt, and Robert M. Gagné which may be considered as prototypes of instructional theories. At the very least, these approaches offer concepts and principles which may lead toward instructional theory based upon what psychologists have been able to establish about learning.

Any complete instructional theory would be guided by (1) the concepts and principles of learning theory and practice and (2) the concepts and principles of human development—both general development and cognitive development. These would provide guidelines not only for how to teach but also when to teach.

Toward a Theory of Instruction—Bruner

Jerome S. Bruner has experimented and theorized in the areas of human perception, concept attainment, and cognitive development. In the provocative book, *Toward a Theory of Instruction,* Bruner has outlined four major features of a theory of instruction (1966, pp. 40-42):

1. A theory would specify the experiences which implant in an individual a predisposition toward learning. What preschool experiences make the child able to learn when he enters school?
2. A theory would specify how a body of knowledge should be structured (organized) so that it may be understood by the learner.
3. A theory of instruction would specify the most advantageous sequence in which to present the materials.
4. A theory would also specify the nature and pacing of reinforcement in learning and teaching. The ultimate goal would be shifting away from extrinsic reinforcement toward the intrinsic reinforcement which results from learning the material. That is, as the person progresses in learning ma-

Concepts Associated with Theories of Instruction

terial such extrinsic rewards as praise and reproof would be removed. The rewards intrinsic to learning a skill or puzzle solving would replace the extrinsic reinforcers.

Bruner's primary statement about teaching is "any idea or problem or body of knowledge can be presented in a form simple enough so that any particular learner can understand it in recognized form" (1966, p. 44). The techniques of simplifying content involves what Bruner terms the three modes of representation: enactive, iconic, and symbolic.

- *Enactive Representation* involves action—psychomotor activity. An infant may enactively represent a rattle by shaking his hand. Young children demonstrate an understanding of the principles of the lever by adjusting their positions on a seesaw. The principles of leverage in this case are enactively represented. The enactive is a very primitive, concrete mode of representation. Enactive representation involves psychomotor acting out of some idea, concept, or principle.
- *Iconic Representation* involves the use of imagery or graphics to represent the idea, object, or principle. This mode of representation defines the object with more completeness and economy. Drawing a chart or diagram and demonstrating the principles of leverage through these would be an example of iconic representation. It is more abstract than the enactive mode but less abstract than the symbolic mode of representation.
- *Symbolic Representation* uses language to demonstrate the idea, object, or event. It is the most abstract of the three modes of representation. The use of these modes appears to follow developmental trends. That is, young children tend to use enactive modes, and as they grow older they make greater use of the symbolic mode. The complexity or difficulty of material may cause any of us to return to the less abstract modes of representation. When we attempt to solve a difficult problem and cannot through the symbolic mode—language—we may draw diagrams, charts, etc. This regression and translation to iconic representation seems to aid us in puzzle solving.

By "translating" ideas in symbolic modes into iconic or enactive ones, Bruner (1966, pp. 59ff) believes that anything can be taught at any age. He has demonstrated, for example, teaching quadratic equations to young children through the less abstract modes.

A teacher following Bruner's system would carefully analyze the material to be learned so that the mode or modes of representation would be appropriate to the difficulty of the material and the developmental level of the learner. Attention would also be paid to the student's predisposition to learn and the student's experience with functioning in the different modes.

The major focus of Bruner's writings from 1959 to 1970 was on the necessity of understanding and teaching the structure of knowledge. That is to say, how knowledge in the various sciences, arts, and disciplines is organized is of primary importance. If a person knows the structures of a science, that person can rapidly learn the concepts and data, and at times even generate concepts and data from the structures. During that decade, Bruner recommended a curricular focus on subject matter—content—specifically the structures of that content. In 1971, he recommended a curricular focus that would initiate within students a deep, long-term desire to learn and a lasting commitment to learning. This focus also included the inculcation of a strong desire to use that learning for the benefit of society and the redress of social wrongs.

The Psychology of Meaningful Verbal Learning—Ausubel

David P. Ausubel is one of the more influential educational psychologists of modern time. The main idea of his instructional system is that what a person already knows and how this knowledge is personally structured are the two most crucial variables in learning and instruction.

Advance Organizer and Subsumption Theory. Some of Ausubel's empirical work has to do with facilitating verbal learning through the *advance organizer*. Prior to presenting the details of the subject matter to be learned, a brief amount of material related to what is to be learned is presented. This brief discourse is the advance organizer. The material in the advance organizer is more general and abstract than the new material to be learned. It provides a structure within which the new material can be acquired, organized, and retained. (Evidence of the value of organization in aiding memory and transfer will be discussed in chapter 5.)

During an experiment involving instructing college students in the metallurgical properties of steel, Ausubel provided a 500-word statement including discourse on the similarities and differences between metals and alloys and their advantages and disadvantages (Ausubel,1960). This material was general, abstract, and inclusive; but it did not contain the same information as that in the material to be taught or tested. The advance organizer was presented prior to the instruction in the new material. Although there is some disagreement of interpretation, such experiments generally find advantages for the use of the advance organizer. The advance organizer mediates

Concepts Associated with Theories of Instruction

between what is already known and what is to be learned. It provides an organizing structure for the new material. Ausubel's experiments have demonstrated the efficacy of this approach for the learning of prose. The placement of brief summaries at the beginning of each chapter of a book or the study habit of reading a summary of a chapter before the chapter itself are recommendations consistent with the idea of an advance organizer.

The advance organizer and the ideas relevant to it are sometimes termed *subsumption theory*. New material is subsumed and organized, with the advance organizer, into the person's existing cognitive structure.

Logical and Psychological Meaningfulness. Coordinate with subsumption theory, Ausubel has developed an explanation of meaning and of meaningful learning. The natures of meaning and of meaningful learning and the processes pursuant to meaningful learning are problems which have plagued psychologists and teachers alike. Ausubel has redefined meaning in learning and helped us to understand the processes of meaningful learning.

Meanings, according to Ausubel, are of two types. First is *logical meaning* which is a property of content or the material itself. Logical meaning

1. Depends only on the nature of the material
2. Contains two properties of relatability
   a) Nonarbitrariness
   b) Substantiveness

Nonarbitrariness has to do with relatedness within the idea, concept, or principle to be learned and relevant corresponding ideas known by a person. In the statement "an equilateral triangle is a triangle with three equal sides"—an example used by Ausubel and Robinson (1969)—the concepts *equilateral triangle* and *triangle* have a nonarbitrary relationship including a relationship between a specific instance and a general case. Each of these concepts within this statement are potentially relatable to each other and to ideas known by the person without arbitrariness. The quality of substantiveness exists if an equivalent wording may be used without altering the ideas, concepts, or principles. The above wording may be changed to "an equilateral triangle is a triangle that has all of its sides equal" without changing the concept or the meaning of the concept. Connected nonsense terms such as *gey-nur* would not be logically meaningful because they do not possess the qualities of relatability. When students do not already know concepts such as *triangle*, they approach learning the above statement in the same manner as they would lists of syllable pairs like *gey-nur*.

The second type of meaning identified by Ausubel is *psychological meaning*. Psychological meaning is the individualized meaning which occurs when logically meaningful material is converted into a person's knowledge (or cognitive structure). It is individualized meaning, incorporated by each person. When new material is experienced and substantively related to ideas the person already knows, it has the quality of psychological meaning.

A person will not relate new ideas to what is already known when approaching the new material with what Ausubel terms a *rote learning set*. A rote learning set is the person's intention to memorize the new material arbitrarily and verbatim (Ausubel, 1968, p. 38). Two factors result in a rote learning set: (1) students know that all too frequently they receive credit only for verbatim statements from many teachers and (2) anxiety and pressure felt by students result in a lack of confidence to learn meaningfully; that is, anxiety and pressure decrease the student's intention and capability to learn meaningfully. We know that it is possible to display glibness with abstract terms without really knowing the underlying concepts. In contrast to the rote learning set is the *meaningful learning set*. This set involves approaching material with the intention to learn it by relating it to what one already knows. The student approaches the material with the notion that the material *can* be meaningful, and thus attempts to relate it to what is already known—with the expectation that it can be done.

Meaningful Learning. The concepts of logical and psychological meaningfulness, and meaningful learning set lead toward an understanding of *meaningful learning*. Meaningful learning is the relating of logical meanings to what is already known. Psychological meaning occurs through the meaningful learning process. For meaningful learning to occur, three conditions must be met:

1. The person must have a meaningful learning set. The person must attempt to relate the new material to concepts already known in a nonverbatim manner.
2. The material must possess the quality of logical meaningfulness.
3. The person must already know the relevant ideas, concepts, and/or principles contained in the new material. Meaningful learning is recombining new and known material into new structures, or in new relationships.

When these three conditions are met, psychological meaningfulness can emerge. Psychological meanings are the product of the meaningful learning process.

Concepts Associated with Theories of Instruction

A teacher following Ausubel's meaningful learning psychology would attempt to do the following:

1. Positively reinforce the meaningful learning set, but never positively reinforce verbatim, glib responses.
2. Take steps to reduce the anxiety which produces the rote learning set.
3. Determine if the person knows the necessary concepts which, individually, constitute the new material. The teacher following stage two in planning for instruction (chapter 1) would teach the necessary prerequisite concepts when deficiencies are noted for individual pupils.
4. Provide practice in student's relating previous knowledge to new material and reinforce responses of this type.
5. Devise and provide advance organizers which will facilitate the learning and organization of new material.

Conceptual Systems Change—Hunt

In his research on teaching, David E. Hunt has followed Lewin's famous formula $B = f(P,E)$, that is, behavior is a function of the person and the environment. A person's behavior will be a joint result of his/her personal characteristics (ability level, needs, etc.) and the characteristics of his/her environment at the time of behaving. Since the teacher is primarily limited to in-class environmental manipulation, Hunt's work is chiefly concerned with the teacher's varying features of the classroom setting.

According to Hunt (1971, 1975), the teacher varies the setting by what he terms *radiating* different in-class environments. Different environments produce different behaviors (in part) and different environments are required to induce change in different people. The teacher must determine which environment is appropriate to attain the specific behaviors relevant to the instructional goal. The teacher then radiates that environment by behaving in certain ways, by supplying appropriate materials, and by controlling the behaviors of the students (which are, of course, also a part of that environment).

Since the range of individual differences is so great, categorizing students is helpful. Thus the teacher groups students according to stages and tries to radiate the appropriate environment. Table 1 describes Hunt's stages and the kind of environment appropriate to persons in each stage.

Students at any one of the three stages require different environments to progress to the next stage. An inherent goal is to get students

Major Concepts from Theories of Learning and Instruction

TABLE 1
Conceptual Systems Change Model:
Stage Characteristics and Optimal Environments for Progression

Stage	Stage Characteristics	Optimal Environment for Progression
Sub I	Impulsive, poorly socialized, egocentric, inattentive.	Accepting but firm; clearly organized with a minimum of alternatives.
Stage I	Compliant, dependent on authority, concerned with rules.	Encouraging independence within normative structure.
Stage II	Independent, questioning, self-assertive.	Allowing high autonomy with numerous alternatives and low normative pressure.

Adapted from: D. E. Hunt, *Matching Models in Education,* The Ontario Institute for Studies in Education, Monograph Series # 101, p. 30, by permission of the author.

to stage II. Persons at stage sub I are characterized as impulsive, etc., so the optimum environment for teaching and for progression to the next stage would be one which is accepting but firm and highly structured. Each succeeding stage represents a step toward autonomy and self-assertion. The highest level of functioning, stage II, provides for creative self-direction. This model seems to be consistent with the ultimate goals of education discussed in chapter 1.

The Conditions of Learning—Gagné
Robert M. Gagné (1970) has developed a challenging approach to organizing what is known about learning with implications for instruction. His key concepts include *eight types and conditions of learning, learning hierarchy,* and *vertical and lateral transfer of learning.* Gagné also has presented a set of *nine components of instruction* (1970, pp. 303ff) and has drawn attention to his view of the instructional implications of the learning hierarchies approach.

Eight Types and Conditions of Learning. Gagné's eight types of learning are largely abstractions similar to the learning theories presented earlier in this chapter. Each type of learning is associated with the *conditions* under which it occurs.

① • The first type of learning is what Gagné calls *signal learning,* which corresponds to classical conditioning, where the appropriate conditions would be *contiguity* of stimulus and response. It is a term for conditioning by contiguity as in Pavlov's and Guthrie's systems. Responses amenable to signal learning are those not typically under voluntary control such as emotional responses.

Concepts Associated with Theories of Instruction

2) • Type two is *stimulus-response* learning for which Gagné basically means Skinner's operant conditioning. Gagné, however, goes beyond "radical behaviorism" in allowing for "mediation" as the paradigm, for this level is not S—, but Ss⟶R, with the "s" standing for internal stimulation to act. These first two types of learning can be called stimulus-response connections or simple conditioning.

3) • The third type of learning in Gagné's model is called *chaining*. This again is an operant conditioning concept involving a sequence of S-R connections where one response produces the stimulus for the next. The learner must learn each S-R "link" in the chain as well as the correct sequence for chaining to occur.

4) • *Verbal association* is the term given to type four learning. This has to do with the formation of new associations between verbal pairs. The stimuli and responses may be nonsense syllables or they may be (potentially) meaningful language terms. However, because both stimulus and response terms are symbolic in nature, and thus unlike the earlier "types"; both must be learned. Verbal association is considered to be a more advanced kind of learning.

5) • The fifth learning type described by Gagné is called *discrimination learning*. This concept is closely related to research in discrimination which has been performed in both the Hullian and operant conditioning traditions. At issue in discrimination learning is learning to make a specific response to a given stimulus and also learning to avoid making that response in a similar but crucially different stimulus situation.

6) • Gagné refers to *concept learning* as type six. Concept learning clearly involves internal processes which could be labelled mediation. Gagné states, "Learning a concept means learning to classify stimulus situations in terms of abstracted properties like color, shape, position, numbers, and others" (Gagné, 1970, p. 51). Concept learning can be considered to be the learning of relationships among a variety of stimuli, and is dealt with in greater detail in chapters 3 and 6.

7) • *Rule learning* is the seventh type of learning. According to Gagné, it is widely applied in formal education. A rule can be considered to be "a chain of two or more concepts" (Gagné, 1970, p. 57). Thus in order for rule learning to take place, concepts must either already have been learned or should take place conjunctively with rule learning.

8) • The eighth and highest level of learning in Gagné's model is *problem solving*. This involves organizing rules into new combinations in order to solve a problem. At this point, Gagné becomes more explicit about events internal to the person. Development of "meta-rules" or rules combining rules necessary for problem solving clearly involves thinking. Table 2 summarizes the types and conditions of

Major Concepts from Theories of Learning and Instruction

learning starting at the second type (stimulus-response connections) and proceeding through the eighth (problem solving).

TABLE 2
Summary of Student Prerequisite Capabilities and Essential Conditions for Each Type of Learning

Learning Type	Prerequisite Capability	External Conditions of Learning
Ss → R Connection	Apprehension of stimulus	Presentation of stimulus so that desired response will be contiguous in time and supply contingent reinforcement.
Motor Chain	Individual connections	A sequence of external cues, stimulating a sequence of specific responses contiguous in time; repetition for selection of correct response-produced stimuli.
Verbal Chain	Individual connections, including "coding" links	A sequence of external verbal cues, stimulating a sequence of verbal responses contiguous in time; repetition may be necessary to reduce interference.
Discrimination	Individual connections, or chains	Practice providing contrast of correct and incorrect stimuli; or, practice providing progressive reduction in stimulus differences.
Concrete Concept	Discriminations	Responding to a variety of stimuli differing in appearance, belonging to single class.
Rule, including Defined Concept	Concepts	External cues, usually verbal, stimulate the formation of component concepts contiguously in a proper sequence; application is made in specific examples.
Higher-Order Rule—Problem Solving	Rules	Self-arousal and selection of previously learned rules to achieve a novel combination.

NOTE: Reprinted by permission of the author and the publisher from R. M. Gagné, *The Conditions of Learning,* 2nd ed. (New York: Holt, Rinehart & Winston, Inc., 1970), p. 334. Copyright (c) 1965, 1970 by Holt, Rinehart & Winston, Inc.

Learning Hierarchy and Transfer. A learning hierarchy is a detailed, sequenced analysis of prerequisite learnings for any task or problem. The learning hierarchy for a complex task will often include prerequisite skills involving several of the eight types of learning described above. Mastery of prerequisite skills may facilitate

Concepts Associated with Theories of Instruction

learning of the new task and when this occurs, the process is called *vertical transfer of learning*. Vertical transfer can be distinguished from *lateral transfer of learning* which is transfer from one task to another of about the same complexity or, in other words, at the same level in a learning hierarchy.

Nine Components of Instruction. Gagné has also described nine components of instruction which form categories of teacher behaviors. Most of these functions are subsumed under stages three, four, and five of the planning for instruction sequence presented in chapter 1. The value of Gagné's list of components lies in its specific teacher behaviors in terms of pupil learning.

1. Gaining and controlling attention. An external stimulus arouses the appropriate attentional set.
2. Informing the learner of expected outcomes. Communication, usually verbal, tells the learner about the kind of performance he will be able to do after he has learned.
3. Stimulating recall of relevant prerequisite capabilities. The learner is reminded of the relevant intellectual skills, and also verbal knowledge, he has previously learned.
4. Presenting the stimuli inherent to the learning task. The particular stimuli to which the newly learned performance will be directed are displayed.
5. Offering guidance for learning. Usually by verbal communications the learner's thinking is directed by prompts or hints until the essential performance is achieved.
6. Providing feedback. The learner is informed of the correctness of his newly attained performance.
7. Appraising performance. Opportunity is provided for the learner to verify his achievement in one or more situations.
8. Making provisions for transferability. Additional examples are used to establish increased generalizability of the newly acquired capability.
9. Insuring retention. Provisions are also made for practice and use of the new capability so that it will be remembered.*

Of the four approaches to instructional theory presented, Gagné's may come closest to incorporating the fruits of the learning theories introduced earlier in this chapter.

A Brief Synopsis of Instructional Theory

It is obvious that instructional theory draws heavily from learning theory. As examples, Bruner accents the role of reinforcement and Gagné recognizes respondent behavior (Pavlovian conditioning) and operant conditioning (Skinnerian conditioning) as basic types

---

*Reprinted by permission of the author and the publisher from R. M. Gagné, *The Conditions of Learning*, 2nd ed. (New York: Holt, Rinehart & Winston, Inc., 1970), p. 304. Copyright (c) 1965, 1970 by Holt, Rinehart & Winston, Inc.

of learning. These basic types of learning are then matched with Gagné's nine components of instruction. The correspondences between cognitive maps and the Gestalt emphasis on organization with the concept of *organization* in subsumption theory are equally apparent.

Considering these correspondences it is not difficult to expect that instructional theorists and learning theorists will continue to interact even though the learning theorist will tend to focus on the learner while the instructional theorists will focus on curriculum, on learning environment, and on teaching acts and teachers.

Some other basic ideas of the instructional models presented may be added to Bruner's four major features of an instructional theory and are listed here:

1. Curriculum content must be examined for its logical meaningfulness and its logical structures. An adequate instructional theory would result ultimately in the organization of instruction around material which met Ausubel's criteria for logical meaningfulness. An adequate instructional theory would provide guidelines for highlighting the logically meaningful material.
2. Instructional theory would also provide guidelines for the development of advance organizers and psychological meaning.
3. Instructional theory would also provide a technology of anxiety reduction (or optimizing) which would increase the potential for meaningful learning.
4. A comprehensive instructional theory should also include guidelines for learning environment–cognitive style matching. This may also include learning environment–student personality matching along the lines established by Hunt and other theorists and researchers.
5. An instructional theory will be more comprehensive and productive if it reflects a recognition of different types of learning and possible instructional components to accompany each.

One area of research in the past ten years or so is the area of classroom observation. In the future this research should significantly influence instructional theory and practice. This emphasis is consistent with recent trends to get instructional research out of the laboratory and into its natural setting—the classroom itself. The value of and basic procedures in research in natural settings is expertly discussed in Brandt (1972). Research in classroom observation is reviewed and evaluated in Dunkin and Biddle (1974).

An Overview of Educational Implications of Learning and Instructional Theory

The implications of learning theory for education may be viewed in terms of stimulus factors, organismic or person characteristics, and response factors.

From learning theory it is known that stimuli are very important in instruction. Thus a teacher should analyze the stimuli in learning situations. In planning for instruction the teacher should carefully consider the sources of stimuli expected in the learning situation—the curricular content, the teacher's own actions, and the actions of the other students as well as the physical environment which influences the learning of individual students.

Some stimuli will help promote desirable responses and some will be distracting. The teacher should analyze these stimulus factors and attempt to control stimuli as carefully as possible.

Reinforcers are also stimuli. Desirable responses must be positively reinforced by the teacher. The principle of successive approximation suggests that teachers may view correctness of responses in a relative way and reinforce responses which are closer and closer to correctness.

Since the teacher's own behaviors are potential stimuli to students, modeling should be used. Correctly modeled behaviors are essential features of instruction. When the student imitates those correct responses the student should be reinforced.

In terms of person characteristics, the teacher must carefully attend to how the student organizes the material learned. More on this will be discussed in later chapters.

In terms of response factors, teachers should conduct an analysis of the desirable student responses in the learning situation. It should be determined what student responses are necessary so that the instructional situation can be designed to encourage those necessary responses.

Recent instructional theories support many of the practical ideas inherent in learning theory. Some practical suggestions from instructional theory are as follows:

1. When students are having difficulty learning abstract material try to represent the material in a concrete manner.
2. The teacher should analyze students' predispositions toward learning. Are the students ready to learn the material?
3. The teacher should provide advance organizers for material—readings, discussions, and lectures.
4. The teacher should attempt to reduce excessive anxiety.

Major Concepts from Theories of Learning and Instruction

5. The teacher should try to find out if students think the material is meaningless and only worth learning by rote.
6. The teacher should carefully analyze and select the curricular content for its meaningfulness. Also, is it logical?
7. The teacher should get to know individual students and try to radiate learning environments which match the student's characteristics.

Conclusion

In this chapter, several theories of learning and models of instruction have been introduced with a view toward identifying some of the key concepts of each. Hopefully the reader is now familiar with many of the major concepts in learning theory and is developing ideas of some of the major requirements for an operational instructional theory. Instructional theory is in a relatively embryonic state at this time. The models presented here incorporate some of the knowledge gained from learning theory but are not sufficiently inclusive to be considered as fully developed theories. Chapter 7 presents, in somewhat more detail, another model which was recently proposed for classroom instruction called *mastery learning*. Teachers should seek to develop their own models of instruction incorporating both learning theory and what is known about instruction as well as the many inferences which can be drawn from their own teaching and learning experiences. Hopefully, teachers will also give consideration to the behavior model presented in the next chapter and use it as they develop their own understanding of human behavior.

Discussion Questions

1. How might the various theorists described in the text approach the question of drill in learning (e.g., how necessary is drill)? Which theorists would take similar views? Which would take opposing views?
2. Recall a short sequence of behavior that resulted in some actual learning taking place. Describe what took place from a reinforcement theorist's point of view, then from a Gestalt-field-perceptual theorist's point of view.
3. Many laboratory experiments in learning have involved animals such as pigeons, rats, cats, and monkeys. Suggest some reasons why such research may be important to an

understanding of human learning. What problems are involved in these respects?
4. How many ways can you think of to distinguish between operant and classical conditioning? How do these ways look in actual classroom learning situations?
5. How might one go about trying to extinguish such behaviors and attitudes as smoking or racial prejudice?
6. How do theories of learning differ from theories of instruction? How does the "science of learning" relate to the "art of teaching"?
7. What are some advantages to each schedule of reinforcement? How might each of the five appear in classroom learning?
8. Why is the variable ratio reinforcement schedule believed to be NOT generally applicable in classroom learning situations, even though it is associated with high levels of performance?
9. How are Guthrie's and Tolman's explanations of learning similar? How are they different? Which one makes more "sense" to you? Why?
10. Is social learning theory more like reinforcement theories or more like Gestalt-field theories? Why? What would social learning look like in a classroom?
11. Which of the learning theories do you see incorporated in Gagné's conditions of learning and components of instruction? How do you see a teacher making use of these?
12. What is missing from the instructional theory models of Bruner, Ausubel, Hunt, and Gagné that you think needs to be dealt with in a theoretical or systematic manner?
13. Identify one of the theoretical concepts that you are reasonably sure *does not* apply in classroom learning situations. Can you defend this position?
14. It has been said that the *science of learning* describes how reinforcement produces acquisition of the behavior being reinforced, whereas the *art of teaching* involves knowing and acting on what is reinforcing and to whom and under what conditions. Do you agree with this statement? Defend your answer.

Recommended Readings

Bigge, M. L. *Learning theories for teachers.* (2nd ed.) New York: Harper & Row, 1971, 366 pp. Ideas are developed related to the learning theories discussed here and others with implications for school learning. The author takes a strong cognitive-field theory point of view and contrasts this with the stimulus-response psychology. (Paperback)

Biggs, J. B. *Information and human learning*. Glenview, Illinois: Scott, Foresman & Co., 1968, 135 pp. An information processing approach to learning. Develops notion of human coding processes and cognitive styles. (Paperback)

Gagné, R. M., & Rohwer, W. D., Jr. Instructional psychology. In P. H. Mussen & M. R. Rosenzweig (Eds.), *Annual Review of Psychology*, 1969, 20, 381-418. A review of research into such topics as attention, feedback, retention, and transfer, including vertical transfer.

Glaser, R., & Resnick, L. B. Instructional psychology. In P. H. Mussen & M. R. Rosenzweig (Ed.) *Annual Review of Psychology*, 1972, 23, 207-76. A more recent review on related topics but complements the Gagné and Rohwer article (above) more than it obviates it.

Hackett, M. G. *Success in the classroom: An approach to instruction*. New York: Holt, Rinehart & Winston, 1971, 109 pp. Applies Gagné's model of instruction directly to the tasks of the classroom teacher. (Paperback)

Keller, R. S. *Learning: Reinforcement theory*. (2nd ed.) New York: Random House, 1969, 182 pp. A concise presentation with examples of seventeen reinforcement concepts in learning. (Paperback)

Kong, S. L. *Humanistic psychology and personalized teaching*. Toronto: Holt, Rinehart & Winston, 1970, 144 pp. Presents what the title implies—a cognitive-humanistic approach to instruction. (Paperback)

Popham, W. J., & Baker, E. L. *Systematic instruction*. Englewood Cliffs, N.J.: Prentice-Hall, 1970, 166 pp. A behavioral objective-based approach to instruction. (Paperback)

Stephens, J. M. *The process of schooling—A psychological examination*. New York: Holt, Rinehart & Winston, 1967, 168 pp. Develops the theory of spontaneous schooling—there is no one correct way to teach. A variety of instructional stances suited to the personalities of those involved is advocated. (Paperback)

Stiles, L. J. *Theories of teaching*. New York: Dodd, Mead and Company, 1974. Discussion by fourteen scholars from a variety of disciplines about teaching and learning theories.

References

Ausubel, D. P. *Educational psychology: A cognitive view*. New York: Holt, Rinehart & Winston, 1968.

References

Ausubel, D. P. The use of advance organizer in the learning and retention of meaningful verbal material. *Journal of Educational Psychology,* 1960, *51,* 267-72.

Ausubel, D. P., & Robinson, F. G. *School learning.* New York: Holt, Rinehart & Winston, 1969.

Bandura, A. Vicarious processes: A case of no-trial learning. In L. Berkowitz (Ed.), *Advances in experimental social psychology.* Vol. 2, New York: Academic Press, 1965.

Bandura, A., & Walters, R. H. *Social learning and personality development.* New York: Holt, Rinehart & Winston, 1963.

Birch, H. G. The relation of previous experience to insightful problem solving. *Journal of Comparative Psychology,* 1945, *38,* 367-83.

Brandt, R. M. *Studying behavior in natural settings.* New York: Holt, Rinehart & Winston, 1972.

Bruner, J. S. The process of education revisited. *Phi Delta Kappan,* 1971, *53,* 18-21.

Bruner, J. S. *Toward a theory of instruction.* Cambridge: Harvard University Press, 1966.

Dunkin, M. J., & Biddle, B. J. *The study of teaching.* New York: Holt, Rinehart & Winston, Inc., 1974.

Estes, W. K. Statistical theory of spontaneous recovery and regression. *Psychological Review,* 1955, *62,* 145-54.

Estes, W. K. Toward a statistical theory of learning. *Psychological Review,* 1950, *57,* 94-107.

Ferster, C. B., & Skinner, B. F. *Schedules of reinforcement.* New York: Appleton-Century-Crofts, 1957.

Gagné, R. M. *The conditions of learning.* (2nd ed.) New York: Holt, Rinehart & Winston, 1970.

Guthrie, E. R. *The psychology of learning.* (Rev. ed.) New York: Harper & Row, 1952.

Hilgard, E. R., & Bower, G. H. *Theories of learning.* (3rd ed.) New York: Appleton-Century-Crofts, 1966.

Hill, W. F. *Learning—A survey of psychological interpretations.* (Rev. ed.) Scranton, Pa.: Chandler, 1971.

Hull, C. L. *A behavior system: An introduction to behavior theory concerning the individual organism.* New Haven: Yale University Press, 1952.

Hunt, D. E. *Matching models in education.* Toronto: Ontario Institute for Studies in Education, Monograph No. 10, 1971.

Hunt, D. E. Person-environment interaction: A challenge found wanting before it was tried. *Review of Educational Research,* 1975, *45,* No. 2, 209-30.

Köhler, W. *The mentality of apes.* New York: Harcourt, Brace, 1925.

Lewin, K. *Principles of topological psychology.* New York: McGraw-Hill, 1936.

Nuttin, J., & Greenwald, A. G. *Reward and punishment in human learning: Elements of a behavior theory.* New York: Academic Press, 1968.

Pavlov, I. P. *Conditioned reflexes.* London: Oxford University Press, 1927.

Rock, I. The role of repetition in associative learning. *American Journal of Psychology,* 1957, *70,* 186-93.

Skinner, B. F. *Science and human behavior.* New York: Free Press, 1953.

Thorndike, E. L. *Animal intelligence.* New York: Macmillan, 1911.

Thorndike, E. L. *Selected writings from a connectionist's psychology.* New York: Appleton-Century-Crofts, 1949.

Tolman, E. C. Principles of purposive behavior. In S. Koch (Ed.), *Psychology: A study of a science.* Vol. 2. New York: McGraw-Hill, 1959.

Underwood, B. J., & Keppel, G. One trial learning? *Journal of Verbal Learning and Verbal Behavior,* 1962, *1,* 1-13.

Watson, J. B., & Raynor, R. Conditioned emotional reactions. *Journal of Experimental Psychology,* 1920, *3,* 1-14.

Wertheimer, M. *Productive thinking.* (Rev. ed.) New York: Harper and Brothers, 1959.

Wilson, J. A. R., Robeck, M. C., & Michael, W. B. *Psychological foundations of learning and teaching.* (2nd ed.) New York: McGraw-Hill, 1974.

Practical Organizer for Chapter 3

A student acts and reacts not so much in terms of stimulus events which occur at the moment of the action but in terms of private meanings, interpretations, and intentions at the frame of reference, account for a great part of the massive individual differences which teachers observe during instruction.

These individual differences comprise the most problematic features of education, especially for the individual teacher. The teacher must respond to these individual differences hour by hour each and every day. Perhaps the best the teacher can do is to try to understand these individual frames of reference by getting to know each individual student as much as possible.

The teacher must both understand and appreciate the influence which the student's concepts, structures, affects values, needs, and interests exert on the student's perception, learning, and thinking.

Thus, frame of reference theory can provide the educator with a perspective through which the student can be observed and through which instructional strategies can be conceptualized. This theory can also provide an interesting idea for instructional evaluation. In the final analysis, effective instruction will markedly change the individual student's frame of reference.

The Frame of Reference: A Cognitive Relativistic View of General Behavior and Learning

3

It is widely known that internal characteristics greatly influence behavior. As you know, these internal, individual characteristics are a result of both genetic and environmental factors. In this chapter we enumerate the major internal factors which influence behavior and learning. We discuss the literature and research which indicate the powerful influences of a person's concepts, structures, affect values, needs, and interests on perception, learning, and thinking.

Frame of Reference: Cognitive Relativistic View of General Behavior and Learning

That human behavior, learning, and instruction can be exceedingly complex is apparent as one examines material such as that discussed in chapter 2. Our most general purpose in chapter 3 is to present a cognitive relativistic model of behavior. This model is complex, as you will see; but we hope that you will find it helpful in understanding your own behavior and the behavior of your students. These understandings should also help you as you teach.

In chapter 1 two major tendencies of human behavior were noted. First is the tendency toward behavioral change as the requirements and context of behavior change. The second is the tendency to resist change, to persist in utilizing old responses which have "worked" in the past. In chapter 2 it was noted that an instructional theory should provide guidelines for overcoming resistance. In this chapter the authors will analyze resistance to change. The basic tenet discussed here is that a person's previous experience leaves residues which continue to influence that person's behavior long after the experience. These residues frequently are as important in understanding and predicting behavior as the environmental stimuli present at the moment of behavior. It is these parts of the person's history—the residues of experience—which partially determine behavior. The person makes interpretations of current stimuli in terms of one's personal history and behaves in ways consistent with those interpretations. These interpretations mediate the impact of current environmental stimuli. Many individual differences in behavior are the result of learnings related to such individualized interpretations.

One of the most urgent concerns of psychologists involves cause-effect relationships. The behaviorist-stimulus response approaches to behavior analysis appear to imply a cause-effect philosophy of science. "Stimulus" is more or less synonymous with cause and "response" with effect. Thus the learning theories discussed in chapter 2, with the exception of Gestalt and field theories, are cause-effect theories. To continue to study the complexities of human behavior only through cause-effect analysis is to oversimplify human behavior. Modern psychology appears to be moving away from this conception of behavior.

Relativism

Two relatively recent modes of scientific thinking are beginning to influence modern psychology. These modes, discussed here, emerge from modern quantum physics and relativity theory.

Modern quantum physics provides a context for the examination of the notion of causality. In quantum physics "detailed causality is

Relativism

replaced by statistical law" [March & Freeman, 1963, p. 157]. The difference between eighteenth and nineteenth century classical physics and the modern concept of causality centers on the interpretation of the concept of "state" (p. 159). Classical physics formulated "state" as a condition determined by values of measured properties in a system. In modern quantum physics a "state" is a momentary, transient condition of the system. The "state" is not determined by and does not correspond to definite values of every variable. Modern physicists have utilized statistics to describe probabilities of delineating values of measurements. Initial "states" are described in statistical probabilities and future probabilities of "states" are calculated based on these initial probabilities.

Extrapolating these ideas to the study of the behavior of living organisms requires two psychological assumptions. The first is that the person's immediate environmental situation constitutes a "situational life system." Assuming this, the psychologist relinquishes any preference for complete descriptions of the "state" of the organism and its situation at any moment in the system's history, even the moment of initial observation. The psychologist also questions the exactness of predictions of future "states." Any state is described in terms of probabilities and thus not fully determined.

A second assumption which is necessary is that the term "state" implies a static fixedness. A language of nouns is somewhat misleading for nouns emphasize the static fixedness. A noun symbolizes a moment of the past which corresponds more to a statement about a historical reality than to ongoing experience. This leaves one with an inadequate vocabulary of progressive-tense verbs. Psychological studies of organismic characteristics are influenced by the error of assumption of stasis in a relativistic sense. Thus, the second assumption is one of process as opposed to stasis. The organism *is* processing, not just "in process."

Heisenberg (March & Freeman, 1963) advanced what he termed the "uncertainty principle" in which it is observed that our methods of measurements tamper with the object of measurement. Neither the psychologist nor the physicist can ever really know whether or not measurements released energy into the system and changed the object of observation (Webb et al., 1966; West, 1967).

The processing nature of an organism also seems amenable to a perceptual set which includes not only a quantum mechanics redefinition of "state" but also a relativistic reinterpretation of the effect of all psychological variables. Within the relativistic context, the impact of each psychological variable derives its existence and function from its relationship to every other impacting variable in the system. We then must view the person and his milieu relativistically (Kagan, 1967).

Frame of Reference: Cognitive Relativistic View of General Behavior and Learning

When a psychologist extracts from among all of the environmental phenomena specific stimuli which relate to behavior and expects a specific stimulus to be related to identical future behavior, he may be accurate. But, it may be maintained that those same stimuli will never recur exactly the same again. The stimuli probably will occur in a different context and in different combinations. Certainly the person will not be exactly the same again. These ideas contrast traditional cause-effect analyses.

As Bigge (1964) states it, "The central idea of relativism is that a *thing derives its qualities from its relationship to other things*" [p. 68]. Admittedly, a human, a "thing," derives its qualities from its relationships to other things. But one must not overlook the fact that the qualities of those "things" are also derived from relationships to many other "things." These "other things" also include the person. In psychology then, even the external stimulus is relative to other external stimuli as well as the state of the individual.

The Frame of Reference and Its Relationship to Cognitive Behavior

In this section we will discuss the person's frame of reference and its relationship to cognition. The discussion centers on six components of the frame of reference and how these components are involved in resistance to change, as well as inducing change through cognition. The general principle followed here is that what we perceive depends on the internal frame of reference components. The frame of reference may contrast with new input and thus create resistance, or it may be consonant with new input and increase the receptivity of the person to the input.

Cognition is a generic term referring to any process involving an organism's coming to know or becoming aware of *events* (English & English, 1958). The processes of cognition are those involved in obtaining knowledge and extrapolating beyond that knowledge (an example would be thinking). The processes include such psychological functions as sensing, perceiving, judging, and reasoning. It is not unusual for psychologists to also classify learning within the processes of cognition. Much of human activity consists of efforts to obtain knowledge of specific parts of the world—objects within the world, and of phenomena occurring within the world.

Some difference must be noted between the term "event" and the term "phenomenon." Traditionally, in philosophy (and this distinction is very helpful here) the term "event" denotes what happened (whatever it was); whereas the term "phenomenon" denotes what appears to have happened. The term "phenomenon" implies *appearing* or human sensation. This distinction helps to avoid the

The Frame of Reference and Its Relationship to Cognitive Behavior

naive assumption that humans can directly sense events. What we sense of the external world are internal energy exchanges which are set off by ambient energy in our environment, and this internal energy may not be the same as the energy around us. Remember that these *internal energy exchanges* are the bases of perception and other cognitive operations.

A model describing important variables which influence a person as knowledge will be discussed in the next section. The world external to the human is the source for an infinite amount of potential information embedded in natural phenomena. The amount of information itself constitutes a major variable influencing cognition, since each observer must select for observation specific phenomena from among others, and extract specific information from the selected phenomena. A second important variable is related to the characteristics of the phenomena. A third variable is the person, in that one projects one's training, one's history, and one's characteristics into the observation. The individual's frame of reference constitutes a significant aspect of the third variable. The following section is an attempt to explain the impact of the individual's frame of reference.

The Individual's Frame of Reference

Stimulation, the initiation of sensory impulses within an organism, occurs from sources both external and internal to the organism. Cognitive processing begins with stimulation from either of these two sources. Hebb (1949) developed a meaningful description of the human's capacity of internal stimulation. Internal stimuli consist not only of impulses from the automonic nervous system which maintains biological balance, but also consist of impulses which are generated by the frame of reference. The frame of reference continuously stimulates the organism and is continuously projected on the external environment to influence, delimit, and select the external variables or factors which have the potential of stimulating the person. That is, some environmental events become stimuli and some do not.

The frame of reference results in selective attention with respect to external stimulation. It must not be assumed, however, that one's frame of reference can negate all stimuli from external sources. Some external stimuli are so intense that activity is initiated within a person nonselectively. For example, a person with normal hearing will hear a high intensity sound despite adverse internal conditions. On the other hand, sounds of lesser intensity are frequently selectively ignored. Humans typically ignore many visual, auditory, and tactile potential stimuli at any given moment—peripheral movements and objects during visual focusing; sounds such as the ticking of a clock, the roaring of a furnace or air conditioner; and the skin surface pressures attendant with holding a book or pencil or sitting in a chair. Fortunately or unfortunately, as the case may be, relatively few of the stimuli introduced by the teacher in the instructional situation have very high intrinsic attention potential. It should be remembered that events in the external world are not to be considered stimulus material per se. Stimulation occurs only when activity is initiated within the individual. Again, it is via stimulation that events in the external world become information. External and internal stimuli are the beginning points of cognition.

The frame of reference influences whether or not particular events or attributes of events are attended to, the manner in which the person attends and responds, and the degree to which the person attends and responds. The frame of reference consists of the following six components: concepts, structures, affects, values, interests, and needs. Each of these six components influence sensation, perception, and thinking. Each may interact with others to produce a cumulative influence. The components represent convenient constructs which reflect "state" or characteristics of persons at any given moment as well as dynamic, processing dimensions of human existence.

A Summary of Some Central Ideas in the Frame of Reference Theory

1. Stimulus reception and perception is selective. The six components of the frame of reference act as selectors or filters (see figure 3) on external stimuli.
2. The six components of the frame of reference are primary generators of internal stimuli. (See figure 3.)
3. Internally generated stimuli may override external stimuli.
4. The person interprets external stimuli in terms of the frame of reference. In other words, the impact of external stimuli frequently is relative to the frame of reference.
5. Perception (how the person interprets stimuli and attaches meaning to them) is of basic importance in behavior.

In the following pages literature and research will be described which provide support for the notion that the six components of the frame of reference exert influence on the psychology of input (e.g., recognition, sensation, and perception), on the psychology of cognitive processing (e.g., memory, thinking, reasoning, and learning), and output (e.g., behavior).

Six Components of the Frame of Reference

POTENTIAL EXTERNAL STIMULI

The Frame of Reference

Concepts
Structures
Affects
Needs
Values
Interests

Internal Stimuli

BEHAVIOR

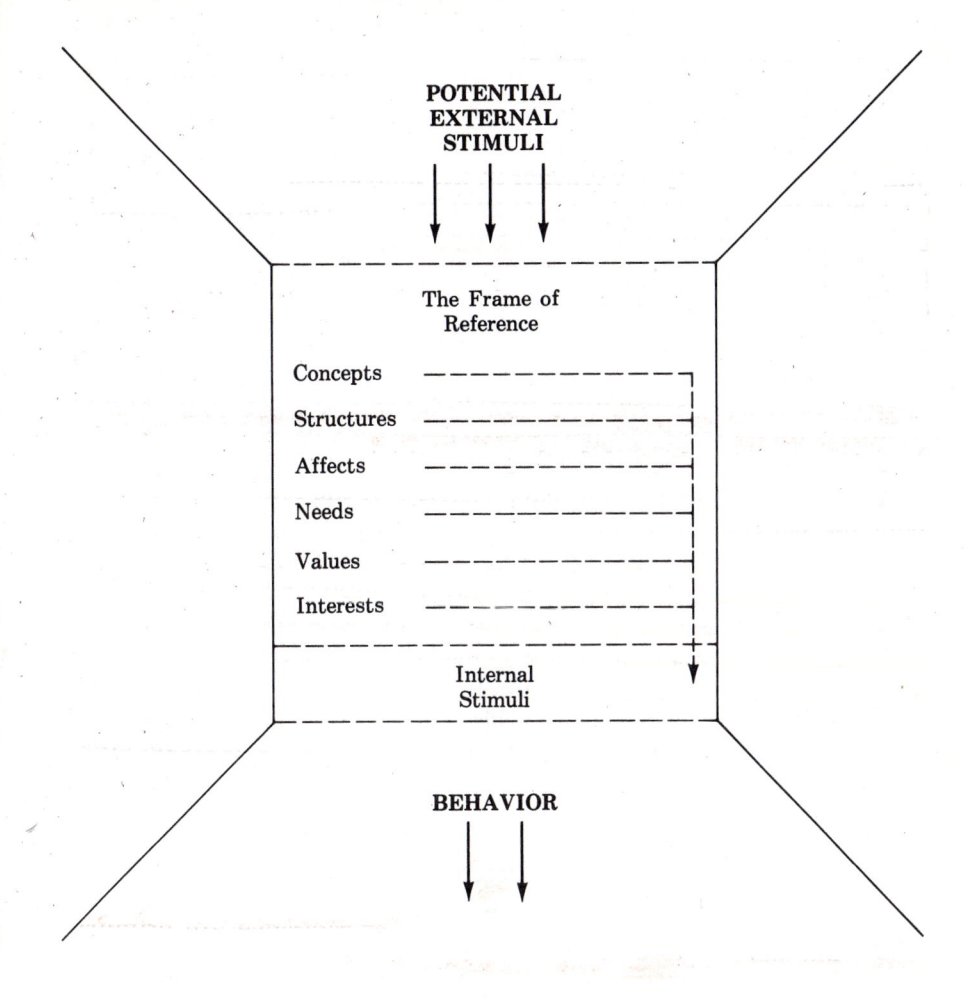

Figure 3. The Selective and Generative Effect of the Frame of Reference

Six Components of the Frame of Reference

Concepts

The term "concept" is usually defined as a discrete object of awareness together with its meaning or significance. A concept implies a rule for categorizing objects according to similarity or commonness among them and is thus abstract and general to a degree. The term

61

Frame of Reference: Cognitive Relativistic View of General Behavior and Learning

"table" is a name of a concept. Certain similar characteristics of objects (e.g., tables) are shared. Our common agreement about these shared characteristics enables us to recognize (characterize and differentiate among) individual objects and to communicate our awareness to one another.

Much of man's knowledge is of the nature of concepts. Concepts are abstract by their very nature, and by the symbolic nature of knowledge and memory. Concepts can be said to represent degrees of abstractness; for instance, "cow" is less abstract than is "mammal." And concepts like "honesty" and "democracy" are more abstract than "hardness" or "tabular."

Previously learned concepts influence the ways a person senses, perceives, and thinks about new phenomena. Psychological research from a variety of points of view support this contention. Judson, Cofer, and Gelfand (1956) had subjects learn lists of words in serial order prior to solving Maier's (1930) two-string problem. The problem involves bringing two strings together which are suspended from a ceiling so far apart that subjects could not grasp one string and then the other to bring them together. One solution consists of making a pendulum of one string by tying some object to the end and setting it in motion, then bringing the other as close as possible and grasping the pendulum as it swings near. Those subjects whose list of words included the words "rope-swing-pendulum" in that order were more efficient at solving the problem than the control group. The task may seem simple but Maier (1930) demonstrated the difficulty of this problem. Very few of Maier's subjects solved the problem without some guidance. This study illustrates the impact of previous learnings in the form of concepts on problem solving. A concept may facilitate learning and thinking in very specific ways.

Another related series of experiments has been conducted on the influence of labels on recognition. Several investigations support the idea that the provision or formation of a label prior to a recognition task facilitates recognition (Campbell & Freeman, 1955; Gaydos, 1956; Katz, 1963; and Kurtz & Kooland, 1953). Some labels may be considered to be names of concepts if they come to stand for a class of objects with some common characteristics.

Cantril (1950) and Ittelson and Cantril (1954) discuss the role of experience and knowledge (much of which is conceptual) in establishing *expectations* which are of primary importance in interpreting stimuli. A person's experience which includes concepts also has an impact on the *recognition* of stimuli (Bagby, 1957). Bagby used a stereoscope, in which one picture was presented to the left eye and another to the right eye. In one pair of slides a picture of a baseball player was presented with the picture of a bullfighter. Most Anglo-Americans tested recognized the baseball player whereas most

Mexicans recognized the bullfighter. This line of research indicates that knowledge obtained over an extended period influences sensation and perception. A predisposition to perceive in one way over another is termed a perceptual set.

The study of Judson, Cofer, and Gelfand (1956) as well as other investigations (Carmichael, Hogan, & Walter, 1932; Haselrud, 1959; Immergluck, 1952; Murray, 1933; Saugstad, 1955; and Siipola, 1935) indicate that such sets may be induced just prior to the experimental period, and that these sets influence sensation, perception, and cognition. Bruner and Minturn (1955) induced expectations in subjects to see either numbers or letters. Subjects who were expecting letters of the alphabet saw "13" as a "B" and those expecting numbers saw "B" as "13." In yet another study, Bugelski and Alampay (1961) presented two groups of drawn figures to subjects. One group consisted of drawings of animals and the other group consisted of drawings of faces of people. One common drawing was included in both groups. If the common drawing was presented with drawings of animals it was most frequently seen as a rat; if presented with drawings of human faces it was most frequently seen as a man's face.

Structures

The term "structure" is used here in two ways. First, the various sciences, arts, and disciplines each contain structures of which we may be aware. In this sense a structure is a conventional—usually logical—way of organizing and interrelating information or concepts included within that science, art, or discipline. These conventions are shared by many persons within that field of knowledge. Structures of this type are learned along with other information and concepts. Rules of grammar are examples of this type of structure in a language; the taxonomic systems in biology and zoology are other examples. Structures of the second type are those personal, relatively individualized, ways of organizing and interrelating information, phenomena, and concepts which the person encounters in present experience or in memory. Each of these types of structures thus may include few or many concepts, and is subjective by definition.

Structures and Learning, Memory, and Problem Solving. It is widely accepted that one's knowledge of the structures within a subject matter field influences ability to learn new material in the field. As noted in chapter 2, Ausubel (1968) distinguished two kinds of meanings which correspond with the two types of structures: logical and psychological meaning. Logical meaning is symbolic in that it consists of nonarbitrary and substantive relationships within the material. Psychological meaning is the product of an individual meaningful learning experience. The person idiosyncratically develops psychological meaning—by relating potentially (logical) meaningful material nonarbitrarily and substantively to relevant ideas within the cognitive structure. Material can only be learned meaningfully when material is logical as well as relatable to the person's cognitive structure (Ausubel, 1968, pp. 37-45). Ausubel states that one of the crucial factors within the person which influences learning ability is the person's cognitive structures. "Since subject-matter knowledge tends to be organized in sequential and hierarchical fashion, what one already knows in a given field, and how well one knows it, obviously influences one's readiness for related new learnings" [p. 26]. Ausubel (1960) has demonstrated the usefulness of providing general structures (logically meaningful material), or advance organizers, which mediate between what students already know and that which students are to learn.

Few psychologists would deny that humans can learn rote (unmeaningful, i.e., unrelated to previously learned structures) material. However, there is general acceptance that (1) it is more difficult to learn rote material, (2) rote material is more quickly forgotten, and (3) material learned by rote usually is not positively transferable, that is, things learned by rote in one situation do not readily transfer to new situations.

Numerous studies illustrate the influence of structures on learning, retention, transfer, and problem solving. Reynolds (1966) concludes that organized perceptual structure may aid new learning. Other research (Postman, 1954) indicates that learning rules of organization facilitates rote learning. Still other studies (Ausubel, 1960; Ausubel & Fitzgerald, 1961, 1962; Merrill & Stolurow, 1966) indicate that providing general organizers which correspond to previously existing ideas of the person will facilitate both learning and retention of meaningful material. When one has a structure to which one can anchor, or subsume the new material within, learning and retention are facilitated (Ausubel, 1968). Some studies (Judd, 1902; Overing & Travers, 1966) also imply that making a general principle available will aid transfer. Several other studies (Hilgard et al., 1953; Hilgard et al., 1954; and Katona, 1940) point out that knowing a general principle will result in better problem-solving performance on a class of problems than memorizing the solution.

During every waking moment humans are exposed to numerous, somewhat unrelated bits of potential information or phenomena. The number of unrelated bits which can be retained is limited, and Miller (1956) suggests that seven plus or minus two (five to nine) is the limit. What happens when the number of bits to which one is exposed, but is expected to remember, exceeds the span of retention? Evidence is quite clear that humans can develop organizing schemes to aid memory. Bousfield (1953) reports "clustering"; Miller (1956), "chunking"; Jenkins and Russell (1952), "structuring"; Mandler (1966), "organizing"; and Katona (1940), "grouping." The organizing scheme enables one to extend the number of bits remembered.

Miller (1956) argues that the limitation holds with qualification for making judgments about, or discriminating among, the bits. He also speculates that this limit extends to perception of the bits. Should this be a valid speculation, the structures not only aid memory but also facilitate and extend the number of discriminations among the bits of potential information. Also structures should enable one to perceive and discriminate attributes of an object and to increase or limit the number and quality of attributes perceivable. A person, encountering a large number of potential bits of information, is able to discriminate and remember from five to nine of the bits (or whatever one's limit is for that task) within some organizational scheme. Each of the discriminations made within the original organizational scheme may become a basis for expanding the limits of the discrimination, for extending perception of the bits, and finally aiding both memory and recognition.

Origins of Structure. Generally speaking, the human ability to develop efficient structure for bits of information increases with age, up to maturity. The bases of structures used generally become more seminal and symbolic during middle childhood. Olver and Hornsby (1966) and Bruner and Olver (1963) note that younger children group arrays through imagery; that is, they are dependent upon moment-to-moment perceptual vividness. After about age six most children begin to symbolically or linguistically relate items in the array. The child under six tends to structure along the lines of perceptually obvious characteristics of color, shape, or size. The older child tends to structure according to function and symbolic commonness.

Investigations such as those just mentioned lead one to surmise that thinking and learning (cognitive) abilities depend primarily on both linguistic skills and the ability to organize and structure—two highly related sets of skills. According to the eminent Swiss psychologist, Jean Piaget (see Piaget & Inhelder, 1969), a person's repertoire of structures are of primary importance in cognition. Some of these structures are called groupings, which are those systems of simple or multiple class inclusion typical of children at the stage of concrete operations (roughly between the ages of seven or eight to age eleven or twelve).

The following description of one of Piaget's experiments should provide the reader with some grasp of a structure which the older, but not the younger, child will use to solve a problem. The subject is told that a substance g, when combined with liquid from two of four beakers of different liquids, will produce a yellow solution. A child younger than 11 or 12 will set out to discover in a random fashion which combination will produce the yellow solution. The child will attempt various combinations in an unsystematic manner—by adding $g + 1 + 4$, $g + 3 + 4$, $g + 1 + 2$. There is no order to the combinations, and combinations may be repeated. The random approach takes longer. An older child may systematically try all possible combinations in an orderly fashion—by adding $g + 1 + 2$, $g + 1 + 3$, $g + 1 + 4$, $g + 2 + 3$, $g + 2 + 4$, $g + 3 + 4$—one of which will be the correct combination (Inhelder & Piaget, 1958). Imposing such structures on problems enables the person at the stage of formal operations (roughly 11 or 12 or older) to solve problems quickly and efficiently.

According to Piaget the person's repertoire of structures increases in developmental stages. At the stage of concrete operations the structural repertoire is limited, and these structures enable the young person to deal primarily with concrete instances rather than higher level abstractions. The person can perceive and operate on the concrete, but cannot operate on the potential—that which the "here and now" might imply logically. Upon reaching the stage of formal operations the structures are more numerous and complete, and the person is able to visualize and operate on the possible or the potential. The person can "escape" the perceptually concrete, is not bound up in the limits of the concrete, and can fit the more symbolic dimensions of problems and problem arrays into even more sophisticated structures. Hewson (1971) has shown that among first-year university students some do not seem to function at the level of formal operations. This and other evidence suggests caution in interpreting too literally the age designations of Piaget's stages. Piaget's studies do show how cognitive structures emerge and develop from birth to maturity. The emphasis should be placed on the sequentiality of stages and not the specific age designations.

Structure and the Reception of New Information. While it is widely accepted that structures influence acquisition (original learning), retention, and problem solving, less agreement exists as to the influence of the structures on reception—recognizing, sensing, and perceiving. There is some evidence indicating that the way a person organizes bits of information and the habitual way similar bits have been organized influences perception and recognition of potential bits of information. Bruner and Potter (1964) and Potter (1966) investigated this issue. Their data indicate that when persons are confronted with unfocused photographs and asked to identify the object in the photograph as it is gradually focused, the early hypotheses tend to interfere with later correct identification. The subjects appeared to be unwilling to change these hypotheses about the object photographed and this delayed the identification. Apparently, when a person encounters an ambiguous array of potential information, the tendency is to impose on it some structured meaning from previous experience and the person is unwilling to give up that meaning. When structures are in error, they inhibit accurate recognition. This is clearly a form of resistance to change which can impede learning.

Summary. This section has presented investigations which indicate the influence of previously learned structures on original learning, transfer, problem solving, and recognition (both sensation and perception). To summarize, the following principles appear to be supported by the evidence adduced:

1. Persons will impose a previously learned structure on ambiguous stimuli.
2. Humans tend to organize even unrelated material, when there is a requirement to remember, and the organization facilitates short-term memory. This organization obviously emerges from previous learning.
3. Optimum conditions for learning exist when the structures are both logically and psychologically meaningful.
4. Structures aid positive transfer and problem solving.
5. Generally speaking, some previous knowledge involving at least minimal structuring is desirable, if not necessary, to recognition.

Recognition implies perceiving something relatable to previous learnings. Recognizing something "new" involves bringing to bear previously learned material in a "new" combination—fitting the new into some organizational structure, some interrelated set of already internalized meanings. The interaction between old and new, however, is dynamic. New material, if processed, can change the structure (Anderson & Ortony, 1975).

During the discussion of concepts and structures, it may have seemed at times arbitrary to have distinguished between the impact of concepts and structures on human cognition, since it may be argued that some of the psychological studies discussed may illustrate the impact of either discrete concepts or structures, or just simply previous knowledge. The authors think that this distinction can be useful. The distinction holds, for example, when one considers the proposition that concepts may exist only within psychological and logical structures. The logical and psychological meaning attached to every object, phenomenon, characteristic, or attribute can only exist within some interrelationship with meanings attached to other objects or phenomena.

Affects

English and English (1958, p. 15) define affect as "a class name for feeling, emotion, mood, temperament." Without doubt, affect is difficult to separate from the other five classes of behavior variables in that it continuously interacts with all of these. Affect is involved in the acquisition and maintenance of attitudes and values. Affects are aroused in connection with our interests and needs. Psychological literature reflects no small disagreement on interrelationships between affect and a variety of other constructs. It should suffice here to note that there is affective or emotional arousal in connection with affect (including biases and prejudices), beliefs, values, interests, and needs. Humans value those objects and contexts with and within which needs are met, and interests are exercised and expressed thereto.

Affective arousal occurs during the process of meeting needs, expressing interests, and maintaining values. Nor can affect be completely divorced from our concepts and structures (our knowledge); we value what we know and can feel threatened when others challenge our explanations. A person who already has formed a concept about an event will usually affectively resist revising that concept. Affect can be considered to be a basis of reinforcement in the sense of emotional satisfaction or dissatisfaction with consequences of behavior.

There are some influences of affect on sensation, perception, learning, and thinking and these should be mentioned at this point. While there is much evidence to support an argument that there are such influences, the evidence of such is beclouded by methodological and inferential problems—see for example Schultz (1974) and Wyer (1975). The most scientific approach would be to regard statements of such influences and relationships as hypotheses—which may be supported or challenged by various findings. Psychologists are not in agreement on affective influences. Fishbein (1967), for example, notes that attitudes, as conventionally measured, do not predict behavior very well; and he regards attitude and affect as nearly synonymous (p. 478), as does Thurstone (1931). It would seem that, in light of the above hypotheses, one can show relationships between affect and the cognitive processes without being required to predict exactly what the person will *do* in a specific situation. While the affective arousal of two persons to an object may be roughly the same, overt responses may be very different as the two persons may have learned to behave differently to the similar feelings.

Although the authors include six components within the frame of reference, strict distinctions between affect, value, interest, and need are not possible. However, some useful distinctions can be made in attempts to communicate behavioral integration and wholeness

Six Components of the Frame of Reference

rather than fragmentation. During this discussion on affect and the following sections on the other components the reader may well believe that one study illustrates the impact of values, while the authors purport that it illustrates the impact of affect. When a study has been traditionally regarded as illustrating an influence of a need, value, or interest on cognitive processes we have tried to include it within the appropriate section.

Several points may be made which will illustrate the global influences of affect on behavior.

1. A person given some autonomy will tend to seek or approach an object, a task, or a situation for which there is positive affect.
2. A person will tend to avoid that for which there is negative affect.
3. If a person is forced to perform a task in a situation which has negative affect, that person will tend to avoid similar tasks and situations later.

These tendencies continuously operate to place a person in contextual settings which provide relative continuity to perceptions and which support concepts and structures.

Anxiety and the Cognitive Processes. One specific area of affect—anxiety—has been shown to have a debilitating influence on cognitive processes (Harleston, 1962; Ruebush, 1960; Sarason et al., 1960; West et al., 1969) although the effects of the nature of the task and other variables such as intelligence cannot be discounted. Some anxiety also appears to have a motivating influence, while anxiety in excess is detrimental. Combs and Snygg (1959) argue that anxiety narrows perception. West et al. (1969) present evidence that high test anxiety decreases one's ability to select relevant from irrelevant information. One could tentatively conclude that extremes of anxiety either high or low are associated with lower performance than are more moderate levels. Moderate anxiety is related to motivation in that it appears to aid performance.

Affect and Cognitive Processes. There seems to be agreement that affect influences the cognitive processes. Some evidence exists that affect may have specific effects on sensation and perception. Findings from a series of studies (Cowen & Beier, 1952; Fulkerson, 1957; McGinnies, 1949) indicate that "taboo" words (words which have negative affective connotation or are "socially unacceptable") are more difficult to recognize than affectively neutral words. It may be that subjects in these studies recognized the words, but were reluctant to say them. Tomkins (Tomkins & Izard, 1965) presented subjects with contrasting pictures in a stereoscope. A photograph with a smiling face was presented on one side of the stereoscope and a photo of the same person with a contemptuous face on the other. Subjects with a humanistic orientation and positive feelings about themselves and others tended to see the smiling face. Subjects with more negative feelings about themselves and others tended to see the contemptuous face.

Projection, the imposition of one's own characteristics on stimuli, exemplifies the influence of affect on what is sensed and perceived. During the administration of the Rorschach ink blots (a projective test) examiners note that subjects "project" or "see" that which is consistent with their feelings, fears, etc. The same phenomenon occurs with other projective techniques. Frequently subjects' reports from item to item are on a related theme—the person who feels threatened reports "seeing" threatening people and situations. These observations and the above findings lend support to the hypothesis that affect influences sensation and perception, that we see what is consistent with our idiosyncratic frame of reference.

Bugelski (1956) and McGeoch and Irion (1952) note some consensus in psychology as to the influence of affect on learning and retention. Apparently affectively charged material is retained better than more neutral material, and pleasant topics often better retained than unpleasant topics.* Kleinsmith and Kaplan (1963, 1964) found that high arousal inhibited immediate recall of paired associates, but facilitated long-term retention when compared to low-arousal associates. Earlier Worchel (1955) found that associates with negative affective material are not retained as well as associates with neutral material. Izard et al., after a series of investigations, conclude

> Pictures with different affect scale ratings evoke significantly different cognitive performances (learning rates). ... Both intensity *and* quality of affect are significant factors in altering behavior. ... The relationship or relevance of the affect-inducing stimuli (e.g., whether they are figure or ground) to concomitant or subsequent cognitive processes (e.g., learning) is of great importance in determining the influence of affect on performance [Tomkins & Izard, 1965].

There is also evidence which indicates that problem solving is influenced by affective variables. The question primarily is "What is the effect of emotional content on reasoning?"

Janis and Frick (1943) investigated the influence of subjects' attitude on solving syllogisms. Sixteen syllogisms, eight valid and eight invalid, were presented. Syllogisms were selected with a minimum of neutral content so as to arouse agreement or disagreement. There

---

*Dutta and Kanungo (1975) in a series of recent investigations report that retention of affective material is a function of the intensity of the affect rather than the quality (pleasant or unpleasant) of the affect.

were four categories: valid with agreement or disagreement and invalid with agreement or disagreement. Subjects were told to judge the syllogisms as to whether or not the conclusions followed logically from the premises. After judging the syllogisms, subjects were given an attitude test made up of the conclusions of the syllogisms. Subjects reported whether they agreed or disagreed with the statements. The investigators found more agree-valid errors and more disagree-valid errors than disagree-invalid errors. This supports the notion that people are more likely to accept invalid conclusions if they agree and are more likely to be critical of valid conclusions if they disagree. In later studies (Frase, 1966; Kaufmann & Goldstein, 1967; Lefford, 1946) support was found for this same conclusion.

Thistlewaite (1950) constructed test items so that they were nearly identical except for the variation in emotional content. College-age groups from various regions of the United States were tested. Statistical interpretation indicated less error on the neutral items than on the emotionally toned items.

In summary, considerable empirical evidence exists indicating the impact of affect on the basic processes involved in human cognition. The residues of experience which result when a person encounters an event—with resulting stimulation—is not only a function of the event itself and its stimulating potential but also the affective state of the person.

Chapter 9 presents a discussion of attitude learning in the school context.

Values

By value we mean a relatively enduring sense of worth or "goodness" attributed to classes of experiences, behaviors, and beliefs. In this section we will discuss the impact of human values and valuing on how we think, sense, and perceive. In the section on affect, it was noted that values are related to affect. If we value something, affect obviously is involved. We also invest value in our concepts and structures and seek to maintain them. This consistency is another source of stability and resistance to change.

Rokeach (1968) has drawn a distinction between terminal and instrumental values. Terminal values are characterized as desirable *end states of existence,* and instrumental values are desired *modes of behavior.* Values are more general than affects or attitudes which are tied to specific objects and settings in that they constitute standards by which to judge the worth of classes of behaviors and goals. Thus, while a person may learn hundreds and thousands of attitudes throughout a lifetime, that person may acquire relatively few, perhaps only a few dozen, values.

Postman, Bruner, and McGinnies (1948) found that subjects recognized tachistoscopically presented words related to their highly prized values more rapidly than they would recognize words related to values not so highly prized. In another study, Bruner and Goodman (1947) found support for an influence of value on perception. The task for members of an experimental group of ten year olds was to adjust the size of a light spot by turning a knob until the spot was the same size as the subjects thought coins to be. The experimental subjects first estimated from memory the size of coins from a penny to a half dollar. The control subjects followed the same procedure, but were told to estimate the sizes of cardboard disks cut to the same size as the coins.

The results indicated that the coin size was overestimated significantly in comparison to the judgment of the cardboard disks. The percentage of overestimations ranged from 15 percent of the penny to nearly 40 percent of the quarter with 35 percent overestimations of the half dollar. The neutral stimuli were not subject to overestimation. Moreover youngsters from "poor homes" drastically overestimated the size of coins compared to children from "rich homes." In yet another study by Ashley, Harper, and Runyon (1951) subjects were shown a metal slug. They were told that the slug was lead, silver, white gold, or platinum. The subjects' estimations of the size of the slug were positively correlated with the "value" (or what they were told about value) and the amount of overestimation.

Political values appear to be a source for "distortion" in cognition. Edwards (1941) noted that political orientation influenced recognition. In another study, Levine and Murphy (1943) found evidence that political values influence original learning and, later, retention of material. Procommunist and anticommunist college students were identified. Each group read and reproduced both pro- and anticommunistic prose passages. The procommunist students learned the anticommunist material more slowly and forgot the material more rapidly. Procommunist students learned the procommunist material more rapidly and forgot it more slowly than the anticommunist students.

Rokeach (1971) reports results of a series of three studies on the experimental modification of values, attitudes, and behaviors of college students. His concern was with the terminal values of freedom and equality, attitudes toward civil rights and actual participation in civil rights activities. Through a clever procedure whereby students were caused to become aware of discrepancies between their values, attitudes, and behaviors, tendencies to change in the direction of consistency were noted. Moreover these changes persisted over periods of time ranging up to twenty-one months.

Six Components of the Frame of Reference

In the same set of investigations, Rokeach noted the interesting result that value change typically preceded attitude change. These findings taken together suggest that attitudes (i.e., evaluations) of specific beliefs about things may vary or be altered only within the scope of a more general value system. That is, a person's values limit the range of specific attitudes that person may hold. And furthermore, in order for major shifts in attitudes to occur, for example, from a strong pro-civil rights to a strong anti-civil rights position, changes in the corresponding values are indicated. Clearly more research is needed to determine the necessary and sufficient conditions for attitude and value change.

In general then, evidence suggests that values influence perception, judgment, recognition, learning, and memory. It is also probable that there is a great deal of resistance to responding in ways that are inconsistent to values. There is evidence that *forcing* individuals to behave in ways that are inconsistent with their values will have the effect of producing motivation for change. The tendency is toward consonance between values and behavior. We will, when relatively free, respond in ways consistent with our values. When forced to respond in ways inconsistent with our values, we experience pressure to change our values, behavior, or beliefs, or all three (Deutsch & Collins, 1951; Festinger, 1957; Festinger & Carlsmith, 1959; Rokeach, 1971).

Allport and Lindzey (1960) developed an instrument called the *Study of Values* which is based on the theoretical work of the German philosopher, Spranger. One's value orientations are indicated by forced choice responses to preferred activities and beliefs. Keyed values include theoretical, economic, political, aesthetic, social, and religious, and ipsative (personal profile) scores can be obtained for relative positions of a person's responses on these six value factors.

Research in values indicates that individuals form associations more rapidly when they are congruent with their own values (Bousfield & Samborski, 1955) and are more efficient in grouping and retaining such congruent items (Mayzner & Tressalt, 1955).

Based upon his experiences in psychotherapy as contrasted with laboratory research findings, Carl Rogers (1964) has concluded that our values and valuing processes have effects on how we "utilize all the richness of our cognitive learning and functioning." He further states, "Man has within him an organismic basis for valuing. To the extent that he can be freely in touch with this valuing process in himself, he will behave in ways which are self-enhancing" [p. 21].

Thus it appears that theory, research, and clinical experience support the notion that values play important roles in influencing cognition, along with the other factors in the frame of reference.

Needs

Several investigators indicate that an organism's basic needs in part influence perception. Levine, Chein, and Murphy (1942) deprived humans of food for one, three, six, and nine hours. Subjects reported what the objects were in pictures distorted through a ground glass screen. There were pictures of food, miscellaneous household articles, and meaningless figures. There was a relationship between the length of deprivation and the frequency of the identification of food objects. That is, those subjects deprived of food for longer periods tended to identify any of the pictures as photographs of food objects.

In one study involving cats (Hernández-Péon et al., 1956) the experimenters were able to record signals from the brains of cats. When a clicking sound was made the neural record indicated a change in the cat's brain. A jar containing two live mice was placed before the cat. Again the clicking sound was made near the cat's ear, but the neural record in the brain indicated no change. Apparently the animal was attending so closely to the mice that the signal did not reach the brain. Similarly, these investigators found that a strong olfactory stimulus—fish odors—was sufficient in distracting the cat's attention to block off the auditory input to the brain.

Postman and Crutchfield (1952) found that needs act as a device in the selection of stimuli in a problem-solving task. Those stimuli which "fit" a need are attended to over other potential stimuli.

McClelland and Atkinson (1948) also studied the effects of food deprivation on responses to neutral stimuli. The investigators projected ambiguous stimuli on a screen and required the subjects to make associations to them. As the time of deprivation increased, the number of food-related responses increased. A related effect was found by Atkinson and McClelland (1948) in the area of thematic apperception. Subjects wrote stories about eight ambiguous pictures after one, four, or sixteen hours of food deprivation. A positive relation was found between hours of deprivation and the number of food deprivation themes written by the subjects. Expressed need for food and activity for overcoming deprivation also increased with increased deprivation.

Maslow (1968) has presented an explanation of needs consistent with his theories of *motivation and self-actualization*. According to Maslow it is necessary to satisfy needs lower in the hierarchy before the higher ones can come to motivate behavior. The first four needs in Maslow's list are termed *deficiency needs* in that a person is motivated to behave in order to fulfill some lack. The last two are characterized as *being needs* related to self-directed behavior.

Six Components of the Frame of Reference

In ascending order the six needs Maslow posits are:

1. Physiological needs (hunger, thirst, sex, etc.)
2. Safety needs (health, shelter, and physical protection)
3. Love and belonging needs (affiliation)
4. Esteem needs (achievement and recognition)
5. Self-actualization needs
6. Needs to know and understand

Another way of distinguishing between the deficiency (1-4) and being needs (5 and 6) is in terms of dependency upon one's environment and other people within it. The being needs involve a considerable amount of self-sufficiency, whereas the individual motivated by love, belonging, and esteem needs is dependent upon others for approval and recognition—social "nourishment." It is probably difficult to get a hungry child (level 1) to study algebra (unless one uses food as a reinforcer!). Once levels 1 and 2 needs are met, people will move for social acceptance and approval. It is probably somewhat easier to make recognition a consequence of studying algebra than it is to use food reinforcers. However, it could be argued that a goal of education is to have people move in the direction of self-actualization, a condition in which other persons are not merely objects to be used in satisfying needs at levels 3 and 4. Thus a person motivated by the higher level needs would be more free and able to accept others as individuals.

The theory appears to be plausible, but there has not yet been a sufficiently large body of empirical evidence to test it. In order to investigate properly the hierarchy, it will be necessary to provide operational definitions of the constructs, especially at the higher levels 5 and 6.

Interests

No specific study known to the authors isolates the influence of interests on sensation, perception, and cognition. However, the evidences for affect, value, and need noted above are related to this issue in that humans are interested in those things they feel strongly about—things which they need and value. We may say then that at least indirect psychological evidence does exist for such an influence. A person's everyday experience should provide some support for the notion that interests influence sensation and perception.

Blair, Jones, and Simpson (1975, pp. 202ff) refer to interests as specific positive attitudes with a motivational component. They regard interests as causes of seeking behavior. Interests may be based on needs in that in response to a need an individual might be expected to become interested in activities which lead to satisfaction of that need. Thus a pupil's interest in sports might reflect needs at a variety of levels in Maslow's hierarchy such as level 2 (e.g., health and fitness needs), level 3 (e.g., team camaraderie), level 4 (e.g., recognition), etc.

Anecdotal evidence may be cited to show that when some event occurs in our immediate environment which is consistent with our interests we may be more likely to sense and perceive it. The first author's son Kenyon by age three had developed a consuming interest in trains. During an automobile drive many "attention worthy" objects were available to him, but trains and train-related objects were selected for attention. The author or his wife may not have noticed a train or track (with semaphore!) nearby, but the reader may rest assured that train-related stimuli were brought to their attention. Likewise if Kenyon were watching television, or playing with friends, he might not hear a call to dinner. How much of the latter illustration is due to selective attention and how much is attributable to other factors is a matter for conjecture.

All normal people have the ability to concentrate on those things in which they are interested and this reduces the salience of other potential stimuli. In other terms of problem solving and thinking such channelization is necessary, for one does not have the capacity to respond simultaneously to every potential internal and external stimulus. If such were not the case, sustained and complex behaviors such as problem solving could not occur.

The total influence of interest tends to place us in situations in which we will perceive stimuli that are consistent with those interests as well as channelizing our attention in certain directions—fixing our attention on certain stimuli out of all the potential stimuli which constantly surround us all. There is also the cumulative effect of these two. Over the years of experience what has been learned in terms of concepts, structures, and affect may serve to intensify the influence of interests on sensation, perception, and cognition.

Strong (1943) has done extensive work in the measurement of vocational interests. Strong's work involved the improvement of job placement counseling by assessing a person's interests by comparing them to those of persons successful in different occupations. Long-term job success predictions have been made on the basis of such assessments of interests (Strong, 1955). It seems that only fairly recently has an emphasis been placed upon pupil interests in planning instructional programs and materials despite the obvious motivational values of such practices.

Summary of the Frame of Reference Model

In the foregoing sections the influence of the six components of the frame of reference on cognition has been discussed. It has been shown how these six components serve to direct that which stimulates humans, that which evokes human responses, and that about which humans think.

The following formula serves to summarize the model.

$$Bp = f(Ie, Si, Bc)$$

Where Ie = external stimuli
    Si = internal stimulation (Si = Sie + Sip)
    Sie = internal stimuli evoked by external ambient energy
    Sip = internal stimuli present (not Ie based interests, needs)
    Bc = behavioral capability or capacity of the person in that class of behaviors
    Bp = the probability of a specific behavior

A pure stimulus-response formula following Skinner's model would be B = f (Se) (see figure 4) or behavior is a function of external stimulation. Reinforcements in Skinner's model are based in the environment. Reinforcement (Se) controls behavior. This would be strictly a linear, cause-effect explanation of behavior. Lewin's model B = f(P,E) (behavior is a function of the person's characteristics and abilities and his environment) is much more relativistic than B = f (Se). (See figure 5.) Lewin's model is very general but it does highlight

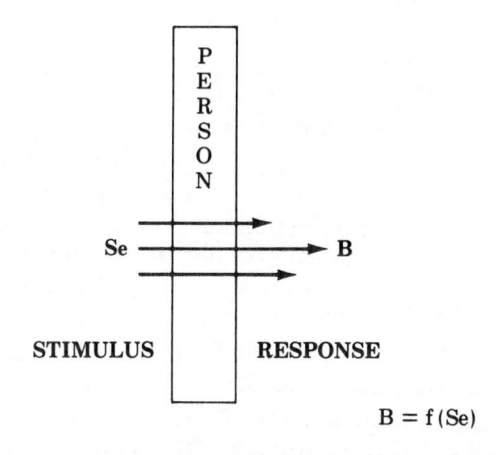

Figure 4. Skinner's explanation of behavior in which behavior (B) is a function (f) of stimuli emanating from the environment (Se).

$$B = f(P, E)$$

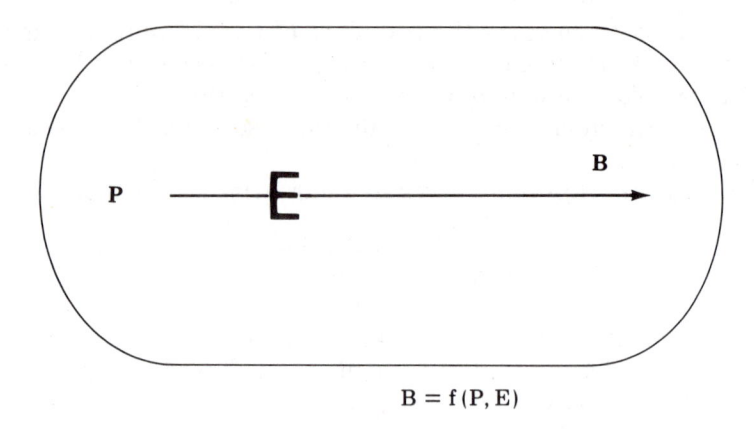

Figure 5. Lewin's field theory showing that behavior (B) is a function (f) of the person (P) and the environment (E).

the interaction of the person's characteristics with enrironmental variables (E) in explaining behavior (B).

Our formulation may be considered an extension of Lewin's in which personal characteristics are specified more clearly. In our model (figure 6) the probability of a specific behavior is a joint, interacting function of the internal energy evoked by external ambient energy (energy outside the person or Ie) plus the internal stimuli (Si) which are the stimuli internal to the person—stimuli emerging from the autonomic nervous system—and the six states-processes plus the response capabilities of the person—his repertoire of skills and abilities. Si is composed of stimuli of two classes: (1) Sie or internal stimuli evoked by or habitually associated with specific external stimuli and (2) Sip, those internal stimuli present in the person but not evoked by specific external stimuli. For example, the sight of the United Nations building may evoke in a person specific memories (internal stimuli, Sie). However, these may not be the only internal stimuli present at that moment for the person may also be stimulated at that time by some physiological need such as hunger. Figure 6 shows some of the topics discussed herein. Behavior would be a result of interaction between the components noted in figure 6.

It should be noted that Rotter (1954, pp. 108-10) and Dulany (1967) have presented similar formulation attempts to provide for the prediction of behavior or behavior potential. In the former case, Rotter's constructs were expectancy and reinforcement value. These can be considered to be specific instances of what we have called *Sip* and *Sie*, respectively. In addition, Rotter has posited a concept of need

Six Components of the Frame of Reference

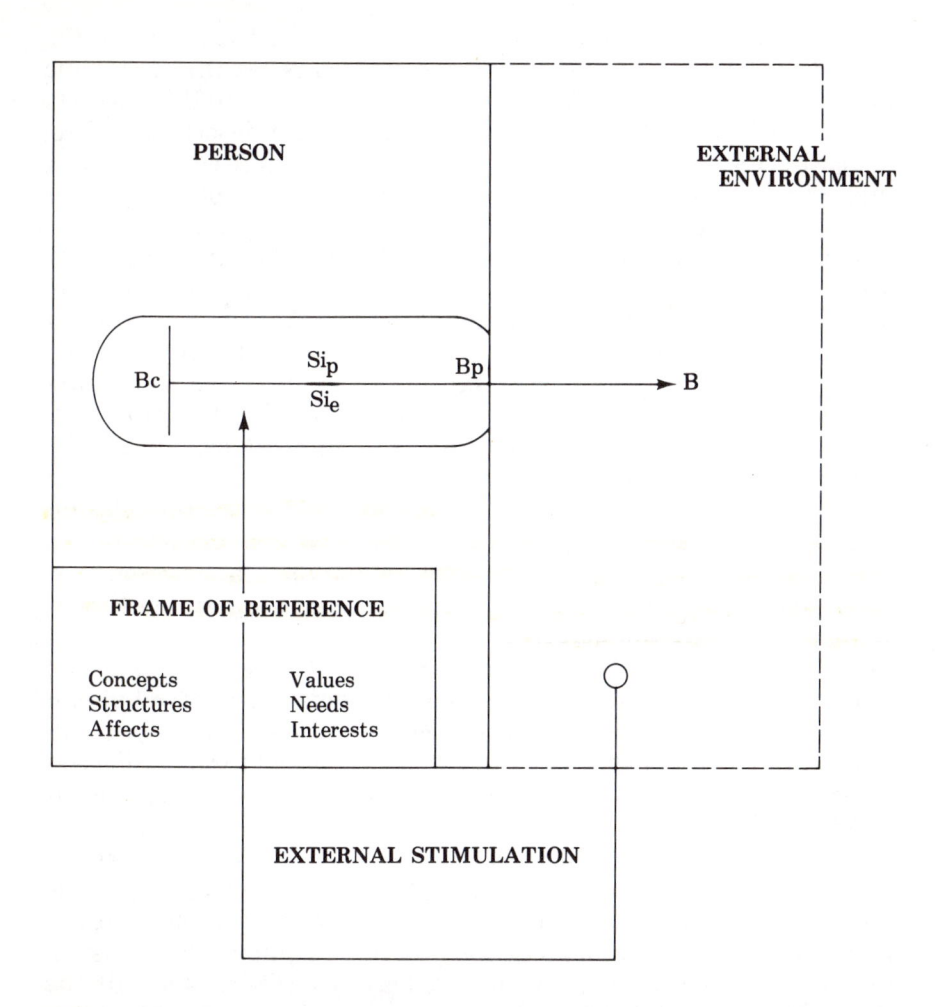

Figure 6. The probability of a specific behavior (Bp) is a function (f) of external stimuli (Ie), internal stimulation (Si), and behavioral capacity (Bc) of the person for that class of behavior. Internal stimulation (Si) consists of the internal stimuli evoked by external ambient energy (Sie) and internal stimuli present (Sip).

potential as a function of freedom of movement and need value. The constructs are closely related to the section of the frame of reference which we have called needs.

Dulany (1967), on the other hand, has used the constructs *behavioral hypothesis* (what a person thinks he should do), as well as the *hypothesis regarding the distribution of reinforcement* (the likely

79

consequences of specific alternative acts), and the *hypothesis of the significance of a reinforcer*. This last construct is like the need value notion of Rotter, and the first two relate respectively to the interests and structures aspects of the frame of reference described before. Using this formulation, Dulany has found some impressive results in improving upon stimulus-response theory in attempts to predict specific behavior in laboratory situations.

All three of these models, ours, Rotter's, and Dulany's, represent attempts to add cognitive components to the understanding and prediction of behavior. They are in a sense reactions to the strict external stimulus binding of behaviorist stimulus-response theory.

This is, of course, a complex picture of human behavior, but behavior is, in fact, much more complex. This model, like the others to which we have referred, represents a drastically simplified attempt to integrate the topics typically studied by psychologists attempting to explain learning and behavior. The frame of reference provides an historical continuity to the individual's behavior, but its six aspects are best viewed as sets of continuous variables and not fixed entities. The frame of reference is dynamic and ever-changing; it is only that the dynamism has a continuity.

One caution is appropriate. This frame of reference model contains only in a small way the possibilities of the social bases of individual behavior. So much of our behavior is socially rooted. Indeed it is difficult at times to know if we are viewing the world through our personal, individual eyes or if we are only reflecting social perceptions. It is known that group judgements and even perceptions do influence individual judgements and perceptions (Asch, 1956; Sherif et al., 1961). The apparently normal individual may respond very inhumanely when under group pressure to do so (Milgram, 1964). We are all swayed in relative degrees by group perceptions, judgements, norms, and pressures. This model may leave you, the reader, with the idea of the stalwart, lonely individual separate and distinct from his social, cultural context. Such is not the case. Supporting this caution lies the truism that the frame of reference is embedded in the many general sociocultural bases and is shaped in part by society in the form of persons who influence some control over the individual's behavior through reinforcement, response guidance, and imitation processes.

Educational Implications

This model of learning and behavior has implications for education at each stage of instruction. Each component of the frame of reference should be considered during goal setting, during the assessment of students' capabilities and inclinations, during the planning and

Educational Implications

conducting of learning experiences, and during evaluation. The complexity and the dynamism of behavior which are accented by the model should also be considered at each stage of instruction.

At the first stage of instruction, goal setting, the planners should carefully consider the frames of reference of the students. The goals should be based in part on the concepts and structures already attained by the students. Also the affects, values, needs, and interests should be considered carefully. Hopefully goals should be selected which are congruent with these components of the frame of reference.

At stage two, preassessment, a direct evaluation of capabilities (concepts and structures) and of inclinations (affects, values, needs, and interests) must be made to determine the readiness of the students. Unless the students have the concepts and structures to build upon and expand, the instruction may be futile. The other four components not only help to determine readiness but also determine motivation. The teacher should attempt to relate to students how the instruction relates to their affects, values, needs, and interests.

At the third and fourth stages of instruction, the six components of the frame of reference may suggest that the planned experiences be directed not only toward cognitive change (concepts and structures) but also toward attitudinal, valuational, and emotional change. Experiences should be planned which touch on the student's affects, needs, values, and interests. Experiences should be planned which help the student to relate the concepts and structures to the other components of the frame of reference. For example, in units on American government, students might be given opportunities to discover and relate the impact of government on their own personal lives and how governmental actions theoretically at least are designed according to the values, affects, needs, and interests of the citizens.

During these two stages—selecting and guiding the experiences—the teacher must be sensitive to *selective* attention which comes about as a result of the frame of reference. The student tends to perceive and process new stimuli in terms of the frame of reference. The teacher must check with individual students periodically and note how the student is perceiving and interpreting the information and experiences.

At the final stage of instruction (evaluation) each component of the frame of reference suggests points for the evaluation of instruction. The component of concepts consists of the more or less isolated concepts presented in the program. Here the teacher may list the concepts taught and sample the student's knowledge of them. The same is true for the structure or the general principles and organized groupings or concepts which were taught. (How well did the students organize and relate the concepts to one another?) The teacher should also focus on affects, values, and interests. (To what extent did attitudes, values, and interests change as a result of the unit?) Also, the extent to which the unit influenced the needs of the student and the extent to which needs were met by the unit should be ascertained.

Discussion Questions

1. Have you been able to identify examples of resistance to change in pupils and examples of overcoming resistance to change on the part of teachers? Do you observe any consistency in these examples (within your group)?
2. What is the significance of "residues of experience" in pupils for educational decision making on the part of teachers?
3. Consider the parts of the frame of reference separately. Which of these does a teacher influence most? Which least? Which can a teacher use to best advantage?
4. If people idiosyncratically develop psychological meaning (e.g., have their own private world), how is communication possible at all?
5. Some argue that education is essentially an intellectual pursuit of truth and beauty. Others say that it needs to be intensely practical. Can you distinguish between *education* and *training* on these terms? Is there room in schools for both? In schools of education?
6. How can anxiety be shown to have a debilitating effect on performance in some studies and a facilitating effect in others?
7. What is a tachistoscope? How has it been used in psychological research? How could it be used in education?
8. Does a teacher have anything to do with the learning of attitudes and values? What?
9. Rokeach (pp. 72-73) found that for a major shift in attitudes to take place, values had to change first. How do you make sense of this?
10. Look at Maslow's hierarchy of needs (p. 75). Of what uses can these ideas be to teachers?
11. Imagine that you are a classroom teacher in a subject area of your choice. Name three behaviors (specific) that you expect your pupils will not have at the beginning of your class (unit) that you would like them to have (be able to do) at the end. Name three that they *can* (or may) be able to do at first that you would like to extinguish (have them stop doing) before the end. Specify the situations under which these occur.

12. In question 11, what procedures will be necessary to accomplish the desired learning and extinction effects?
13. What is the probable origin of the behaviors noted in question 11?
14. What part does motivation play in questions 11, 12, and 13?

Recommended Readings

Bridgman, P. W. *The nature of physical theory.* Princeton: Princeton University Press, 1964.

Coleman, J. A. *Relativity for the layman.* New York: Signet, 1954.

Danto, A., & Morgenbesser, S. (Eds.) *Philosophy of science.* New York: World Publishing Co., 1960.

Frank, P. *Modern science and its philosophy.* New York: Collier, 1961.

Gregory, R. L. *Eye and brain, the psychology of seeing.* New York: McGraw-Hill, 1966.

March, A., & Freeman, I. M. *The new world of physics.* New York: Vintage, 1963.

Pepper, S. C. *World hypotheses.* Berkeley, Calif.: University of California Press, 1972.

Wilman, C. W. *Seeing and perceiving.* New York: Pergamon, 1966.

References

Allport, G. W., Vernon, P. E., & Lindzey, G. *A study of values.* Boston: Houghton Mifflin, 1960.

Anderson, R. C., & Ortony, A. On putting apples into bottles—a problem of polysemy. *Cognitive Psychology,* 1975, *7,* 167-80.

Asch, S. E. Studies of independence and conformity: 1. A minority of one against a unanimous majority. *Psychological Monographs,* 1956, *70,* Whole No. 416.

Ashley, W. R., Harper, R. S., & Runyon, D. L. The perceived size of coins in normal and hypnotically induced economic states. *American Journal of Psychology,* 1951, *64,* 564-72.

Atkinson, J. W., & McClelland, D. C. The projective expression of needs II: The effect of different intensities of the hunger drive on thematic apperception. *Journal of Experimental Psychology,* 1948, *38,* 643-58.

Ausubel, D. P. *Educational psychology: A cognitive view.* New York: Holt, Rinehart & Winston, Inc., 1968.

Ausubel, D. P. The use of advance organizers in the learning and retention of meaningful verbal material. *Journal of Educational Psychology,* 1960, *51,* 267-72.

Ausubel, D. P., & Fitzgerald, D. The role of discriminability in meaningful verbal learning and retention. *Journal of Educational Psychology,* 1961, *52,* 266-74.

Ausubel, D. P., & Fitzgerald, D. Organizer, general background, and antecedent learning variables in sequential verbal learning. *Journal of Educational Psychology,* 1962, *53,* 243-49.

Bagby, J. W. A cross-cultural study of perceptual predominance in binocular rivalry. *Journal of Abnormal and Social Psychology,* 1957, *54,* 331-34.

Bigge, M. L. *Learning theories for teachers.* New York: Harper & Row, 1964.

Blair, G. M., Jones, R. S., & Simpson, R. H. *Educational psychology.* (4th ed.) New York: Macmillan, 1975.

Bousfield, W. A. The occurrence of clustering in the recall of randomly arranged associates. *Journal of General Psychology,* 1953, *49,* 229-40.

Bousfield, W. A., & Samborski, G. The relationship between strength of values and the meaningfulness of value words. *Journal of Personality,* 1955, *23,* 375-80.

Bruner, J. S., & Goodman, C. D. Value and need as organizing factors in perception. *Journal of Abnormal and Social Psychology,* 1947, *42,* 33-44.

Bruner, J. S., & Minturn, A. L. Perceptual identification and perceptual organization. *Journal of General Psychology,* 1955, *53,* 21-28.

Bruner, J. S., & Olver, R. R. Development of equivalence transformation in children. *Monograph of the Society for Research in Child Development,* 1963, *28,* 125-41.

Bruner, J. S., & Potter, M. C. Interference in visual recognition. *Science,* 1964, *144,* 424-25.

Bugelski, B. R. *The psychology of learning.* New York: Holt, Rinehart & Winston, 1956.

Bugelski, B. R., & Alampay, D. A. The role of frequency in developing perceptual sets. *Canadian Journal of Psychology,* 1961, *15,* 205-11.

Campbell, V., & Freeman, J. Some functions of experimentally induced language in perceptual learning. *Perceptual and Motor Skills,* 1955, *5,* 71-79.

References

Cantril, H. *The why of man's experience.* New York: Macmillan, 1950.

Carmichael, L., Hogan, H. F., & Walter, A. A. An experimental study of the effect of language on the reproduction of visually perceived form. *Journal of Experimental Psychology,* 1932, *15,* 73-86.

Combs, A. W., & Snygg, D. L. *Individual behavior.* (Rev. ed.) New York: Harper & Row, 1959.

Cowen, E. L., & Beier, E. G. A further study of threat expecting variables in perception. *American Psychologist,* 1952, *7,* 320-21.

Deutsch, M., & Collins, M. E. *Interracial housing: A psychological evaluation of a social experiment.* Minneapolis: University of Minnesota Press, 1951.

Dulany, D. E. Awareness, rules and propositional control: A confrontation with S-R behavioral theory. In T. R. Dixon, & D. L. Horton (Eds.), *Verbal behavior and general behavior theory.* Englewood Cliffs, N. J.: Prentice-Hall, 1967, pp. 340-87.

Dutta, S., & Kanungo, R. N. *Affect and memory: A reformulation.* Oxford: Pergamon, 1975.

Edwards, A. L. Political frames of reference as a factor in influencing perception. *Journal of Abnormal and Social Psychology,* 1941, *36,* 34-50.

English H. B., & English, A. C. *A comprehensive dictionary of psychological and psychoanalytical terms.* New York: David McKay Company, 1958.

Festinger, L. *A theory of cognitive dissonance.* Evanston, Ill.: Row, Peterson, 1957.

Festinger, L., & Carlsmith, J. M. Cognitive consequences of forced compliance. *Journal of Abnormal and Social Psychology,* 1959, *58,* 203-10.

Fishbein, M. (Ed.) *Readings in attitude theory and measurement.* New York: Wiley, 1967.

Frase, L. T. Validity judgments in relation to two sets of terms. *Journal of Educational Psychology,* 1966, *57,* 239-45.

Fulkerson, W. The interaction of frequency, emotional tone, and set in visceral recognition. *Journal of Experimental Psychology,* 1957, *54,* 188-94.

Gaydos, E. J. Intersensory transfer in the discrimination of form. *American Journal of Psychology,* 1956, *11,* 107-10.

Harleston, B. W. Test anxiety and performance in problem-solving situations. *Journal of Personality,* 1962, *30,* 557-73.

Haselrud, G. M. Transfer from context by sub-threshold summation. *Journal of Educational Psychology,* 1959, *50,* 254-58.

Hebb, D. O. *Organization of Behavior.* New York: Wiley, 1949.

Hernández-Péon, R., Scherrer, H., & Jouvet, M. Modification of electric activity in cochlear nucleus during "attention" in unanesthetized cats. *Science,* 1956, *23,* 331-32.

Hewson, M. G. A'Beckett. A Piagetian analysis of intellectual performance on first-year university physics examinations. (Unpublished Master's Thesis) Vancouver: The University of British Columbia, 1971.

Hilgard, E. R., Edgren, R. D., & Irvine, R. P. Errors in transfer following learning with understanding: Further studies with Katona's card trick experiments. *Journal of Experimental Psychology,* 1954, *47,* 457-64.

Hilgard, E. R., Irvine, R. P., & Whipple, J. E. Rote memorization, understanding, and transfer: An extension of Katona's card trick experiments. *Journal of Experimental Psychology,* 1953, *46,* 288-92.

Immergluck, L. The role of set in perceptual judgement. *Journal of Psychology,* 1952, *34,* 181-89.

Inhelder, B., & Piaget, J. *The growth of logical thinking from childhood to adolescence.* New York: Basic Books, 1958.

Ittelson, W. H., & Cantril, H. *Perception: A transactional approach.* Garden City, N. Y.: Doubleday, 1954.

Janis, V., & Frick, F. The relationship between attitudes toward conclusions and errors in judging validity of syllogisms. *Journal of Experimental Psychology,* 1943, *33,* 73-77.

Jenkin, N. Affective processes in perception. *Psychological Bulletin,* 1957, *54,* 100-27.

Jenkins, J. J., & Russell, W. A. Associative clustering during recall. *Journal of Abnormal and Social Psychology,* 1952, *47,* 818-21.

Judd, C. H. Practice and its effects on the perception of illusions. *Psychological Review,* 1902, *9,* 27-39.

Judson, A. J., Cofer, C. N., & Gelfand, S. Reasoning as an associative process: II. Direction in problem solving as a function of prior reinforcement of relevant responses. *Psychological Reports,* 1956, *2,* 501-07.

Kagan, J. On the need for relativism. *American Psychologist,* 1967, *22,* 131-41.

Katona, G. *Organizing and memorizing.* New York: Columbia University Press, 1940.

Katz, P. Effects of labels on children's perception and discrimination learning. *Journal of Educational Psychology,* 1963, *66,* 423-28.

Kaufmann, H., & Goldstein, S. The effects of emotional value of conclusion upon distortion in syllogistic reasoning. *Psychonomic Science,* 1967, *7,* 367-68.

References

Kleinsmith, L. J., & Kaplan, S. Interaction of arousal and recall interval in nonsense syllable paired-associate learning. *Journal of Experimental Psychology,* 1964, *67,* 124-26.

Kleinsmith, L. J., & Kaplan, S. Paired associate learning as a function of arousal and interpolated interval. *Journal of Experimental Psychology,* 1963, *65,* 190-93.

Kurtz, K., & Kooland, C. The effects of verbalization during observation of stimulus objects upon accuracy of recognition and recall. *Journal of Experimental Psychology,* 1953, *45,* 157-64.

Lefford, A. The influence of emotional subject matter on logical reasoning. *Journal of General Psychology,* 1946, *34,* 127-51.

Levine, J. M., & Murphy, G. The learning and forgetting of controversial material. *Journal of Abnormal and Social Psychology,* 1943, *38,* 507-17.

Levine, R., Chein, I., & Murphy, G. The relation of the intensity of a need to the amount of perceptual distortion: A preliminary report. *Journal of Psychology,* 1942, *13,* 283-93.

McClelland, D. C., & Atkinson, J. W. The projective expression of needs: I. The effect of different intensities of the hunger drive on perception. *Journal of Psychology,* 1948, *25,* 205-22.

McGeoch, J. A., & Irion, A. L. *The psychology of human learning.* (2nd ed.) New York: Longmans, 1952.

McGinnies, E. Emotionality and perceptional defense. *Psychological Review,* 1949, *56,* 244-51.

Maier, N. R. F. Reasoning in humans: I. On direction. *Journal of Comparative Psychology,* 1930, *10,* 115-43.

Mandler, G. Organization and memory. In K. W. Spence and J. T. Spence (Eds.), *The psychology of learning and motivation.* New York: Academic Press, 1966.

March, A. M., & Freeman, I. M. *The new world of physics.* New York: Vintage, 1963.

Maslow, A. H. *Toward a psychology of being.* (2nd ed.) New York: Van Nostrand, 1968.

Mayzner, M. S., Jr., & Tresselt, M. E. Concept span as a composite function of personal values, anxiety and rigidity. *Journal of Personality,* 1955, *24,* 20-33.

Merrill, M. D., & Stolurow, L. M. Hierarchical preview versus problem oriented review in learning an imaginary science. *American Educational Research Journal,* 1966, *3,* 251-62.

Milgram, S. Group pressure and action against a person. *Journal of Abnormal and Social Psychology,* 1964, *69,* 137-43.

Miller, G. A. The magical number seven plus or minus two: Some limits on our capacity for processing information. *Psychological Review,* 1956, *63,* 81-96.

Murray, H. A. The effect of fear upon the estimates of the maliciousness of other personalities. *Journal of Social Psychology,* 1933, *4,* 310-29.

Olver, R. R., & Hornsby, J. R. On equivalence. In J. S. Bruner et al., *Studies in cognitive growth.* New York: Wiley, 1966.

Overing, R. L. R., & Travers, R. M. W. Effect upon transfer of variations in training conditions. *Journal of Educational Psychology,* 1966, *57,* 179-88.

Piaget, J., & Inhelder, B. *The psychology of the child.* New York: Basic Books, 1969.

Postman, L. Learned principles of organization in memory. *Psychological Monographs,* 1954, *68* (Whole No. 374).

Postman, L., Bruner, J. S., & McGinnies, E. Personal values as selective factors in perception. *Journal of Abnormal and Social Psychology,* 1948, *43,* 142-54.

Postman, L., & Crutchfield, R. S. The interaction of need, set and stimulus structure in a cognitive task. *American Journal of Psychology,* 1952, *65,* 196-217.

Potter, M. C. On perceptual recognition. In J. S. Bruner et al., *Studies in cognitive growth.* New York: Wiley, 1966.

Reynolds, J. H. Cognitive transfer in verbal learning. *Journal of Educational Psychology,* 1966, *57,* 382-88.

Rogers, C. R. Toward a modern approach to values: The valuing process in the mature person. *Journal of Abnormal and Social Psychology,* 1964, *68,* 160-67. (Reprinted in C. R. Rogers, & B. Stevens, *Person to person: The problem of being human. A new trend in psychology.* New York: Pocket Books, 1971, 4-21.)

Rokeach, M. *Beliefs, attitudes and values: A theory of organization and change.* San Francisco: Jossey-Bass, 1968.

Rokeach, M. Long-range experimental modification of values, attitudes and behavior. *American Psychologist,* 1971, *26,* 453-59.

Rotter, J. B. *Social learning and clinical psychology.* New York: Prentice-Hall, 1954.

Ruebush, B. K. Interfering and facilitating effects of test anxiety. *Journal of Abnormal and Social Psychology,* 1960, *60,* 205-12.

Sarason, S. B., Davidson, K. S., Lighthall, F. F., Waite, R. R., & Ruebush, B. K. *Anxiety in elementary school children: A report of research.* New York: Wiley, 1960.

Saugstad, P. Problem-solving as dependent upon availability of functions. *British Journal of Psychology,* 1955, *46,* 191-98.

Schultz, C. B. Information seeking following the confirmation or contradiction of beliefs. *Journal of Educational Psychology,* 1974, *66,* 903-10.

References

Sherif, M., Harvey, O. J., White, B. J., Hood, W. R., & Sherif, C. W. *Intergroup Conflict and Cooperation: The Robbers Cave Experiment.* Norman: Institute of Group Relations, University of Oklahoma, 1961.

Siipola, E. M. A group study of some effects of preparatory set. *Psychological Monographs,* 1935, *46* (Whole No. 210), 27-38.

Strong, E. K., Jr. *Vocational interests 18 years after college.* Minneapolis: University of Minnesota Press, 1955.

Strong, E. K., Jr. *Vocational interests in men and women.* Stanford, Calif.: Stanford University Press, 1943.

Thistlewaite, D. Attitude and structure as factors in the distortion of reasoning. *Journal of Abnormal and Social Psychology,* 1950, *45,* 442-58.

Thurstone, L. L. The measurement of social attitudes. *Journal of Abnormal and Social Psychology,* 1931, *26,* 249-60.

Tomkins, S. S., & Izard, C. E., Eds. *Affect, cognition and personality: Empirical studies.* New York: Springer, 1965.

Webb, E. J., Campbell, D. T., Schwartz, R. D., & Sechrest, L. *Unobtrusive measures: Nonreactive research in the social sciences.* Chicago: Rand McNally, 1966.

West, C. K. Theoretical and instrumental intervention or the "medium is the message." *Perceptual and Motor Skills,* 1967, *24,* 753-54.

West, C. K., Lee, J. F., & Anderson, T. H. The influence of test anxiety on the selection of relevant from irrelevant information. *Journal of Educational Research,* 1969, *63,* 51-52.

Worchel, P. Anxiety and repression. *Journal of Abnormal and Social Psychology,* 1955, *50,* 201-05.

Wyer, R. S. *Cognitive Organization and Change: An Information Processing Approach.* New York: Wiley, 1975.

Practical Organizer for Chapter 4

Three of the most important considerations for an instructor involve motivation, reinforcement, and imitation. The effective instructor must be aware constantly of the effects of motivation. Put most succinctly, the instructor has to initiate student action, direct or channelize it, and maintain that action. During many occasions motives or factors internal to the student will suffice to initiate, direct, and maintain the necessary student action. These occasions comprise, perhaps, the times when teaching is least difficult and most productive.

On other instructional occasions, the necessary student action will occur only through instructor-manipulated forces external to the student. At these times the instructor must have a thorough knowledge of reinforcement. The large array of available reinforcers which are presented in this chapter will be of great use to the instructor.

These reinforcers together with the potential imitative influences should, in most instructional situations, provide the necessary external control for the desired student action. An instructor should remember that not only the teacher can be an effective model but also successful students may serve as models for desirable action.

Motivation, Reinforcement, and Imitation 4

In this chapter we discuss interrelated psychological topics—motivation and reinforcement. We will show how the six components of the frame of reference are related to motivation and reinforcement and introduce some new and related research and literature. In view of the educational implications of imitative learning, and since imitation is interrelated with motivation and reinforcement, we will also discuss imitation.

Motivation, Reinforcement, and Imitation

Motivation, reinforcement, and imitation are three extremely important concerns in the psychology of learning. The study of motivation is important because it aids the understanding of why people behave in the ways they do, even when external conditions might seem to direct them into other patterns of behavior. Motivation and the frame of reference are the bases for the conceptualization of humans as dynamic and self-regulating beings. Studies of motivation also aid in understanding the apparent diversity and deep commitments which are characteristic of human behavior. Motivation and stimulation are the two avenues through which behavior is initiated, directed, and maintained.

Reinforcement* is also very important for it is a primary way that persons have of obtaining feedback as to their behavior's effectiveness. The nature of that feedback has much to do with human needs and motives. It is for this reason that reinforcement and motivation are discussed in the same chapter.

Single responses as well as chained behaviors may be learned not only through reinforcement, but also through imitation and combinations of reinforcement and imitation. The knowledge of having more or less accurately copied certain behaviors of prestigious models may be reinforcing. Many reinforcers occur in a social setting seminal for the occurrence of imitation. For these reasons, a discussion of imitation is also included in this chapter.

Motivation

Motives are internal factors related to energizing a person for action, providing direction to a person's behavior, and sustaining the level of activities. The topic of motivation for teachers thus involves students' internal conditions which are related to the five stages of instruction (as discussed in chapter 1).

External conditions (or variables) which are related to behavior are external stimuli. The teacher has two avenues through which appropriate behaviors are induced in students—avenues via motivation and avenues via external stimulation. When the teacher varies external conditions to initiate, direct, and sustain pupil behavior the teacher is stimulating the student with incentives to action. When the teacher uses incentives it is with a view toward appealing to the student's internal motives to initiate, direct, or sustain behavior. The

---

*The reader may wish to refer to chapter 2 for a review of reinforcement in the work of Pavlov and Skinner.

Motivation

teacher is attempting to motivate the student. It is important to note that one does not actually "motivate" another person. One person stimulates another. The difference between motivation and external stimulation is analogous to the difference between established momentum and required push. Differences between "cookie-obtaining behaviors" (motivated behavior) and "room-cleaning behaviors" (externally stimulated behavior) of a five year old are illustrated in the following example.

When Henry at age five wants a cookie, very little pushing, prodding, or nagging is necessary to initiate, direct, or maintain cookie-obtaining behavior. Henry may exhibit very complex patterns of responses in his quest for cookies with very little external stimulation. (Although later we will see that external stimulation is involved and that few, if any, human response patterns are due solely either to motivation or external stimulation—see Figure 7.) Henry may search for a short stool, a chair, or a bar stool which will give him the necessary height. He will place the chair carefully, climb to the counter, crawl several feet to the proper cabinet and search diligently if the cookie jar has been moved. In the case of "cookie-obtaining behavior," motivation is almost sufficient to explain Henry's behavior.

On the other hand, what is necessary for "room-cleaning behavior"? Moderate to massive amounts of external stimulation (bribery, prodding, shouting, nagging) may be necessary even to initiate this behavior. If Henry's mother is fortunate (or if she has taught well), the gentle command, "clean your room," will suffice to get Henry to turn toward his room and perhaps even to take several steps in that direction. The amount of external stimulation necessary may become massive as Henry, instead of actually placing the toy cars scattered throughout his room in his toy box, "drives" them casually in the general direction of the box. Strong external stimuli such as "PLEASE PUT THEM IN THE BOX!" may be necessary.

Such response chains as "room-cleaning behaviors" may be primarily initiated, directed (channelized), and maintained by external stimulation. Yet even that response chain involves a modicum of motivation. Doubtless Henry is motivated to please his mother or to avoid unpleasant consequences to some extent. In the case of "cookie-obtaining behaviors," primarily explainable by motivation, external stimulation played a minor, yet important role, in that sensory input and feedback aided in the location of the chair or the bar stool as well as the location of the cookie jar itself. Some incentive external stimulus, such as a television ad showing a cookie may even have initiated the response chain. Thus it may be seen that both types of forces play important roles in these two response chains. This must be the case for practically all human action.

93

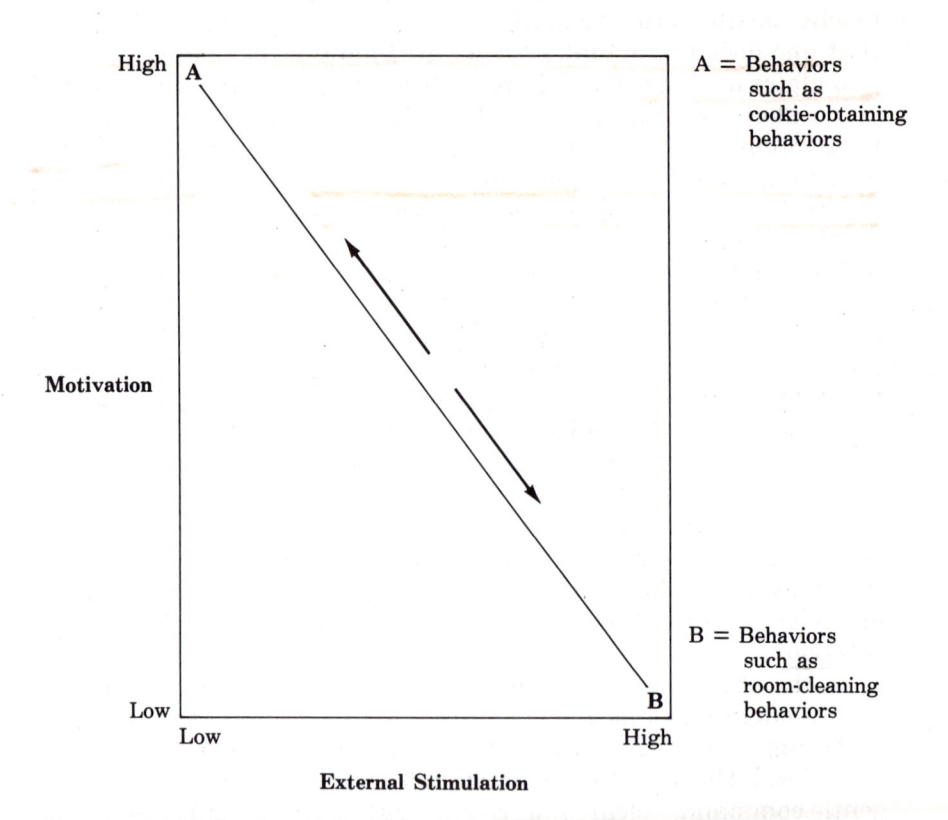

[Figure: A graph with "Motivation" on the y-axis (Low to High) and "External Stimulation" on the x-axis (Low to High). A diagonal line runs from point A (high motivation, low stimulation) down to point B (low motivation, high stimulation), with double arrows along the line. A = Behaviors such as cookie-obtaining behaviors. B = Behaviors such as room-cleaning behaviors.]

Figure 7. Relationship between Motivation and Stimulation

In figure 7, any behavior a person performs may be plotted at some point on the line *AB*. A behavior may be attributable primarily to motivation or to external stimulation, but it is seldom attributable to one or the other alone. It may be that the process of learning involves "moving" responses toward the *A* point of the continuum.

Motivation and the Frame of Reference

While reading chapter 3, the thoughtful reader may have ascertained that the discussion on the frame of reference presented material pertinent to motivation. That is the case. The six components of the frame of reference serve as motives for human action. Humans appear to be motivated to behave consistently with what they know (concepts and structures) as well as by the various affective aspects of their lives (affects, values, interests, and needs). This is true even though the discussion in chapter 3 primarily centered on the influence of the frame of reference on cognition—especially the *input* and *inter-*

Motivation

nal processing dimensions of cognition. The frame of reference as initiating action is depicted in figure 3 in chapter 3.

Persons generally are motivated to (1) maintain and extend their concepts and structures; (2) maintain and proselytize values, beliefs, and interests; and (3) meet the great number and variety of needs which seem necessary to human life.

Needs

Needs have traditionally been defined as "the lack of something which, if present, would tend to further the welfare of the organism or species . . . " (English & English, 1958, p. 338). Without doubt needs are major motives of human behavior. (We will see later that most reinforcers are related to specific postulated needs.) Needs are internal factors which initiate, direct, and sustain activity.

The question then arises: What are the human needs which motivate? Many classification systems have been developed which group needs (see, for example, Maslow, 1954; Murray, 1938). Human behavior appears so diverse in relatively autonomous situations that many different needs must be inferred to help explain the diversity. The existence of such diversity of apparent needs makes a classification system very helpful. Table 3 represents our own conceptualizations of the range and extent of human needs. This classification system seems to more or less exhaust the classes of needs except for aesthetic and religious types of needs.

The Class I needs are those which are basic to living. Unless these needs are satisfied, the organism perishes. In evolutionary and survival terms, the person is aware that these Class I needs are often met in social settings. Man apparently evolved in a social setting. The social setting was apparently not developed *after* the evolution of man. Class II needs are derivable from Class I needs. These secondary needs (Class II) have motivating value of their own. A person may be motivated by these needs whether or not Class I needs are met, although in general these needs decrease in motivating value when Class I needs are not met.

Humans are also aware that Class I needs must be met in the future. What they can learn, know, and understand about themselves and their environment aids them in meeting Class I and Class II needs in the present and in the future. In this sense, needs exist having to do with the maintenance and extension of cognitive life (Class III). The survival and evolutionary value of Class II and Class III needs are apparent.

The tertiary needs may be as basic as any of the primary and secondary needs. In chapter 1, for example, it was seen that continuing external stimulation is necessary, for without it the central

TABLE 3
Three Classes of Human Needs With Appropriate Immediate Reinforcers

Needs	Reinforcers
I. Maintenance of biophysiological life	
A. Food	Meals, snacks, candy, cookies, etc.
B. Water	Needs B through F do not seem appropriate as bases for reinforcers in schools.
C. Oxygen	
D. Elimination	
E. Sex	
F. Shelter	
II. Maintenance and extension of personal and social life	
A. Affection (Murray, 1938)	Isolation from peers, peer contact; teacher acceptance or rejection; feedback on correctness or incorrectness of modeling attempts, etc.
B. Acceptance	
C. Approval	
D. Self-actualization (Maslow, 1954)	
E. Achievement (Atkinson, 1966; Maehr, 1974; Weiner, 1967, 1974)	Praise or reproof. Knowledge of degrees of success and failure.
F. Competence (White, 1959)	Appropriate feedback on how well or how poorly the student has developed, matured, achieved, etc., from teachers, parents, and peers; highly specific and appropriate successes and failures in achievement and personal/social interaction.
G. Adequacy (Combs and Snygg, 1959)	
H. Personal comfort	Attention and respect.
III. The maintenance and extension of cognitive life	
A. Cognizance (Murray, 1938)	Novelty, variety of activity, specific student-generated questions and problems resolved individually or in groups, manipulation of complex objects and ideas, knowledge of correctness of response, *knowing* that one knows, etc.; highly specific and appropriate successes and failures in learning and problem solution.
B. External stimulation (Lilly, 1956; Shurley, 1960)	
C. Curiosity (Berlyne, 1960; Butler, 1953)	
D. Meaning (Frankel, 1963)	
E. Comprehension (Maslow, 1954)	

nervous system ceases to "operate" properly. Exactly *which* need or class of need is basic is a difficult question. One may be required to *know* a great deal before obtaining food, or one may need to be socially accepted before obtaining food in a given situation. Thus it is in-

Motivation

appropriate to rank any one class of needs as more important than any other class.

The reader may not be familiar with some of the psychological terms in table 3. *Achievement motives* are those which have to do with "... an active impulse to undertake a particular achievement-oriented activity" (Maehr & Sjogren, 1971, p. 144). Important variables of the achievement motive are the perceived probability of success, the relative value of the incentives involved, the perceived probability of failures, and pride in achievement (Maehr & Sjogren, 1971). *Self-actualization* (Maslow, 1954) has to do with the development of one's potential and self-acceptance. *Competence* (White, 1959) and *adequacy* (Combs and Snygg, 1959) were discussed in chapter 1.

In the Class III category, *cognizance* (Murray, 1938), *meaning* (Frankel, 1963), and *comprehension* (Maslow, 1954) simply name a desire to learn, know, and find meaning. The needs for *external stimulation* (Lilly, 1956; Shurley, 1960) and *curiosity drive* (Berlyne, 1960; Butler, 1953)—sometimes called the exploratory drive—were also discussed in chapter 1.

Needs of these three classes are internal stimuli which motivate the person. Activities which allow a person to meet one or more of these needs have a high probability of engaging a person's attention and activity.

The Transient and Specific Nature of Motivation

A note on the transitory and specific nature of motivation is in order. A person may be motivated to engage in one activity at one time and another activity at another time. Of course, the teacher may observe general patterns in the motivation of the student. The very specificity of the enumerated needs in table 3 indicates the specificity of motivation. When one need is temporarily satisfied, the attention of the person is turned to the satisfaction of another need. Maslow (1954), for this reason, posited a hierarchy of needs. Under this system, "higher" needs such as self-actualization and comprehension would not be apparent until the person met the more basic needs. As discussed before, the authors' classes of needs are interrelated.

The process of formal schooling offers potential opportunities for students to meet many of the Class II and Class III needs as well as some of the Class I needs. Students may also learn ways of meeting any of the needs. Perhaps the main reasons that this potential is not attained are that (1) school personnel have not consciously developed reinforcers appropriate to each of the Class II and Class III needs, (2) students and teachers are not keenly aware of all of their needs, and (3) students do not perceive schools as meeting many of those needs of which they are aware.

Motivation and Instruction

Since one does not motivate another person, how is the teacher to use his knowledge of motivation for instructional purposes? At this point the reader should review briefly the material on the five stages of instruction in chapter 1. Motivation should be a concern of the teacher during all five stages of instruction.

At stage one, objective setting, the decisions about what is to be taught should be based on the needs of students as enumerated in table 3. Notice that it is not necessarily recommended that the student be initially aware of the needs to which the instruction corresponds. If such is the case, the student can be made aware of those needs during the instruction.

The second stage of instruction directly involves motivation together with pupil ability. In this stage, ability and predispositions (prior learnings including motivation) are assessed. This assessment may be formal or informal and is an important aspect of what is termed *formative evaluation* (as discussed in chapter 9). The teacher should attempt to evaluate directly the extent to which the students are motivated to engage in activities designed to master the objectives. At times it may be necessary to postpone the attainment of an objective until students are appropriately motivated. Postponement may not be convenient in many circumstances. If so, the lack of motivation may be approached during the third stage of instruction, selecting and sequencing activities (experiences).

Usually, an objective of instruction may be attained by a number of different activities. If one activity does not possess sufficient incentive value, perhaps another will. A need may be met by one activity but not by another. The mandate for the teacher during the third stage of instruction is to select and sequence the most highly motivating types of activities for the greatest number of students or to individualize instruction if possible when it is necessary. Alternative activities should be developed prior to the actual instruction so that the students can engage in alternatives which may be consistent with individual motivational consideration.

Some of the differences between the sexes in the elementary school on reading skill may be due to motivational differences between sexes. Asher and Markell (1974) found that if reading material is highly interesting to boys, they read as well as girls.

During the fourth stage of instruction, the teacher should try to assess periodically pupil motivation. During this stage some or all of the alternative activities may be employed which were planned during stage three.

The main motivational activity for both stages four and five involves evaluation. In the last stage, teachers should note again the likes and dislikes, interests and preferences, of the students. Hopefully, the students will be more interested in and will more highly regard the instructional content and the circumstances under which it occurred. If students dislike or are uninterested in the content, the teacher should attempt to ascertain the reasons for this and then attempt to revise the instructional program accordingly. Revision at this point may not aid the students instructed at that time; but revision may help students who participate in a similar program at some later time.

Reinforcement

Operant conditioning psychology (discussed in chapter 2) provides a definition of reinforcement as any response contingent event (a stimulus) that increases the probability of a response occurring again. More broadly, through reinforcement of specific responses, persons are provided knowledge as to the appropriateness of their actions. It is necessary that external and internal events (reinforcers) occur which inform the person as to the appropriateness of responses. According to operant conditioning psychology, reinforcement plays important roles in both original learning as well as maintaining and strengthening behavior. Reinforcement may be internal in that the subjective consequences of behavior—for example, awareness that a prestigious model has been correctly emulated—may be satisfying (Kanfer, 1965). Or reinforcement may be external, for example, being told of an error on a multiple-choice test item. Many different reinforcers have been shown to be operative in human learning studies.

Even cursory reviews of reinforcement experimentation reveal the variety of reinforcers actually shown to be reinforcing in infrahuman research. The material shown in table 4 is a simple illustration of variety. The point is that for even infrahuman species a variety of reinforcers operates in experimental settings which have little to do with Class I needs.

There are also many kinds of events which serve as reinforcers for human subjects. Bijou and Sturges (1959) identify five classifications of reinforcers:

1. *Consumables* such as food
2. *Manipulatables* such as toys
3. *Visual and auditory stimuli* such as lights and bells
4. *Social stimuli* such as praise and reproof
5. *Tokens* to be exchanged for such items as are desired

Consumables are clearly need satisfiers and are the only reinforcers which are definitely related to Class I needs. The other types of rein-

TABLE 4
Varieties of Reinforcers Identified through Research with Animals Other than Man

Reinforcer (event, stimulus)	Organism	Investigator(s)
Access to a running wheel	Rats	Kagan and Berkun (1954)
Self-applied electronic brain stimulation	Rats	Pliskoff, Wright, and Hawkins (1965)
Briefly viewing scenes such as the experimenter moving toy objects	Monkeys	Butler (1953)
The disassembly of mechanical puzzles	Monkeys	Harlow (1950)
Body contacts	Monkeys	Harlow (1960)

forcers are primarily related to Class II and Class III needs. (See table 3.)

It is our position that the needs or motives in table 3 are related to specific reinforcers. Perhaps a reinforcer is a reinforcer because it satisfies a motive or need. Of course the point of view represented in operant psychology overrides this inference. The inference also raises the issue of an incentive. The incentive is an external object or condition which, it is inferred, arouses a motive. The differences between an incentive and a reinforcer are slight. A cookie may be seen as an incentive which arouses a motive and resultant action. It may be a reinforcer, however, when it is actually received.

The reinforcement classifications of Bijou and Sturges (1959) and the reinforcers matched with the three categories of needs (table 3) may suggest to the teacher a great variety of reinforcers for use in the classroom. Teachers use these reinforcers and those suggested in table 3 in ways which make the student aware that, at specific times, one must either (1) exhibit a certain response, (2) modify a response or a sequence of responses to increase their appropriateness, or (3) refrain from making a response or a sequence of responses which are inappropriate.

Individual differences exist in regard to what is reinforcing to a person at any given moment (Lintner & Ducette, 1974). These indi-

Reinforcement

vidual differences may be understood through a consideration of the six components of the frame of reference. Instances of confirmation or nonconfirmation (feedback) of one's concepts and structures may be reinforcing. So also will be events which are consistent with a person's affect, values, interests, and needs.

Consequences of behavior may be either positive or aversive in nature. Aversive consequences may involve the removal of some punishing event contingent on the person's making a response. This is termed *negative reinforcement*. Negative reinforcement is thus associated with an increase in the likelihood of the occurrence of the response(s) that immediately preceded the termination of the aversive condition. Whereas the application of some aversive stimulus to reduce the probability of a response recurring or to inhibit an undesired response is called *punishment*.

It is generally recommended that teachers refrain from the use of punishment. Punishment may be interpreted by the student as more than an instance of failure. Through social learning, punishment may help a student learn that brutality is an acceptable form of behavior since teachers or principals are permitted to be brutal. Many instances of failures may damage the student's academic performance (Lazarus et al., 1952). Failure also leads to a lowering of the student's level of aspiration (Child & Whiting, 1949). (Success leads to raising the level of aspiration.) Other possible outcomes of punishment are: school absenteeism, dropping out, vandalism in schools, excessive anxiety, fear, and excessive conformity (Meacham & Wiesen, 1969, pp. 64-65). Some detrimental influences of excessive anxiety on cognitive processing, for example, are noted in chapter 3. In other words, the negative affective responses made by the pupils to the punishment may well generalize to objects which are in connection with the negative experiences, for example, school, books, studying, or teachers.

There is probably such an ample potential for punishment and disastrously unintentional negative reinforcement in formal schooling, and in the informal social interactions concomitant with schooling, that teachers should minimize or eliminate their overt use of negative reinforcement, especially punishment. Of course, a teacher should provide appropriate knowledge of correctness or incorrectness of responses; but this should be presented to students in ways which minimize the probability of inculcating feelings of failure and inadequacy. It is important that the student continue to perceive self as one who *can* (eventually) perform the assigned task well. This is an important dimension of establishing and maintaining a predisposition to learn in formal educational settings. One may present any number of "reinforcers," any number of stimulus events which *may* serve as reinforcers. Yet, what is reinforcing to one student's behavior may not reinforce that of another student. Nor may that same stimulus event serve to reinforce the same behavior on another occasion. Needs and motives vary in their preeminence within the person from time to time. Of course, if one adheres strictly to the operant conditioning definition, one does not need to recognize individual differences in reinforcement. A reinforcer increases the probability of a response occurring again. If the probability of response recurrence does not change, there has been no reinforcement.

Premack (1965) recommends that the teacher use time to engage in favorite activities as a reinforcer. The teacher must first become aware of some of the student's favorite activities. Then the teacher can allow the student to perform those activities as a reinforcer for other responses.

In some experimental schools the *Premack Principle* is used in conjunction with a token system. The student might, for example, be given a token as a reinforcer for cooperative classroom behavior (if classroom management is the central problem) which then may be traded for five minutes on the basketball court. The *Premack Principle* involves determining a number of reinforcers for individual students. First the teacher finds out what reinforces the individual student and then uses those reinforcers when the student responds correctly. As noted before, favorite student activities may be used as reinforcers (see, for example, Hosie et al., 1974).

Some authorities are adamant in stating that reinforcement must occur immediately after the response whether the reinforcer is praise, reproof, or knowledge of correctness. Immediacy of reinforcement appears to be generally necessary in experiments according to reviewers of research in animal learning (Renner, 1964; Terrell, 1965). These same reviews reflect a lack of consistency of any detrimental influence of delayed reinforcement in human learning. This may be partly explained by human abilities to expect and covertly "rehearse" events or by some other form of subjective reinforcement involving cognition.

Kulhavy (1971), in a carefully designed experiment, found that delaying knowledge of results in a prose test situation was more productive of learning than immediate knowledge of results. He concludes that knowledge of results need *not* be reinforcing and that delaying corrective feedback gave the subjects an opportunity to forget errors. Basic to this position is the notion that people learn to do what they do. This same position is basic to programmed instruction in that frames are designed to minimize error. An error made is an error learned as it were.

In the reinforcement point of view, the teacher may be seen primarily as a dispenser of reinforcements. Of course, this task may be assigned to teaching machines! Thus the teacher will be free for other

Reinforcement

activities (Skinner, 1968). In actual practice teachers appear to dispense reinforcements at a low rate (Byalick & Bersoff, 1974). Other than the tasks of sequencing experiences and arranging the school atmosphere, the teacher's job is to reinforce the specific behaviors of students on appropriate occasions. If one is appreciative of the role which imitation plays in performance and learning, the psychological tasks of the teacher increase in number.

In general terms, reinforcement may be employed by the teacher to strengthen, weaken, or maintain behaviors. Melton (1950) refers to this general area in learning as fixation (fixing the learned response). Performing the response initially is termed *acquisition*. Why are the desired responses performed initially? This original performance (acquisition) may occur in a variety of ways. The following four ways are not mutually exclusive. The teacher's own direct actions may be effective in 2 and 3. The main role, however, of the teacher in 1 and 2 is waiting and arranging the situation to facilitate 1 and 2. Teachers play their most active roles in response guidance (3) and imitation (4).

1. *Self-initiated*—The student may already know how to perform the response and then become motivated at some point to emit the behavior. Many learnings fall into this category (see, for example, the discussion of Hull [chapter 2, pp. 27 to 28] in which the person's tendency to perform is changed, yet the behavior itself is not changed. In this manner the original performance is acquired as an influence of motivation. Reinforcement procedures may then be brought to bear to strengthen and maintain the behavior.
2. *Discovery*—The original performance may be discovered through group inquiry procedures or through individual inquiry procedures—discovery, trial and error, etc. The literature on learning by discovery is voluminous (see Shulman & Keislar, 1966; Strike, 1975). After reviewing the literature on discovery learning versus expository learning, Ausubel (1968, pp. 497-504) reports that the question of relative superiority of these two types of techniques remains unresolved. Nonetheless, a response may be discovered by an individual alone, or with peer or teacher guidance. As the student performs the response, reinforcement may again be brought to bear to strengthen or maintain it. Of course, the awareness of the discovery may be reinforcing of itself.
3. *Response guidance*—Another general method by which a student may acquire the behavior is through teacher guidance, either verbal or nonverbal—and again, some form of reinforcement is brought into play to strengthen and maintain

the behavior. Very generally, any external stimulus or sequence of external stimuli may guide or force a person to elicit a response the first time. See chapter 2 and the discussion of shaping for an explanation of one kind of response guidance.
4. *Imitation*—Imitation is the act of copying the behavior of another. The student may observe the teacher or another student performing a behavior and may copy that behavior. Again, reinforcement may be required to maintain and strengthen the behavior.

Imitation

An introduction to imitative behavior is included in chapter 2 within the topic of social learning theory. A person's frame of reference has a great influence on his choice of models and his choice of *which* of the many behaviors of a model are emulated. As previously discussed, imitation is one of the means whereby a response is acquired originally. It may also be a means of fixing (strengthening and maintaining) a response when the model performs a response already known by the learner. Some form of internal (vicarious) or external reinforcement may also follow the response of the learner in the imitative situation. Bandura (1969, p. 120ff.) identified three modeling influences:

1. *Observational learning*—The acquiring of new responses which were not in the learner's repertoire (an infant sees someone clap hands, the infant claps as well).
2. *Inhibitory or disinhibitory effect*—Increasing or decreasing the reluctance of the learner to perform a response pattern not socially sanctioned already in his behavioral repertoire (a delinquent boy stops shoplifting when his adult friend is caught and punished [inhibitory]; or he increases his shoplifting because his friend profited [disinhibitory]).
3. *Response facilitation effect*—A response already in the observer's repertoire is performed as a result of a model's influence (a model gazes at the sky, others do also).

Two related explanations exist in the literature on imitation. First is the theory advanced by Miller and Dollard (1941) in which a model is observed. If the learner responds exactly as did the model, the learner is thereby reinforced.

A second explanation is that of Mowrer (1960) in which the model performs some action and is reinforced. The observer learns even if the model is the one who is reinforced (empathic learning). Note that both explanations include reinforcement as a necessary condition. In the first explanation (Miller & Dollard, 1941), the learner is reinforced for copying and in the second the model is reinforced (Mowrer, 1960). In the Mowrer explanation, the learner experiences the feeling components of the reinforcement. The research of Aronfreed (1968) supports Mowrer's stressing of the role of affect in imitative learning.

The research of Bandura and his associates has rapidly advanced our understanding of imitative behavior. His work generally has not followed the practice of Miller and Dollard (1941) of directly reinforcing the learner (observer). Bandura and his associates most frequently have used an indirect form of reinforcement to enhance any learning effect of the observation itself. That is to say, the observer views the model being reinforced and is thus vicariously reinforced (Bandura & Harris, 1966; Bandura, Ross, & Ross, 1963).

Bandura (1969, pp. 148-49) has indicated that modeling results in learning for different kinds of behaviors such as aggression, dramatic play patterns, teaching styles, most social behaviors, and language acquisition. Bourdon (1970) concludes that practical application of imitation in counseling and therapy have great potential. Numerous classes of behaviors have been experimentally modified through imitation. This intimates that a great deal of what is learned, such as attitudes, in nonexperimental, natural, social situations may be learned by imitation.

Naturally occurring social situations such as classrooms generally contain a plethora of models. Peers are frequently imitated as well as teachers. There is an increasing use of peers as models in learning in classroom instruction. Hamblin and Hamblin (1972) successfully used a combination of peer tutoring and token reinforcement to teach disadvantaged preschoolers to read. See also DeVries and Edwards (1973). The behaviors of models may be rewarded or punished or ignored. Observers who imitate, likewise, may be richly rewarded, or soundly punished, or be ignored. The observer may "provide" his own reinforcement through his internal affective processes; or the reinforcement, if it occurs at all, may be administered by a group, by a very specific model, or by a third person in the situation.

What happens when the model also dispenses reinforcers to the observer contingent upon imitation? The evidence is clear that relatively rapid advances are made in the treatment of those maladjustments which are amenable to remediation through learning (Lovaas, 1966; Risley & Wolf, 1967; Sloane, Johnston, & Harris, 1968). In these investigations, the model exhibits the desired behavior and then reinforces the observer *if* the behavior is correctly imitated. Both parents and teachers will frequently use this approach in natural settings. That is, the model also provides the reinforcement directly to the observer.

The nature and extent of the reinforcers obtained by models and vicariously experienced by observers give rise to explanations as to why the behavior of some persons is emulated. Research indicates that the characteristics of the model make a difference as to which models are emulated. Models who reward others, who are prestigious and competent, who have high status, and who possess control of the consequences of their behavior are more likely to be emulated (Bandura & Walters, 1963, p. 107). Also Garrett and Cunningham (1974) found that first-grade children imitate a same sex teacher more than an opposite sex teacher.

Not only do the characteristics of the model make a difference in imitative learning, so also do the characteristics of the observer. Such characteristics as high dependency tendencies (Jakubczak & Walters, 1959) and lack of self-esteem (de Charms & Rosenbaum, 1960) seem to increase the likelihood of emulation. It is highly probable that the characteristics of the observer and the model, the aspects of the situation, and the behavior to be learned all interact to influence the learning outcomes.

An Overview of Practical Applications

The following practical ideas are consistent with the literature and research discussed in this chapter.

1. There are many kinds of reinforcers (suggested by Bijou & Sturges, 1959). Other reinforcers are consistent with the needs classification in table 3. Teachers should find out what events are reinforcers for which students and then use those reinforcers accordingly.
2. Most students want to be competent or successful and to avoid failure. Teachers should think "successive approximation" and build up feelings of success for problem students.
3. Puzzle solving can be motivating. Try beginning units of instruction with a problem. Successful puzzle solving can be reinforcing.
4. Use peer teaching with good students teaching poor students. The positive effects are probably attributable to modeling, motivation, and to a one-on-one response guidance.
5. Students may be motivated not only by the curricular material but by the context of learning. Try to vary the context of learning through large group teaching, one-on-one teaching (by peers, and at times, by working with single students), and by small group work. Let peers teach small groups at times. Develop cooperative contextual approaches as well as competitive situations in planning for instruction. At times students

Discussion Questions

will enjoy competition and at times they will enjoy cooperative efforts.
6. Search for interesting material. Provide for novelty of material to gain students' attention.

Conclusion

Three major topics of importance were discussed in this chapter. Motivation was treated as the study of forces internal to the person which initiate, direct, and sustain activity. Motivation was contrasted with external stimulation which also includes the study of external forces which initiate, direct, and sustain activity. During instruction, the teacher uses both types of forces.

One of the teacher's manageable ways of externally stimulating students during instruction is through techniques which use the process of reinforcement. It was shown that reinforcement is concomitant with human needs and is thus directly connected to motivation. Specific reinforcers were suggested consistent with various needs.

Reinforcement and imitation were discussed as the two primary ways people learn. The initial acquisition of a learned response and the strengthening of a response already in the person's repertoire may both be influenced by imitative learning. Obviously, the literature on imitative learning points up the necessity of providing appropriate models during school learning.

Discussion Questions

1. What relationships do you see between motivation, reinforcement, and imitation?
2. Is reward or praise always reinforcing? Explain.
3. Distinguish among motives, needs, and incentives. Which are learned, which inherited? How does learning override inheritance? Give examples.
4. What would the term "no trial learning" mean in a social learning situation?
5. Explain the old ideas of "intrinsic" and "extrinsic" motivation in terms of the frame of reference model.
6. How would you employ the principles of positive and negative reinforcement in a classroom situation to achieve some desired learning? Describe the situation including grade level and the pupils and subject matter in question to illustrate your answer.
7. Contrast the frame of reference, self-starting behavioral model, with an external stimulation model such as Skinner's. Which do you prefer? Why?

8. In your high school, which teachers appeared to be emulated most frequently? Why? Which students seemed to imitate teachers most frequently?

Recommended Readings

Atkinson, J. W. *An introduction to motivation.* Princeton, N.J.: D. Van Nostrand, 1964.

Bandura, A. *Principles of behavior modification.* New York: Holt, Rinehart & Winston, 1969.

Banduar, A. *Social learning theory.* New York: McCalbe-Seiler, 1971.

Becker, W. C., Thomas, D. R., & Carnine, D. *Reducing behavior problems: An operant conditioning guide for teachers.* Urbana, Ill.: Educational Resources Information Center, Clearinghouse on Early Childhood Education, 1969.

Cofer, C. N. *Motivation and emotion.* Glenview, Ill.: Scott, Foresman and Company, 1972.

Givner, A., & Graubard, P. S. *A handbook of behavior modification for the classroom.* New York: Holt, Rinehart & Winston, 1974. (Paperback)

Logan, F. A., & Wagner, A. R. *Reward and punishment.* Boston: Allyn and Bacon, 1970.

Maehr, M. L. *Sociocultural origins of achievement.* Monterey, Calif.: Brooks/Cole, 1974.

Meacham, M. L., & Wiesen, A. E. *Changing classroom behavior: A manual for precision teaching.* Scranton, Pa.: International Textbook Co., 1970.

Wiener, D. N. *Classroom management and discipline.* Itasca, Ill.: Peacock, 1972.

References

Aronfreed, J. *Conscience and conduct.* New York: Academic Press, 1968.

Asher, S. R., & Markell, R. A. Sex differences in comprehension of high- and low-interest reading material. *Journal of Educational Psychology,* 1974, *66,* 680-87.

Atkinson, J. W. Mainsprings of achievement oriented activity. In J. D. Krumboltz (Ed.), *Learning and the educational process.* Chicago: Rand McNally, 1966.

References

Ausubel, D. P. *Educational psychology: A cognitive view.* New York: Holt, Rinehart & Winston, 1968.

Bandura, A. *Principles of behavior modification.* New York: Holt, Rinehart & Winston, 1969.

Bandura, A., & Harris, M. B. Modification of syntactic style. *Journal of Experimental Child Psychology,* 1966, *4,* 341-52.

Bandura, A., Ross, D., & Ross, S. A. Vicarious reinforcement and imitative learning. *Journal of Abnormal and Social Psychology,* 1963, *67,* 601-07.

Bandura, A., & Walters, R. H. *Social learning and personality development.* New York: Holt, Rinehart & Winston, 1963.

Berlyne, D. E. *Conflict arousal and curiosity.* New York: McGraw-Hill, 1960.

Bijou, S. W., & Sturges, P. S. Positive reinforcers for experimental studies with children—consumables and manipulatables. *Child Development,* 1959, *30,* 151-70.

Bourdon, R. D. Imitation: Implications for counseling and therapy. *Review of Educational Research,* 1970, *40,* 429-57.

Butler, R. A. Discrimination learning by rhesus monkeys to visual-exploratory motivation. *Journal of Comparative and Physiological Psychology,* 1953, *46,* 95-98.

Byalick, R., & Bersoff, D. N. Reinforcement practices of black and white teachers in integrated classrooms. *Journal of Educational Psychology,* 1974, *66,* 473-80.

Child, I. L., & Whiting, J. W. M. Determinants of level of aspiration. Evidence from everyday life. *Journal of Abnormal and Social Psychology,* 1949, *44,* 303-14.

Combs, A. W., & Snygg, D. *Individual behavior.* (Rev. ed.) New York: Harper & Row, 1959.

de Charms, R., & Rosenbaum, M. E. Status variables and matching behavior. *Journal of Personality,* 1960, *28,* 492-502.

DeVries, D. L., & Edwards, K. J. Learning games and student-teams: Their effect on classroom process. *American Educational Research Journal,* 1973, *10,* 307-18.

English, H. B., & English, A. C. *A comprehensive dictionary of psychological and psychoanalytical terms.* New York: David McKay, 1958.

Frankel, V. E. *Man's search for meaning.* New York: Washington Square Press, 1963.

Garrett, C. S., & Cunningham, D. J. Effects of vicarious consequences and model and experimenter sex on imitative behavior in first-grade children. *Journal of Educational Psychology,* 1974, *66,* 940-47.

Hamblin, J. A., & Hamblin, R. L. On teaching disadvantaged preschoolers to read: A successful experiment. *American Educational Research Journal,* 1972, *9,* 209-16.

Harlow, H. F. Learning and satiation of response in intrinsically motivated complex puzzle performance in monkeys. *Journal of Comparative and Physiological Psychology,* 1950, *43,* 289-94.

Harlow, H. F. Primary affectational patterns in primates. *American Journal of Orthopsychiatry,* 1960, *30,* 676-84.

Hosie, T. W., Gentile, J. R., & Carroll, J. D. Pupil preferences and the Premack Principle. *American Educational Research Journal,* 1974, *11,* 241-47.

Jakubczak, L. F., & Walters, R. H. Suggestibility as dependency behavior. *Journal of Abnormal and Social Psychology,* 1959, *59,* 102-07.

Kagan, J., & Berkun, M. The reward value of running activity. *Journal of Comparative and Physiological Psychology,* 1954, *47,* 108.

Kanfer, F. H. Vicarious human reinforcements: A glimpse into the black box. In L. Krasner & L. P. Ullman (Eds.), *Research in behavior modification.* New York: Holt, Rinehart & Winston, 1965.

Kulhavy, R. W. *The delay retention effect with meaningful material.* Unpublished doctoral dissertation, University of Illinois, 1971.

Lazarus, R. S., Deese, J., & Osler, S. F. Effects of psychological stress upon performance. *Psychological Bulletin,* 1952, *49,* 293-317.

Lilly, J. C. Mental effects of reduction of ordinary levels of physical stimuli on intact, healthy persons. *Psychiatric Research Reports,* No. 5, 1956, 1-28.

Lintner, A. C., & Ducette, J. The effects of locus of control, academic failure and task dimension on a student's responsiveness to praise. *American Educational Research Journal,* 1974, *11,* 231-39.

Lovaas, O. I. A program for the establishment of speech in psychotic children. In J. K. Wing (Ed.), *Early childhood autism.* Oxford: Pergamon, 1966.

Maehr, M. L. Culture and achievement motivation. *American Psychologist,* 1974, *29,* 887-96.

Maehr, M. L., & Sjogren, D. D. Atkinson's theory of achievement motivation: First step toward a theory of academic motivation. *Review of Educational Research,* 1971, *41,* 143-61.

Maslow, A. H. *Motivation and personality.* New York: Harper & Row, 1954.

Meacham, M. L., & Wiesen, A. E. *Changing classroom behavior: A manual for precision teaching.* Scranton, Pa.: International Textbook Company, 1969.

References

Melton, A. W. Learning. In W. S. Monroe (Ed.), *Encyclopedia of educational research.* (Rev. ed.) New York: Macmillan, 1950.

Miller, N. E., & Dollard, J. *Social learning and imitation.* New Haven: Yale University Press, 1941.

Mowrer, O. H. *Learning theory and the symbolic processes.* New York: Wiley, 1960.

Murray, H. A. *Explorations in personality.* Fair Lawn, N. J.: Oxford University Press, 1938.

Pliskoff, S. S., Wright, J. E., & Hawkins, T. D. Brain stimulation as a reinforcer: Intermittent schedules. *Journal of Experimental Analysis of Behavior,* 1965, *8,* 75-88.

Premack, D. Reinforcement theory. In D. Levine (Ed.), *Nebraska symposium on motivation.* Vol 8. University of Nebraska Press, 1965.

Renner, K. E. Delay of reinforcement: A historical review. *Psychological Bulletin,* 1964, *61,* 341-61.

Risley, T., & Wolf, M. Establishing functional speech in echolalic children. *Behavior Research and Therapy,* 1967, *5,* 73-88.

Shulman, L. S., & Keislar, E. R. *Learning by discovery: A critical appraisal.* Chicago: Rand McNally, 1966.

Shurley, J. Profound experimental sensory isolation. *American Journal of Psychiatry,* 1960, *117,* 539-45.

Skinner, B. F. *The technology of teaching.* New York: Appleton-Century-Crofts, 1968.

Sloane, H. N., Jr., Johnston, M. K., & Harris, F. R. Remedial procedures for teaching verbal behavior to speech deficient or defective young children. In H. N. Sloan, Jr. & B. A. MacAulay (Eds.), *Operant procedures in remedial speech and language training.* Boston: Houghton Mifflin, 1968.

Strike, K. A. The logic of learning by discovery. *Review of Educational Research,* 1975, *45,* 461-83.

Terrell, G. Delayed reinforcement effects. In L. P. Lipsett & C. C. Spiker (Eds.), *Advances in child development and behavior.* Vol. II. New York: Academic Press, 1965.

Weiner, B. Implications of the current theory of achievement motivation for research and performance in the classroom. *Psychology in the Schools,* 1967, *4,* 164-71.

Weiner, B. Motivational psychology and educational research. *Educational Psychologist,* 1974, *11,* 96-101.

White, R. W. Motivation reconsidered: The concept of competence. *Psychological Review,* 1959, *66,* 297-333.

Practical Organizer for Chapter 5

Nothing is quite so natural in human learning as the failure to remember or to transfer learning. A knowledge of memory and transfer processes can give us better perspectives and practices for promoting efficient learning. The teacher who wishes to promote long-term memory and transfer must take care that the material is well learned initially. The problem is how to ensure thorough meaningful learning. Recent experiments on the psychology of memory and transfer provide the teacher with a great deal of help in this regard. In this chapter there are many references to concepts and structures. You should review early sections in chapter 3 on concepts and structures to better understand these discussions.

The material on these recent experiments discussed in this chapter emphasizes the importance of six variables which can promote learning for retention and transfer. They are: meaningfulness, generalizability, codability, imagability, familiarity, and structurability. Instructors can make use of these ideas to promote long-term memory and transfer. You might use a mnemonic device to remember these factors. Memorize the following statement and try to form as bizarre a mental picture as possible about it: The mean general codes his unusual images into familiar structures.

The mean	meaningfulness
general	generalizability
codes his	codability
unusual images	imagability
into familiar	familiarity
structures.	structurability

Retention and Transfer in Human Learning

5

In schools it is expected that what is taught will be remembered on a long-term basis and then applied to a number of relatively different situations. In this chapter human memory and transfer of learning are discussed in terms of theory and research in psychology. Problems concerning memory and transfer have been actively investigated throughout this century. Like the other topics in this book the "last word is not yet in." However, a considerable body of evidence exists on which educators can draw.

W*hat* do people remember? *How* do people remember? Do we remember our experiences? All of them? A few of them? Or do we only remember how we perceived and structured those experiences at the time of experiencing? Among that which we remember, what do we apply to new situations? Why do we sometimes fail to apply something which we learned in one situation to another appropriate situation? If one does apply a learned skill to a new situation, how is the application to be explained? How can teachers provide for better retention and application? All of these questions plus others intrigue the student of human learning. In this chapter we shall attempt to approach some of these questions by presenting recent research and literature on memory and transfer and relating these to the frame of reference. The six components of the frame of reference—concepts, structures, affect, values, needs, and interests—influence what the person perceives, learns, and remembers.

The study of *retention* involves how experiences are remembered (stored), retrieved, or reconstructed, as well as the conditions under which these memories occur or do not occur. In classroom learning it is often desired that certain modifications of behavior or of behavioral potential be relatively permanent. It is hoped much of what is learned will be retained on a long-term basis.

The study of the conditions wherein what is learned is applied or not applied to new situations involves *transfer*. That which is learned will not be transferred unless it is remembered. However, the fact that a skill is remembered does not necessarily mean that the skill will be transferred to a specific situation. Thus transfer involves more than memory alone.

This chapter will focus on what is known about how retention and transfer take place in school learning and on aiding retention and transfer. Resistance to change is also discussed. Specific suggestions as to what the teacher can *do* to promote retention and transfer are listed in chapter 10. Knowledge about transfer and retention should aid the educator especially during stages 3 and 4 of planning for instruction.

Retention

The thesis that what a person learns is partially a function of the frame of reference at the time of experiencing was presented in chapter 3. The nature of the experience resulting from that transaction is symbolic. What the person incorporates and takes away from the transaction is symbolic, an abstraction from the experience. To investigate these symbols or abstractions after the experience is to study retention. The person abstracts aspects of the experience, organizes that abstraction into what is retained from previous experience, and later may exhibit retention. What is recalled will be determined by the person's cognitive abstractional and organizational procedures and mechanisms during acquisition and by the details of the transaction as well as by conditions which are present at the time of recall. Wittrock terms such acquisition procedures and mechanisms "generative processes" (1974).

Theories of Forgetting

Three general explanations frequently have been advanced as to why persons fail to retain what they learn, or why they appear to forget what they learn. These explanations have some experimental or experiential basis.

Selective or Motivated Forgetting. From a Freudian point of view we never really forget anything. What appears to have been forgotten is hidden from consciousness by the defense mechanisms of unconscious repression or conscious suppression. Such memories can only be "restored to consciousness" by therapeutic techniques such as hypnosis. Fragmentary aspects of these memories emerge in dreams, humor, and in what appear to be random associations. A painful experience which a person has had may appear later to be "forgotten," but may really only be repressed (or suppressed). The person may selectively forget such an experience because it is unpleasant to remember. According to psychoanalytic theory, many mental illnesses are based on such selective forgetting. The painful experience is termed a trauma.

Trace Decay. Another explanation of forgetting accents the dimensions of time and disuse. According to this explanation a skill is forgotten because a memory trace is established in the brain which, if unused during the passage of time, decays in strength, making it more difficult to recall. Some time must pass before one can speak of retention or forgetting—whether it is three seconds or thirty years. If reductions of recall do occur during this passage of time, there is a tendency to ascribe the forgetting to trace decay. Since the constructs "retention" and "forgetting" involve time, time becomes a necessary but not sufficient condition for explanation of these phenomena. Decay theory is not a widely accepted explanation among experimental psychologists today. The principal reason for this is that since the classic study by Jenkins and Dallenbach (1924), interference has been the prominent explanation of forgetting—receiving the support of numerous research findings (Adams, 1967).

Interference. Most learning psychologists in recent years explain forgetting in terms of *what happens during the passage of time,* rather than simple decay in time. Intervening learnings appear to influence the retaining or forgetting of each other. Learning one skill may facilitate the retention and subsequent performance of a previously learned skill, or it may interfere with it. Generally, it has been shown that the nature of the intervening experience has more to do with forgetting than the passage of time itself.

Interference has been broken down into two types, proactive interference and retroactive interference, depending on the temporal location of the source of the interference with respect to the learning and its subsequent performance. Thus, if an earlier learning interferes with the recall of some later learning, the term is *proactive interference.* The paradigm for this is B-A-A', where "B" represents the learning of some fact, concept, or skill which interferes with the recall of some subsequent learning "A." Many examples of proactive interference in everyday life can be cited. For instance, consider the person who learns to drive a car having a manual (stick) transmission, and subsequently learns to drive a car having an automatic transmission. After a period of time of not driving any cars, that person enters a car with an automatic transmission, but the foot pounds the floor where the clutch *should* be (in the stick shift car) at every stop-start sequence. This is an instance of proactive interference, as a prior learning made retention of a subsequent learning difficult.

The A-B-A' sequence, where B still represents the source of interference, is known as *retroactive interference*. This is where *interpolated* learning (B) occurs between the learning of A and its subsequent performance A', thereby interfering with recall of A at A'. The sequence, then, is A-B-A'. An example of this from everyday life was reported by one of our students in Canada. This student, an avid ice skater, took up roller skating one summer. After a season on the roller skates, she returned to the ice only to discover, her first time out, that when she tried to stop on the ice she used the roller skate movement which, of course, was not appropriate to ice skating. This example of retroactive interference—learn A, learn B, try to perform A, and experience forgetting due to interference from B—is interesting because while retroactive interference has been experimentally demonstrated in verbal learning studies, it is rare in laboratory studies of motor skills learning (Adams, 1967).

These examples are drawn from everyday experience in retention of complex motor skills. Interference is commonly observed in verbal learning as well. Persons who have learned responses which are similar but appropriate in different situations experience interference effects. "I can think of the word for it in Spanish, but I can't remember how you say it in French" is the complaint of an English-speaking

Retention

individual who may be experiencing proactive interference from high school studies of Spanish on recall of college French, when trying to order a meal in a Montreal restaurant. Likewise one's present telephone number can be said to interfere retroactively with recall of former telephone numbers, even though the old responses may have been practiced repeatedly over many years.

Interference explanations of forgetting are widely accepted by experimental psychologists in North America and have to be regarded as modern views of memory which tend to supplant the Freudian and trace decay theories.

Some Modern Views of Memory

Traditional views of memory have tended to concentrate on internal storage and retrieval with an attendant analogy of the central nervous system as a "junk box." That is, the tendency has been to think of the central nervous system as a container where one places and stores treasures. What a person knows is placed in the "box" for storage until it is brought out (retrieved) for some purpose. In recent decades many attempts have been made to revise radically this conceptualization to account for the processes that must occur "in the box" in order for the phenomena of human memory to take place. However, the more "recent" conceptualizations also have a history embedded, in many cases, in pre-twentieth century philosophy.

Shiffrin and Atkinson (1969) have described an information-processing model of human memory which attempts to describe the processes "in the box" based on inferences from research data. Basically there are two kinds of storage—*long-term* and *short-term retention*. As the names imply, these refer to whether information is acquired for immediate use (less than about a minute—as in looking up and dialing a telephone number), or for long-term storage and retrieval (longer than immediate use—up to a lifetime—as in certain language skills, one's telephone number, etc.). Both long-term and short-term memory systems are associated with separate memory banks each of which may be addressed for recall. The characteristic of the short-term memory store is content which is subject to rapid forgetting, whereas long-term storage is characterized by content which is addressable and retrievable for an extended period of time.

In addition there are three other components of the information-processing model which are used to describe the flow of information and what happens to it. The first and third of these components are the *sensory register* and the *response generator*. As the name implies, the sensory register receives information which is then transmitted either to short-term store for rehearsal or directly to the response

117

generator. In the former case (input sent to short-term store), information is either used immediately by a connection to the response generator or coded for long-term storage and passed on to that component. For a stimulus to be transmitted directly to response generator from sensory register, the response would have to be of a reflex nature (e.g., eyeblink, heartbeat) and thus require no processing by the more central short-term or long-term components. A very important part of this model is the second component termed *control processes* which influence the sensory register and both short-term and long-term store. Essentially, the control processes determine where the information goes and what happens to it. They monitor and dictate the links between the other components, the rehearsing, coding, searching, and comparing functions.

Another modern revision of this internal storage focus involves the idea that much of what appears to have been stored internally in the central nervous system is largely embedded in the environment (Ashby, 1964, p. 207). For example, one does not internally store all the information which might appear to be necessary to drive from Urbana, Illinois to Vancouver, B. C., or even to Chicago. One "stores" a few bits of information and response patterns to environmental cues related to those stored bits. One responds to those few cues such as "Turn north on Lincoln Avenue to Highway I-74. Turn west on I-74. Go north on I-57." It might appear that one would need to know thousands of bits of information to arrive in Chicago, when in fact only a few are internally stored. An observer might note thousands of responses made by the driver and attribute most of these responses to memory. Much of the necessary information is in fact "stored" in the environment.

The act of responding to bits of information may produce other cues which are reconstructed or constructed on a momentary basis. Thus, these cues appear to be retrieved from some "storage pool" when in fact they are only reconstructed or constructed through person-environmental transactions. What appears to be functioning memory in that case is really a performance/mnemonic consideration. Neisser's (1967, p. 285) analogy is very apt for mnemonic reconstructive-constructive processing. He likens the processing of memory to the paleontologist who creates (re-creates?) the entire dinosaur form out of a few bone chips. According to this view we store a few bits (chips) but remember (reconstruct or construct) the entire dinosaur! Neisser also applies the "paleontologist" analogy to perception. Perception, too, is an act of construction, not simply "receiving" input.

This example has many parallels in the classroom. If a student knows that Montreal is a port city, he can actually construct and then enumerate many characteristics of the city. It is true that these characteristics are also descriptive of other port cities, but for practical human learning purposes the student "remembers" these characteristics as being pertinent to Montreal, Quebec.

Memory Processes

Many of the modern approaches to memory are represented in figure 8.

Functions of Memory

The first dimension in the processes of memory are the three functions which are termed retrieval, reconstructive, and constructive. What is remembered (forms 1 and 2) may be either a "taking out of storage"

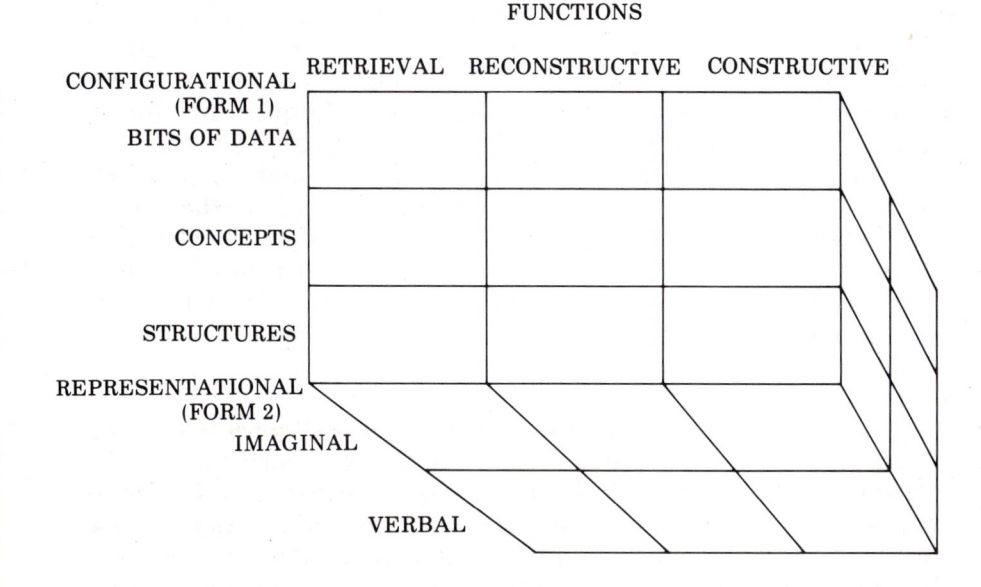

Figure 8. Functions and forms of memory

retrieval process, or a reconstructive "building upon that which is stored" (Bartlett, 1932; Norman, 1969, p. 137), or a purely constructive process (Bartlett, 1932; Norman, 1969). Many writers view this constructive process as a problem-solving function. Doubtless the dividing point between some instances of mnemonic processes and some instances of problem-solving processes is arbitrary. The authors believe that the constructive function of memory borders on problem solving. Problem solving is further discussed in chapter 6.

Configurational Forms

A second dimension of the processes of memory in figure 8 is termed configurative forms (form 1) and consists of "bits" of data, concepts, and structures. "Bits" of data are the most reducible aspects of experience and learning. Bits of information occur in the context of sensory-perceptual input. Concepts and structures have been further identified and discussed in chapter 3. It may be recalled that concepts are relatively small units of knowledge and meanings represented in categories or labels. Structures are larger units of knowledge, organized sets of concepts.

Representational Forms

The third dimension of the processes of memory depicted in figure 8 is the representative dichotomy (form 2); imaginal and verbal (Anderson & Hidde, 1971; Anderson & Kulhavy, 1972; Bandura, 1969; Neisser, 1967; and Paivio, 1970). The results of a recent study by Paivio and Csapo (1969) in which visual imagery was found to facilitate storage of items (bits), but not the storing of sequential information, suggest that the cells in the model *imagery-concepts* and *imagery-structure* should be questioned. Paivio and Csapo (1969) maintain that only the verbal encoding system handles the sequential order input. On the other hand, earlier works exemplified by Köhler (1929) and newer work by Asch (1969) and his associates may be interpreted as indicative that visual imagery is in fact used in conceptual and structural memory. Further research should be conducted on these and related points.

Experimental psychologists frequently study verbal memory in terms of recall of pairs of items, often nonsense syllables, which help to reduce the effects of previous learning for experimental purposes. Such pairs of items are called a *paired-associate task*. *Serial tasks* are also employed whereby persons are asked to memorize lists of items in order. A third approach frequently used in laboratory studies of human verbal memory is called the *free recall task* wherein persons are asked to recall a list of items in any order they wish. This latter approach is useful to study the organization of memory since persons tend to reorder a list to better "fit" it into existing cognitive structure. Numerous tests of interference theory, imagery, cognitive organization, and other aspects of memory have been performed by using such procedures (Adams, 1967).

Bandura (1969, p. 133) also views memory as involving the two representational systems—imaginal and verbal. Although Bandura feels these representational systems are appropriate for imitative learning, they can be also regarded as systems for retention of learnings which are acquired through self-initiated study, discovery, or

Memory Processes

response guidance. During acquisition, that which is learned is coded into images, words, or both. An example of an imaginal mnemonic representation might be your "mental picture" of your home or a "mental picture" of the look on a person's face upon seeing a fly in the soup. An example of a verbal representation might be one's word definition of the term "theory." There must surely be some correspondence between the kind of stimulus involved and the type of code, or representational form. It is difficult to code the meanings of abstract terms such as "theory" or "hypothesis" imaginally. These terms are most amenable to verbal representation. On the other hand, it is difficult to code verbally the memory of some "concrete" items such as the appearance of a friend at last night's party. It may be that some persons tend to "think" in terms of images whereas others tend to think in terms of words. Such cognitive differences may exist and be reflected in individual preferences for one or the other of the mnemonic representational systems.

Population tendencies for one form (thinking in terms of images) over another (thinking in terms of words) may also be reflected in various cultures. Among others, Rohwer, Lynch, Suzuki, and Levin (1967) have used pairs of pictures instead of words or nonsense syllables in studying children's learning. Pictures depicting an interactive relationship between two objects were more easily learned than merely side-by-side pictures. In a careful review of the research literature on imagery in children's learning, Rohwer (1970) concludes that the capacity to derive optimal benefit to learning from verbal forms may develop earlier than from pictural representation.

It has been found that subjects who were given instructions to rank sentences according to their "image-evoking value" retained more than subjects given instructions to rate the pronunciability (Anderson & Hidde, 1971). Bower (1970) instructed subjects to use images and found significant improvement in learning. In another study (Anderson, 1971) those subjects given instructions to "bring to mind a vivid mental image of the event described in each sentence" retained significantly more subject nouns than those who were given instructions to read each sentence aloud as many times as they could during the presentation period.

Anderson and Hidde (1971) attribute their positive findings to the opportunities provided subjects to process material meaningfully. Exactly what meaningfulness and meaningful processing are remains a problem (Johnson, 1975). Paivio (1969) maintains that imagery value may operate independently of any meaningfulness index. When imagery is controlled, Paivio has found that only small effects, if any, are attributable to meaningfulness. This leads us to a closer consideration of *meaningfulness*. Meaningfulness may be defined in a variety of ways. We have already discussed Ausubel's distinctions of logical and psychological meaningfulness in chapter 2. Noble (1952) established an operational index of meaningfulness by having subjects give as many associations to a stimulus word as they could during a one-minute interval. The mean number of associations became the meaningfulness value of the stimulus word. Meaningfulness may also be distinguished from familiarity, the amount of prior contact a person has had with an object.

Material in all three configurational mnemonic forms—bits of data, concepts, and structures—may be considered then to be coded verbally, as well as imaginally (see figure 8). When asked to associate pairs of words, subjects tend to use verbal mediators. For example, when the two stimulus words, *oak* and *pine,* are presented, subjects may use such verbal mediators as *tree, forest,* or *shade* (Marshall & Cofer, 1963, p. 411). As has already been mentioned, many experiences appear to lend themselves to verbal encoding, storage, and recall. Large amounts of information (residues of experience) may be coded in verbal structures. Lesser amounts of information are coded into verbal concepts. Structures and concepts are constructed by chains, arrays, and groupings of "bits." These bits, too, may be verbal or imaginal in nature.

Wood (1967), in a series of five experiments, investigated influences of mnemonic systems on recall of verbal material. Briefly, Wood's findings were that subjects who were provided with a list of memory "peg" words to use as mnemonics, did use them and to advantage over subjects without the "peg list." Learners using mnemonic devices performed better at a slower rate of presentation, suggesting that it takes some time to "work" the mnemonics. Unlike the results of most studies involving the "memorizing" of lists of words, when subjects used a mnemonic device, items from the middle of a list were not more difficult to learn or retain than items from either end. In other words, the use of mnemonics "neutralized" the primacy-recency phenomena in learning.

Some words of caution are appropriate here. First, long-term retention was not studied in Wood's experiments so that it is unclear what the effects of mnemonics are on anything but almost immediate recall. Second, as in most verbal learning studies, very simple materials were used (lists of common words). It is not at all clear if the same results would hold up with complex stimuli and responses. Further, repeated use of the same mnemonic device is likely to lead to proactive and retroactive interference where different responses are being learned. The mnemonics F-A-C-E and Every Good Boy Does Fine are useful for remembering the spaces and lines in the treble clef and are not mutually interfering because they differ in at least two important ways—one is a four-letter word, the other is a five-word sentence.

Memory and the Frame of Reference

The following statements summarize the influence of the frame of reference on memory.

1. The frame of reference includes a person's knowledge (concepts and structures). Thus learning processes and mnemonic processes change the person by changing his frame of reference. What a person already knows is a primary factor in what is learned and how well it is remembered and transferred (Wittrock & Cook, 1975).
2. A person's structures generally help learning and retention. New material will tend to be fitted into previously known structures. When a previously known structure interferes with the learning or retaining of new material, new structures must be learned or existing ones modified.
3. A person's attitudes may influence retention. Negative affective material may not be retained as well as more neutral material (Worchel, 1955).
4. A person's values and needs may influence his retention of material (Levine & Murphy, 1943).
5. Although no research known to the authors specifically illustrates correspondence between interests and retention, it is highly probable that this aspect of the frame of reference does, at least indirectly, influence retention. A person's needs and interests guide many of that person's actions. Aspects of experience resulting from these actions are the bases of memory. A young child, for example, stimulated by the color and drama of volcanos, may develop a lasting interest in this and related phenomena. The child may continue to seek consistent learning experiences for many years. The interest results in much knowledge in later years about volcanos and related phenomena.

Memory and the Characteristics of the Material Recalled

The nature of the material will frequently interact with other variables to influence retention. The following points illustrate the influence of the material's nature.

1. *Meaningfulness.* Material which is meaningful is retained better than that which is not meaningful. Since psychological

meaning is related to previous learning (for example, a word is meaningful because it is at least partially known or a person has some associations "connected" with it), what appears to be acquisition is frequently a "putting together" of several "meanings" not previously brought together. The new organization is meaningful and such organization will be remembered better than less-organized material. The factor of meaningfulness is also confounded by imagery.

2. *Generalizability*. Generalizations are retained better than isolated material. A generalization may be considered as a type of structure.
3. *Codability*. All other factors being equal, material which lends itself to systematic coding will be encoded and then remembered better than material otherwise equivalent (Homan, 1966; Underwood & Erlebacher, 1965). For example, few persons would find it easy to learn and remember this sequence of digits, 14916253649, without coding them in some way. Should the person code them as "the first seven squares" ($1 \times 1 = 1$, $2 \times 2 = 4$, $3 \times 3 = 9$, $4 \times 4 = 16$, etc.) remembering them would be easy. Some material lends itself to coding more readily than other material.
4. *Imagability*. Material which lends itself to the formation of visual images may be retained better. This is probably related to a preference for concreteness over abstraction, such as was described in Bruner's model of instruction in chapter 2. Illustrated materials in texts have been found to promote retention (Peeck, 1974).
5. *Familiarity*. Learning material with which one is already relatively familiar is generally an easier task than learning totally new material. In fact, if material is familiar, it is already known to some extent and the task may be to learn it better.
6. *Structurability*. Material which is organized into the person's cognitive structure, or which may be so organized, will be retained better.

What is retained and transferred depends a great deal on the events surrounding acquisition or the original learning. The degree of learning is partially dependent on attentional processes. In the following sections attention will be discussed briefly.

Memory and Attention

People are highly selective as to what events they attend among the many events which occur at any given time. Persons appear to be unable to *attend to* and *respond to* all potential stimuli in the environment at any given time. Through attentional processes the appropriate stimuli are selected and then encoded. Broadbent (1958) emphasized the limited capacity of the organism to handle stimuli. He also noted the lack of randomness of selectivity. What stimuli are actually selected, perceived, and attended to is a function of both the characteristics of the phenomenon and the person, including the frame of reference.

This selectivity function enables a person to be task oriented. It enables one to attend to the salient external stimuli of the task and the appropriate internal mnemonic stimuli. This latter attentional focus enables a person to "remember" experiences which are appropriate to the task and transfer these learnings to that task.

Attention as it is discussed here is the focusing of the person's sensory-perceptual systems on the input of information. This focusing consists of two stages. The first stage involves *orienting* the person to the salient aspects of the tasks to be learned or the problem to be solved. Some researchers speak of the *orienting reflex* (Sokolov, 1963). Research (Lynn, 1966) has indicated some of the responses characteristic of the orienting stage, which are as follows:

1. Increased sensitization of the sense organs (e.g., pupil dilation)
2. Skeletal muscle movement which directs sense organs (e.g., head turning)
3. Amplitude changes in EKG readings
4. Other body changes (respiratory and heart rate changes)

The second stage of attention is *maintaining contact* with those salient features of the task or problem. Both stages of attention involve external or overt responses as well as internal or covert responses.

The *overt* responses may be such action patterns as postural adjustments; for example, moving the body so that one can look in a certain direction and adjusting the position of the head. Other examples of overt response are looking at a specific word or picture and touching a certain point in a tactile array. Examples of the *covert* responses during both stages of attention are such perceptual/mnemonic responses as "calling to mind" the meaning one has of various attributes of the sensed word or shape, comparing relationships between words, and mental rehearsing of pronunciations.

Attention then should not be seen as some mysterious "faculty" or "ability" or a mysterious investment of psychic energy, but as a composite of numerous overt and covert responses which are involved in the reception and selection of information through the sensory-perceptual systems. Some of the failures to attend to appropriate information in terms of what the inattentive test-anxious person is doing instead of attending to the task (for example, a test item) are enumerated. The test-anxious person attends to self-evaluation and self-depreciation rather than to the task. That person worries about personal performance and about how others are doing. Actions are repetitive. In comparison, the attentive non-test-anxious student is task oriented and only concerned with those things pertinent to that task (Marlett & Watson, 1968; Wine, 1971). The attentive student reads the problem carefully, becomes concerned with only the relevant data and ignores irrelevant data. It is also likely that anxiety, even test anxiety, influences the person's ability to remember previous learnings and to transfer those to the problem immediately confronting him.

That to which a person attends influences what the person learns, remembers, and transfers. Attentional mechanisms "bridge the gap" between a person's frame of reference and what is learned, retained, and transferred. In the following section the transfer of learning is discussed.

Transfer of Learning

In a general sense, practically all new learnings involve transfer to some extent. The process of relating previously known material to new material is itself a form of transfer. Many of the functions of the frame of reference presented throughout the text involve transfer.

Transfer of learning involves the facilitating or disrupting influences of learning from one situation to another. Many laymen believe that if a person knows something, that person can be expected to apply the knowledge to all areas to which it is appropriate. Experimental and naturalistic observations, however, convince us that such is not the case. Applications of a skill do not appear to occur automatically. On the other hand, performance in an initial situation *may facilitate* performance in a later situation. Solving an algebraic equation in algebra class *may* aid the solving of a similar equation in a chemistry exam. A student *may* transfer the learning from algebra class to the chemistry laboratory. Such applications are termed *positive transfer*.

Performance in an initial situation may also interfere with learning in a second situation. Such cases are instances of *negative* transfer. In learning more than one task, facilitation, disruption, or neither may occur. Several different theories emerge in the literature as to the nature of these disrupting and facilitating influences.

Formal Discipline Theory

Psychologists of the nineteenth and early twentieth centuries conceptualized the mind as being composed of faculties (or agencies or

Transfer of Learning

powers). Such faculties as memory, attention, reasoning, and concentration were believed to exist and their effectiveness could be increased by exercise. Supposedly, learning and practice with some subjects such as Greek and Latin sharpen and increase these powers to a greater extent than learning and practicing other subjects. One "trains" one's "mind" by exercising one's faculties on difficult material. Once the "faculty" or "power" is sufficiently exercised and disciplined it may be used on any subject matter. The "power" will transfer to any mental activity. One can find even today statements used to support general education requirements or language requirements for various university degrees based on the idea that knowledge in such areas "disciplines" the mind. Theory and data of empirical psychologists today do not support the formal discipline theory of transfer.

Generalization Theory

Judd (1908) advocated the idea that a generalization formed in one situation may be transferred to another related situation (see also Overing & Travers, 1966). Underwater target shooting tasks were employed by Judd, Overing, and Travers. The tasks involved learning to make an adjustment for the refraction of light when shooting at submerged targets. Subjects who were instructed in the principle of refraction mastered the transfer task more readily than those not so instructed. Moreover, Overing and Travers (1966) established that subjects who verbalized the principle, and subjects who had established a set to respond, experienced greater generalization.

Identical Elements

According to Thorndike (1913), the extent of transfer of training from one situation to another is a function of the sameness of the parts of the two situations. If two situations share identical elements and a response was learned in the first, that response will be used in the second situation. Research done on *task* similarity, *response* similarity, *stimulus* similarity, and transfer helps us to understand more about both the generalization and identical elements theories, because similarities are always the bases for generalizations and identical elements among situations.

Similarity

While observing human behavior one might look to the nature of the task to study similarity relations. Thus, Skaggs and Robinson (Robinson, 1927) focus on the *task* to investigate similarity and transfer. Facilitative transfer under this orientation is more likely to occur when the characteristics of the task are either identical (similar) or opposite. Maximum interference occurs when some characteristics of the task are similar and some are dissimilar.

A specific characteristic of the task is the stimulus, which leads us to Osgood's (1949) notion of *stimulus and response similarity*. Task similarity seems to accentuate the configurational, the total field, whereas the notions of stimulus and response similarity accentuate specific stimuli and specific responses. According to Osgood's analysis, transfer is a function of the extent to which stimuli and responses are similar. In any two given situations both the responses to the situation and the stimuli in the situation may be different or remain the same. If the responses necessary to the situation are the same, the condition of *response similarity* obtains. If the stimuli are the same, *stimulus similarity* obtains. Facilitation and interference are a function of both response similarity (r_s) and stimulus similarity (s_s).

Consider the following examples of the various combinations of response and stimulus similarity as a child learns to read. An example of response similarity when stimuli are different (s_d-r_s) is pronunciation of the words *reed* and *read*. Two different stimuli call for the same vocal response. This is not facilitative. Consider now the last three letters of *reed* and *need*. The stimulus, *eed*, is the same and the response to them (pronunciation) is the same (s_s-r_s). This condition is facilitative. In the case of the words *moot* and *look*, the letters *oo* are the same but call for different vocal responses (pronunciation) (s_s-r_d). This condition is not facilitative. In the case of s_d-r_d the stimulus words *if* and *than* are different and different responses are appropriate. Thus, neither interference nor facilitation is likely to occur.

Learning to Learn

Harlow's famous experiments (e.g., Harlow, 1949) in which monkeys learned to make two-choice discriminations more and more rapidly have introduced the idea that *learning to learn* certain patterns of behavior is possible. Harlow's monkeys became more skillful in making two-choice discriminations with practice. Humans also are able to become more efficient on a specific class of tasks. Providing the learner with practice on the type of task involved increases the learner's efficiency (speed and accuracy) on that task for a short time (Hamilton, 1950; Thune, 1950). This is called the "warm-up effect." According to Thune (1950), learning to learn is a more lasting phenomenon than "warm up."

In recent years learning to learn (sometimes termed nonspecific transfer) has been conceptualized beyond the training on one type of discrimination problem observed by Harlow (1949). Some problem-solving strategies seem to facilitate performance from trial to trial (Davis, 1967; Neimark, 1961). In a very general sense, one may consider the complex structure-strategies described by Inhelder and Piaget (1958), and discussed in chapter 3, as learning/transfer aids in a learning to learn sense. Other problem-solving and concept-formation strategies (Bruner, Goodnow, & Austin, 1956; Miller, Galanter, & Pribram, 1960) also may be regarded as learning/transfer aids.

Degrees or Kinds of Transfer

In the introduction to the transfer of learning facilitating and disrupting influences were mentioned. These influences may be referred to as kinds of transfer.

- One kind of transfer is *positive* or *facilitative.* Facilitation is synonymous with *positive transfer,* the case of learning in one situation aiding the acquisition of skills in another situation.
- Another kind of transfer is *negative transfer* in which learning in one situation disrupts learning in another situation. For example, having learned that "mas" means "but" in Portuguese may make it more difficult to learn that "mas" means "more" in Spanish (negative transfer), but may facilitate the learning that "ma" means "but" in the Italian language (positive transfer).

It is important here to distinguish between *transfer* and *interference.* *Transfer* refers to the acquisition of new learnings being aided or disrupted by previous learnings. *Interference* refers to the recall (or performance) decrement (forgetting) which occurs when two things have been learned, but *one interferes with the recall of the other.*

The distinction between negative transfer and proactive interference thus becomes clear. Since transfer refers to the acquisition or *learning* phase and interference refers to the recall or retention of performance phase, negative transfer involves one learning making the learning of another (similar) thing difficult. Proactive interference involves a difficulty in remembering the second of two learnings because of interference from the first (B-A-A'). Thus, learning that "mas" means "but" in Portuguese may impede learning that "mas" means "more" in Spanish. However, once both these meanings are learned, to use "mas" correctly in Spanish requires overcoming the proactive interference of also having previously learned its Portuguese meaning.

- Another transfer term is *"zero transfer."* In many cases it is impossible to demonstrate either positive or negative transfer. These are conditions then of no transfer, *zero* transfer; the stimuli and responses are unrelated.

This brief overview of the kinds of transfer indicates some of the pitfalls that may be encountered by the educator in planning for instruction. It also indicates the necessity of planning and sequencing experiences carefully in schooling.

Conditions of Original Learning Facilitative of Positive Transfer and Retention

This section attempts to provide an overview of the research on specific conditions of original learning which facilitate retention and positive transfer, and should aid the teacher during stages 3 and 4 of instruction.

Verbalization

Overing and Travers (1966) found that verbalizing generalizations prior to applying the generalizations promotes transfer in problem solving. It is likely that such verbalization aids the learner in focusing attention responses on salient aspects of the task and situation. It is also likely that verbalizing aids the structuring and encoding processes involved in memory, especially verbal memory.

Practice

Practice on a variety of tasks or problems to which a skill is appropriate aids transfer (Duncan, 1958). The degree of learning is important because each problem must be learned well or practice on a variety of tasks will not have a positive influence. The learner must master each varied task or problem before transfer will occur (Morrisett & Hovland, 1959; Paul & Noble, 1964).

Degree of Original Learning

Mandler (1962), after reviewing research on the influence of the degree of original learning on transfer, concludes that greater amounts of practice result in increased positive transfer. This is related to the observation that "higher" degrees of learning result in better retention (Underwood, 1964; Underwood & Keppel, 1963). The term "overlearning" is frequently used to note a condition of learning beyond minimal mastery. Overlearning is generally considered to result in that which is being learned becoming resistant to forgetting.

Individual characteristics which influence acquisition probably also influence transfer and retention, especially by influencing the degree of learning. Such individual difference variables as the various aspects of the frame of reference, intelligence (Flavell & Hill, 1969), motivation, and anxiety will influence the extent of retention and the direction and extent of transfer. For example, a more intelligent student may be able to perceive generalizations and similarities and to verbalize them, and then learn them better. The more intelligent person will also be better able to create meaningful structures which will both strengthen original learning and aid recall.

The factors of structurability, generalizability, meaningfulness, codability, familiarity, and imagability discussed earlier in this chapter interact with verbalization, practice, and degree of original learning to influence retention and transfer. For example, having a student form a structure, verbalize it, and practice employing the structure should enhance the degree of original learning. This should result in better retention and transfer.

One area of research which is applicable to the degree of learning as well as attention is the research arising out of Rothkopf's notion of "mathemagenic" behaviors. "Mathemagenic" behaviors are those actions of the learner which give rise to learning (Rothkopf, 1970). They include attentional responses as well as cognitive processing responses.

One question which has emerged from Rothkopf's notion is, what can teachers and text writers do to stimulate these actions? One idea well researched is that questions could be inserted in written material. These questions would then stimulate attentional responses and cognitive processing responses. Research, in general, has shown that inserted questions do promote better retention and transfer (Walker, 1974; Rothkopf & Billington, 1974). Inserted questions seem to help focus the learner's attention, to stimulate review, to stimulate deeper processing, and to stimulate important inspection of nearby material. It would seem that the effect of inserted questions is to promote "higher" degrees of learning.

Summary

It should be obvious from this discussion of memory, attention, and transfer that these cognitive processes are very complex. Much is known, however, which can aid the person who is teaching or designing instructional materials to promote better retention and to promote positive transfer.

Discussion Questions

1. Does (should) every formal learning experience in school have distinct possibilities for transfer? Give examples.
2. What is the importance of transfer in contemporary society?
3. What do you take to be the key distinction between transfer and interference? How can proactive interference and negative transfer be distinguished?
4. What does the term "meaningful" mean as Ausubel uses it in the studies of "meaningful verbal learning"? What concern is this to teachers?
5. Can you distinguish between "meaningful" and "familiar" and between "meaningless" and "unfamiliar" in terms of learning materials? Devise examples of all four combinations, for example, meaningful familiar materials, or meaningful unfamiliar.
6. Identify some examples of proactive and retroactive interference in memory from your own experience.
7. If proactive and retroactive interference are rampant in school experiences, what can teachers do to counteract these types of forgetting? Be specific in terms of your own intended teaching.
8. Why do some teachers do a good job without ever having heard of transfer or interference? What things are they probably doing on an intuitive level?
9. Try recalling something you learned in school recently using visual imagery. How vivid is this memory? Is it a fact or a concept? A structure? Explain.
10. Think of a portion of a school curriculum in some discipline or subject-matter area which you may some day teach. Can you identify areas of possible positive and negative transfer?
11. In the context of question 10, can you identify items which should be acquired for long-term store by students and other items which may only need to be retained for a short period, forgotten, and may be relearned at some later date when and if needed?

Recommended Readings

Adams, J. A. *Learning and memory: An introduction.* Homewood, Ill.: Dorsey Press, 1976.

Bakan, P. (Ed.) *Attention.* Princeton, N. J.: Van Nostrand, 1966. Some basic studies on attention.

Cermack, L. S. *Human memory: Research and theory.* New York: Ronald Press, 1972.

Ellis, H. C. *The transfer of learning.* New York: Macmillan, 1965. A thorough overview; some basic studies are also reprinted.

Hunter, I. M. *Memory: Facts and fallacies.* Baltimore, Maryland: Penguin, 1957. A good overview of the psychology of memory.

Munsat, S. *The concept of memory.* New York: Random House, 1966. A philosophical analysis of the concept of memory.

Trabasso, T., & Bower, G. H. *Attention in learning: Theory and research.* New York: Wiley, 1968. A basic primer for those interested in reading further about attention.

References

Adams, J. A. *Human memory.* New York: McGraw-Hill, 1967.

Anderson, R. C. Encoding processes in the storage and retrieval of sentences. *Journal of Experimental Psychology,* 1971, *91,* 338-40.

Anderson, R. C., & Hidde, J. L. Imagery and sentence learning. *Journal of Educational Psychology,* 1971, *62,* 526-30.

Anderson, R. C., & Kulhavy, R. W. Imagery and prose learning. *Journal of Educational Psychology,* 1972, *63,* 242-43.

Asch, S. A reformulation of the problem of association. *American Psychologist,* 1969, *24,* 92-102.

Ashby, W. R. Modeling the brain. *Proceedings of the IBM scientific computing symposium on simulation models and gaming.* Yorktown Heights, N.Y.: Thomas J. Watson Research Center, December 7-9, 1964.

Bandura, A. *Principles of behavior modification.* New York: Holt, Rinehart & Winston, 1969.

Bartlett, F. C. *Remembering: A study in experimental and social psychology.* London: Cambridge University Press, 1932.

Bower, G. H. Analysis of a mnemonic device. *American Scientist,* 1970, *58,* 496-510.

Broadbent, D. E. *Perception and communication.* London: Pergamon Press, 1958.

Bruner, J. S., Goodnow, J. J., & Austin, G. A. *A study of thinking.* New York: Wiley, 1956.

Davis, G. A. Detrimental effects of distraction, additional response alternatives, and longer response chains in solving switch-light problems. *Journal of Experimental Psychology,* 1967, *73,* 45-55.

Duncan, C. P. Transfer after training with single versus multiple tasks. *Journal of Experimental Psychology,* 1958, *55,* 63-72.

Flavell, J. H., & Hill, J. P. Developmental psychology. In P. H. Mussen and M. R. Rosenzweig (Eds.), *Annual Review of Psychology,* 1969, *20,* 1-56.

Hamilton, C. E. The relationship between length of interval separating two learning tasks and performance on the second task. *Journal of Experimental Psychology,* 1950, *40,* 613-21.

Harlow, H. F. The formation of learning sets. *Psychological Review,* 1949, *56,* 51-65.

Homan, L. E. *Stimulus coding ability and stimulus predifferentiation.* Unpublished master's thesis, University of New Mexico, 1966.

Inhelder, B., & Piaget, J. *The growth of logical thinking from childhood to adolescence.* New York: Basic Books, 1958.

Jenkins, J. G., & Dallenbach, K. M. Obliviscence during sleep and waking. *American Journal of Psychology,* 1924, *35,* 605-12.

Johnson, R. E. Meaning in complex learning. *Review of Educational Research,* 1975, *45,* 425-59.

Judd, C. H. The relation of special training to general intelligence. *Educational Review,* 1908, *36,* 28-42.

Köhler, W. *Gestalt psychology.* New York: Liveright, 1929.

Levine, J. M., & Murphy, G. The learning and forgetting of controversial material. *Journal of Abnormal and Social Psychology,* 1943, *38,* 507-17.

Lynn, R. *Attention, arousal and the orientation reaction.* Oxford: Pergamon Press, 1966.

Mandler, G. From association to structure. *Psychological Review,* 1962, *69,* 415-27.

Marlett, N. J., & Watson, D. Text anxiety and immediate or delayed feedback in a test-like avoidance task. *Journal of Personality and Social Psychology,* 1968, *8,* 200-03.

Marshall, G. R., & Cofer, C. N. Associative indices as measures of word relatedness: A summary and comparison of ten methods. *Journal of Verbal Learning and Verbal Behavior,* 1963, *1,* 408-21.

Miller, G. A., Galanter, E., & Pribram, K. H. *Plans and the structure of behavior.* New York: Holt, Rinehart & Winston, 1960.

Morrisett, L., Jr., & Hovland, C. I. A comparison of three varieties of training in human problem solving. *Journal of Experimental Psychology,* 1959, *58,* 52-55.

Neimark, E. D. Information-gathering in diagnostic problem-solving. *Psychological Record,* 1961, *11,* 243-48.

Neisser, U. *Cognitive psychology.* New York: Appleton-Century-Crofts, 1967.

Noble, C. E. An analysis of meaning. *Psychological Review,* 1952, *59,* 421-30.

Norman, D. A. *Memory and attention: An introduction to human information processing.* New York: Wiley, 1969.

References

Osgood, C. E. The similarity paradox in human learning: A resolution. *Psychological Review,* 1949, *56,* 132-43.

Overing R. L. R., & Travers, R. M. W. Effect upon transfer of variations in training conditions. *Journal of Educational Psychology,* 1966, *57,* 179-88.

Paivio, A. Mental imagery in associative learning and memory. *Psychological Review,* 1969, *76,* 241-63.

Paivio, A. On the functional significance of memory. *Psychological Bulletin,* 1970, *73,* 385-92.

Paivio, A., & Csapo, K. Concrete image and verbal memory codes. *Journal of Experimental Psychology,* 1969, *80,* 279-85.

Paul, N. T., & Noble, C. E. Influence of successive habit reversals on human learning and transfer. *Journal of Experimental Psychology,* 1964, *68,* 37-43.

Peeck, J. Retention of pictorial and verbal content of a text, with illustrations. *Journal of Educational Psychology,* 1974, *66,* 880-88.

Robinson, E. S. The 'similarity' factor in retroaction. *American Journal of Psychology,* 1927, *39,* 297-312.

Rohwer, W. D., Jr. Images and pictures in children's learning: Research results and educational implications. *Psychological Bulletin,* 1970, *73,* 393-403.

Rohwer, W. D., Jr., Lynch, S., Suzuki, N. S., & Levin, J. R. Verbal and pictorial facilitation in paired-associate learning. *Journal of Experimental Child Psychology,* 1967, *5,* 294-302.

Rothkopf, E. Z. The concept of mathemagenic activities. *Review of Educational Research,* 1970, *40,* 325-36.

Rothkopf, E. Z., & Billington, M. J. Indirect review and priming through questions. *Journal of Educational Psychology,* 1974, *66,* 669-79.

Shiffrin, R. M., & Atkinson, R. C. Storage and retrieval processes in long-term memory. *Psychological Review,* 1969, *76,* 179-93.

Sokolov, E. N. *Perception and the conditional reflex.* New York: Pergamon Press, 1963.

Thorndike, E. L. *Educational psychology, the psychology of learning.* Vol. II. New York: Teachers College, Columbia University Press, 1913.

Thune, L. E. The effect of different types of preliminary activities on subsequent learning of paired-associate material. *Journal of Experimental Psychology,* 1950, *40,* 423-38.

Underwood, B. J. Degree of learning and the measurement of forgetting. *Journal of Verbal Learning and Verbal Behavior,* 1964, *3,* 112-29.

Underwood, B. J., & Erlebacher, A. H. Studies of coding in verbal learning. *Psychological Monographs,* 1965, *79* (whole No. 606).

Underwood, B. J., & Keppel, G. Retention as a function of degree of learning and letter-sequence interference. *Psychological Monographs,* 1963, *77* (whole No. 567).

Walker, B. S. Effects of inserted questions on retroactive inhibition in meaningful verbal learning. *Journal of Educational Psychology,* 1974, *66,* 486-90.

Wine, J. Test anxiety and direction of attention. *Psychological Bulletin,* 1971, *76,* 92-104.

Wittrock, M. C. Learning as a generative process. *Educational Psychologist,* 1974, *11,* 87-95.

Wittrock, M. C., & Cook, H. Transfer of prior learning to verbal instruction. *American Educational Research Journal,* 1975, *12,* 147-56.

Wood, C. Mnemonic systems in recall. *Journal of Educational Psychology Monograph,* 1967, *58* (whole No. 645).

Worchel, P. Anxiety and repression. *Journal of Abnormal and Social Psychology,* 1955, *50,* 201-05.

Practical Organizer for Chapter 6

Educators should know enough about human problem solving and creativity to break through the mystique which surrounds much of the rhetoric about these processes. It is likely that the same forms of acquisition—self-initiation, discovery, response guidance, and imitation—and the same means of response fixation—reinforcement—operate in thinking and creativity as other behavior patterns.

It is true that problem solving and creativity are complex processes, but enough is known about them that the teacher can, at least to some extent, shape these skills.

Suppose, for example, the teacher wishes to encourage thoughtful, critical, reading skills. Appropriate prose passages can be selected and using table 5 as a guide, the teacher could direct the group to locate examples of the typically used illogical devices.

The instructor should select content-related problems for individual students and groups of students and encourage students to acquire similar problem-seeking behaviors. The teacher provides guidance as the group (or the individual) conceptualizes the problem, selects appropriate information, and develops hypotheses about the problem. The techniques of "set breaking" (see list of questions on p. 159) and brainstorming may be used both in problem finding and solving. The teacher may wish to shape skills in both problem identification and creative problem solving using similar content-related problems.

Thinking, Problem Solving, and Creativity

6

Educators frequently are exhorted to teach students to think and to be creative. Those who so exhort are not always familiar with the complex nature of such behavior nor with the difficulty involved in modifying thought and creativity. In this chapter we discuss a wide range of literature and research on the nature of thinking, problem solving, and creativity as well as some ways of teaching these behaviors. Remember that thinking and creativity frequently involve transfer and set.

Many actions involve extensions beyond immediate memory and reactions to external stimuli. Such extensions beyond given information in memory and environment fall within the realms of thought and creativity. Humans seem impelled to analyze the *implications* of what is known as well as generate the *possibilities* from what is known. Indeed, the authors recognize this as being so important that in chapter 4 cognitive needs are considered as being as basic as other needs.

Wallach (1967, p. 46) terms the *analysis of implications* as thinking, and the *expression of possibilities* as creativity. The former tends toward cognitive *convergence* and the latter toward cognitive *divergence* (Guilford, 1967). Guilford (1967) assigns to convergent thinking those cognitive processes which achieve a single right or wrong answer to a problem. Convergent thinking seems to be most typical of those operations used in answering items on achievement and ability (intelligence) tests. On the other hand, divergent thinking appears to be most typical of those cognitive operations resulting in exploring different aspects or possibilities of information. Guilford's (1967) concepts have emerged from factor analysis procedures which reduce intercorrelations among tests and test items to underlying "factors."

Such dichotomies as *convergent* and *divergent* should not be thought of as strictly separate, but as "impure" statistical groupings of responses to test items. Guilford, unlike many previous investigators, has included convergent and divergent thinking (creativity) within a larger category of intellectual operations, thus categorizing creativity and thinking together as mental processes. The authors tend to agree with this organization.

Even though these two psychological constructs may be grouped, it is helpful to examine each separately in order to reflect upon the implications of the research on these topics. Educators are interested in helping persons develop ways of generating correct solutions as well as develop ways of achieving unique, original solutions and ideas. As you read this chapter and consider its contents you should frequently be reminded of the roles of past learning, situational variables, and the frame of reference in thinking and creativity. Thus the probability of occurrence of the creative response in any situation can be considered to be a function of external stimulation, internal stimulation, and behavioral capability as discussed in chapter 3.

In a general sense, thinking involves problem identification, classification, and resolution behaviors. So also does creativity, but it involves solutions and relationships between concepts which are either unique or unusual. Neither thinking nor creativity are the most basic of psychological processes. Both involve more fundamental psychological processes such as sensation, attention, perception, learning, memory, and transfer.

Problem resolutions and classifications also involve transfer. Indeed it is likely that most resolutions involve the application of previously learned material or skills to new situations. Without this transfer, it is unlikely that problem solving would occur at all.

Thinking

The number of different meanings for the verb "to think" reflects the variety of meanings of the term in psychology. Bourne et al. (1971, p. 8) enumerate several usages of the term "think": believe, anticipate, remember, and imagine. Many of these meanings have parallels in the psychological studies of human thought or indicate more basic processes likely to be involved in thinking (such as memory).

The literature on human thought includes two broad research areas: problem solving and concept formation. Generally, problem-solving behaviors involve (1) the attainment of some goal, (2) the failure of initial attempts, and (3) the existence of alternatives (Bourne et al., 1971, p. 9). Problem solving seems to involve *resolution* between an initial state of affairs and a desired state of affairs (Loree, 1965). Examples of resolution problems frequently encountered in the classroom are listed here. Items 1, 3, 4, and 5 are pertinent to discovery methods of teaching in the classroom.

1. Explaining phenomena by laboratory experimentation.
2. Setting of rules of deportment by a group.
3. Deciding how to gather data.
4. Deciding how to evaluate data.
5. Deciding how to use data.

Concept formation primarily involves placing events, phenomena, and objects in a category or a *classification*. Classification problems frequently encountered in the classroom are listed here.

1. Identify central issues (classifying as central or not central).
2. Recognize underlying assumptions.
3. Evaluate evidence or authority (classifying as supportive or nonsupportive).
4. Recognize stereotypes and clichés.
5. Recognize bias and emotional factors in a presentation.
6. Distinguish between verifiable and unverifiable data or argument.
7. Distinguish between relevant and nonrelevant data or argument.
8. Distinguish between essential and incidental data or argument.
9. Recognize adequacy of data (classifying as adequate or inadequate).

10. Determine whether facts support a generalization (classifying fact as supporting or nonsupporting).
11. Check consistency (classifying arguments as consistent or inconsistent).*

Much of human thought involves classification. We process much of the information with the immediate goal of placing it in a category. Bruner et al. (1956, pp. 12-13) enumerate the many functions of categorization, some of which are noted below. By classification:

1. Environmental complexity is lessened
2. Objects are identified
3. Memory is aided (that is, the need for constant, repetitive learning is lessened)
4. Directions for operant behavior are provided

Educators should realize that intellectual functioning is characterized by individual differences. People solve problems in different ways. Research in cognitive style emphasizes patterns of individual differences (Denney, 1974; Ehri & Muzio, 1974; Kagan, 1965; Robinson & Gray, 1974; and Witkin et al., 1962).

Five Approaches to Thinking

There are five different approaches to the study of human thought discussed here: (1) associationism, to include Thorndike's trial and error approach (discussed in chapter 2), (2) logical analysis, (3) Gestalt psychology (also in chapter 2), (4) computer simulation, and (5) cognitive-structural analysis (e.g., Piaget). A description of each approach is included.

Associationism

The history of associationism, its general role in behavior theory, and its more specific role in the psychology of thought is long and complex. This history extends to ancient Greek philosophy and may be seen in the work of Aristotle (Ross, 1942). Aristotle spoke about the mental associations of events and facts to one another through contiguity, or closeness in space and time of the occurrences of events or facts. Associationism may also be traced through Bain (1855), Hume (1912), James (1918), and Mill (1878). Relatively modern psychologists, especially behaviorists, tend to analyze thought into specific conditioned connections (associations) between stimuli

---

*Adapted from T. H. Anderson and D. Essex, *Report to the National Science Foundation on Programs and Plans. An Experiment in Engineering Education*, T. P. Torda, N.S.F. Grant #GY 9300 (undated), by permission of the authors.

Five Approaches to Thinking

(Pavlov, 1927), connections between stimuli and responses (Pavlov, 1927), connections between situations and responses (Thorndike, 1931), and connections between reinforcers and responses (Skinner, 1953). Very generally, associationists have analyzed thinking in terms of different kinds of connections and series or chains of connections.

Skinner (1953), for example, uses a reinforcement paradigm to explain problem solving. Persons emit responses (operants) to situations which include alternatives and some responses are reinforced. When the conflict among the alternatives is ended, the problem is resolved (1953, p. 244). Skinner has not considered this procedure to be the same as Thorndike's trial and error learning (1953, p. 248) primarily because he sees a lack of randomness in operant behavior.

Modern associationist theory involves more than observable stimulus-response associations. Verbal mediators—covert responses—are found to be employed during verbal learning (Adams & Montague, 1967) and in problem solving (Judson, Cofer, & Gelfand, 1956).

The fact that these language or verbal mediators (some are termed *natural language mediators* by Adams and Montague) are found to exist gives impetus to questions about relationships between language and thought (and culture). Sapir (1949) maintains that language is a major determining factor in strategies, styles, and modes of thought and thus influences culture. Students who wish to investigate this area are encouraged to read further (Bourne et al., 1971, especially chapters 13 and 14; Bruner et al., 1966, especially chapter 2; Piaget, 1967, especially chapter 3; Rankin, 1963; Saporta, 1961; and Vygotsky, 1962).

Logical Analysis

A second approach to thinking is logical analysis. There have been numerous attempts to analyze logically the steps or phases involved in problem solving. Perhaps the most often quoted steps in problem solving (reflection) are those of Dewey and are as follows:

1. A felt difficulty
2. Its location and definition
3. Suggestion of possible solution
4. Development by reasoning of the most likely solution
5. Further observation and experimentation leading to solution acceptance or rejection; that is, the conclusion of belief or disbelief [1910, p. 72].

Dewey believed that the first two steps frequently fuse into one. The felt difficulty may have been brought about by (1) a conflict between conditions and an intended result, (2) an attempt to identify the characteristics of an object, or (3) an attempt to explain an unexpected event (pp. 72-73).

Dewey believed that when the felt difficulty came unexpectedly and as a shock the first two stages did not fuse. In these cases there was a need to define the nature of the problem or "make clear the specific character of the problem" (p. 74). It was necessary to define the problem, or the suggestions (frequently called the hypotheses) would emerge in a random fashion (p. 74).

The third stage, "suggestion of a possible solution," involves going from what is "present to something absent" (p. 75). It involves selection of facts and arrangement of those particular facts from which suggestions issue (p. 75). This suggestion constitutes a thought, and cultivating varieties of these thoughts denotes good thinking.

The fourth step involves tracing out the implications of the suggestions. The fifth step involves verification of "experimental corroboration" (p. 77). Dewey believed that thinking mediates observations—the original observations at the beginning of the felt difficulty and the final observations at the resolution (p. 77).

Another logical approach is described by Munn (1956) who presents four stages attributed to Poincaré (p. 360). They are (1) preparation, (2) incubation, (3) inspiration or illumination, and (4) verification or revision. Preparation consists of a variety of activities from training activities such as studying and gathering data to trial and error types of activities. Incubation consists of reflection and very little apparent progress. Inspiration, the third stage, suddenly occurs as a flash of insight. The material suddenly has meaning and the parts of the problem suddenly fit together. The fourth stage, that of verification, or revision, is that of testing out or evaluating the possible solutions which occurred during the point of inspiration.

Gestalt Psychology

A third approach to the study of thinking is that of the Gestalt psychologists. For several decades the Gestalt principle of insight posed the major theoretical alternative to trial and error learning and problem solving. The work of Köhler presented an appealing mentalistic contrast to the rather mechanical trial and error interpretation. Insight (Köhler's ideas are discussed in chapter 2) also presented a wholistic conceptualization which differed from the fragmentation of trial and error association formation.

Max Wertheimer (1959) also researched problem solving from a Gestalt point of view, but articulated an explanation which was like insight but different enough to warrant a brief discussion. To

Wertheimer, problem solving consisted primarily of grasping the structural relationships in a situation (p. 235).

Wertheimer's analysis focused upon the dynamic understanding of the structural features interacting with the processes of grouping which led toward solution. He protested vigorously against the tendency of the associationists to fragment the structural wholistic process of problem solving (p. 237). Wertheimer's ideas had considerable influence on Karl Duncker (1945), who did research in the area of insight. Duncker had subjects "think aloud." His work led to further understanding of the structuring features of problem solving as well as the positive effects of verbalizing and verbal examination of each offered solution. That is, through verbalizing about one alternative one learns (discovers) other alternatives.

Gestalt theory and associationist psychological theories apply insight and reinforcement respectively as explanations of learning and problem solving. Insight and reinforcement (with resulting stimulus and response connections) are coordinate explanations of behavior change. The first times they occur may be considered as problem situations. Learning occurs that first time by either insight or reinforcement. If learning does occur initially, on the next instance the solution may be remembered and applied to a second situation. That is to say, learning and problem solving are involved in the first instance and memory and/or transfer of learning and new problem solving in the second instance.

Computer Simulation

A fourth approach to the study of thinking and problem solving is computer simulation (Feigenbaum & Feldman, 1963; Hovland, 1960; and Reitman, 1965). Computers represent practically the only readily acceptable analogue to the human brain. The factors of input, processing, and output are roughly analogous to stimulation-perception variables, organismic structuring-mnemonic variables, and response variables in human behavior.

Two types of computers are identifiable—the digital and the analog. The digital computer represents information with binary digits or symbols. Symbols, numbers, and instructions are stored and processed in terms of "zeros" and "ones." The digital computer counts digits in discrete units in a series. The pattern of combination of the two figures is crucial to the operation of the computer. This system is compatible with algorithmic situations. Given exact data a correct solution is found. The digital system until recently was not efficient when a large number of variables interact on the outcome of a given solution in terms of probability. The analog computer operates on the basis of heuristics. Information is represented in terms of continuous and varying voltages. It may operate upon "rules" which produce correct solutions more often than not. Wiener (1954) has characterized digital machines as those that *count*, whereas analog machines *measure*.

A typical computer simulation approach is to collect protocol material from human subjects "thinking aloud" as they solve problems in a laboratory situation. Then programs are written which simulate the processes used by the human subjects. For example, Newell and Simon (1961) asked college sophomores to solve symbolic logic problems while "thinking aloud." The computer (the general problem solver) was then programmed to the steps obtained from the data. Newell and Simon concluded that computers use methods of problem solving which parallel those methods used by humans. (Recent research on *artificial intelligence* is much broader in scope than computer simulation of problem solving [Ortony, 1975a, 1975b, 1975c].)

Cognitive-Structural Analysis

The fifth approach to the study of human thought is referred to as cognitive structural. Investigators using this approach accentuate development of internally organized responses. A brief overview of Piaget's work is presented below as the most important example of this approach. This overview is also presented to acquaint the reader with the development of human thought processes from birth to adolescence. To Piaget, cognition, intelligence, and development are inseparable, and learning is an essential dimension of all three.

Piaget and the Development of Human Thought

Piaget and his colleagues have greatly influenced research on human thought throughout the world. Piaget attempts to study thought processes developmentally. Taking only a few subjects, he observes and interviews them in terms of their cognitive development. The subjects' interactions with physical reality and the sequential development of patterns of interaction and their effects on cognitive structures appear to be Piaget's principal problems. Piaget sees cognitive development as an unfolding from simple, naive processes to more complex processes. His detailed explanations help to explain the increasing acceptance of his particular approach. Few cognitive theorists are able to explain in such detailed terms the gradual developments which may be observed. The reader should be able to observe some of these developmental phenomena in children and begin to grasp their educational implications.

Piaget and the Development of Human Thought

Basic Concepts

Several concepts should be discussed in order to understand Piaget's explanations of cognition.

Assimilation and Accommodation. To Piaget cognition consists of two processes, assimilation and accommodation, which are dual interacting aspects of organismic adaptation to environment. Assimilation pertains to the changes produced in respect to the objects of the environment which are "taken in" for the organism's use. Accommodation is the organism's adjustment to characteristics of the environment in order to be receptive to environmental products required for the organism's use. Patterns of behavior or of cognition which result are termed schemata (singular-schema). The relation among assimilation, accommodation, and schemata is like the action, reaction, synthesis sequence in Hegelian dialectics.

Egocentrism. The concept of egocentrism appears to be descriptive of an important dimension of cognitive development which has attained some measure of attention. "Egocentrism" is defined as a confusion of "...his self with the universe, in other words that he is unconscious of his self..." (Piaget, 1963, p. 125). The young child apparently does not differentiate between self and external reality or between that which is self and that which is not self. Egocentrism is characteristic of a world view and of the initial phases of speech development. Egocentrism disappears, according to Piaget, as a result of environmental (including social) interaction. Decentering is the process of the decline of egocentrism—the movement away from egocentrism with respect to objects. It involves being able to see that there are other persons in the world and eventually to see the world from another person's point of view. The decentering process continues until adult roles are assumed (Inhelder & Piaget, 1958).

Action and Equilibration. Other important concepts of Piaget are action and equilibration. Throughout Piaget's research the role the person's actions or responses play in learning and development is paramount. The person's interactions with environment form bases for learning and development. It will be seen in later sections that the simple reflexive, motor *actions* of the infant unfold through individual characteristics and environmental interactions to produce very complex reflective cognitive strategies. The strategies develop through action.

Equilibration is the unifying principle of development, cognition, and intelligence (Furth, 1969, pp. 205-19; Piaget, 1967, pp. 100-13.) (Piaget always makes the point that development, cognition, and intelligence are interactive and inseparable.) Equilibration is an

147

Thinking, Problem Solving, and Creativity

internal, self-regulating mechanism which achieves balance when external factors and other internal factors become imbalanced. Equilibration, in correcting these imbalances, extends the person's cognitive skills (and thus enhances intelligence and development). It is the means for progressing from one developmental level to the next.

Allusions to assimilation and accommodation may help the reader to understand equilibration and its balancing function. As a person assimilates, or produces changes in the environment, that person may be required to develop a new cognitive strategy enabling interaction with that change thus achieving balance or equilibrium. On the other hand, as the person accommodates or changes, balance must also be achieved with environmental factors relating to that internal change.

Piaget's Method

For the most part Piaget's method involves observation of problem-solving behaviors with varying amounts of intervention and situational control by the experimenter. Careful observation of the verbal and nonverbal behavior of the subject is followed by analysis and generalization. There is practically no concern with experimental design in the sense of control and experimental groups or statistical analysis of data.

Piagetian studies usually involve one subject at a time. A problem is posed and, when the subject makes a response, the experimenter poses a new question or a variation of the initial question to delve into aspects of the problem.* The observed verbal behaviors are frequently interspersed with psychomotor responses. In some instances there is no verbal interaction between experimenter and subject. In the studies of very young children, Piaget simply observes, analyzes, and reports their behaviors in given situations. During the later stages of the first period, nonverbal tasks are posed. Later more extensive "interviews" are conducted.

The principal objective is to investigate the cognitive structure of the subject. Subjects of various age levels are studied in order to examine cognitive changes developmentally. Flavell (1963) indicates that most of the information which has been reported on the first period of cognitive development consists of minute observations of Piaget's own three children.

Flavell (1963) notes that Piaget's methods of studying cognitive structure fall into two classes: (1) making careful observations with

---

*Teachers should find such approaches helpful with "problem" students. Observe and interact on a one-to-one basis with students who are having problems. There are times when a problem-oriented interview of a few minutes with one student will have benefit.

Piaget and the Development of Human Thought

no other experimenter intervention and (2) providing stimuli which evoke the behavior studied. The majority of Piaget's studies fall into the latter class whereas the former characterizes his earliest work. Flavell also appropriately notes that logical analysis generally follows observation, and that results are generally interpreted in terms of traditional philosophy. Several overviews of Piaget's work now exist in English other than Flavell's and are recommended to the reader (Elkind, 1970; Furth, 1969; Piaget, 1967; Piaget & Inhelder, 1969; and Wadsworth, 1971; also see the recommended readings at the end of this chapter).

The Periods of Cognitive Development Summarized

Piaget abstracted four major periods of cognitive development from birth to maturity. These stages have approximate ages associated with them, but it should be emphasized that this is a stage theory and the chronological ages are very approximate and not to be generalized to any child. The initial period is from birth to about age two and is termed the *sensorimotor* period. During this period the child's cognitive development involves relatively basic motor and sensory organization and coordination. Such primary skills as eye-hand coordination develop at this time through repetitive and circular behaviors.

The second period is the *preoperational* and *intuitive* period which lasts from about age two until around ages six or seven. Early in this period the child begins to manipulate symbols. The child later develops structural frameworks which are used to order external events and enters the *concrete operational* period (approximately ages seven to eleven or twelve).

The final period is termed the *formal operations* period which lasts from about ages eleven or twelve to fifteen in which the adolescent fully develops complex techniques for not only dealing with the immediate world but the symbolic world of abstraction and possibility. In actuality the onset of formal operations may be delayed considerably and never appear at all in some retarded adults. The age ranges cited are not to be regarded as fixed, rather the emphasis is placed on the invariant sequence of stages.

The Sensorimotor Period

It is during this period that the child establishes contact with external reality and differentiates between self and external objects. Basic sensorimotor skills are developed and coordinated. Toward the end of this period the child is able to represent actions rather than merely to perform them, by symbolic representations other than pure language.

Thinking, Problem Solving, and Creativity

At the end of this period the child recognizes that objects have existence apart from self. With respect to cause, the child has developed a capacity to infer effect when cause is obvious. With respect to time, Piaget believes that time is seen by the child as a factor in which objects and the self can be located with respect to each other. This period, which is divided into six stages, is thoroughly described in Piaget's *The Origins of Intelligence in the Child* (1952b.).

The First Stage. During this stage "the reflex is consolidated and strengthened by virtue of its own functioning." There is "a growing need for repetition" (Piaget, 1952b, p. 32). The infant's reflex of sucking is repetitive and it appears that some searching behavior occurs for the nipple or related objects, especially when the child is hungry.

The Second Stage. Two principal circular reactions (repetitive actions which strengthen the reflex) become evident in the second stage—a systematic protrusion of the tongue and thumbsucking. Signals appear to initiate sucking. These signals are position, optical signals (the mother), and so forth (1952b, p. 49). The child begins to turn to look at sources of sound and react to them.

The Third Stage. This stage appears with the development of the capacity to apprehend visual objects. It is marked by the appearance of secondary circular reactions and intentional behavior. The secondary circular reactions are attempts to maintain changes produced by chance in the environment through repetition (Piaget, 1952b, p. 157). These are attempts to make interesting sensations last. These attempts are cited as evidence to show that the child primitively recognizes the external environment and that actions are no longer related to the child's own body. Repeated dropping of the spoon during mealtime in the months following is a secondary circular reaction familiar to most parents.

The Fourth Stage. This stage begins at about eight to nine months. Marked advances are noted here in the child's recognition of objects. The child becomes capable of seeking objects which disappear. Apparently the child now attributes a reality to objects independent of self (1952b, p. 211). If you have access to an infant of this stage try gaining its attention with some small object. Hide the object immediately in front of the child. Starting at this stage the child will search for it.

The Fifth Stage. This stage begins at about twelve months. The stage is characterized by a search for novelty or a kind of experimentation. Tertiary circular reactions are said to develop at this point in the development of the child. Repetitive acts are still the means whereby the child explores objects, but the tertiary circular reactions are those which the child uses to explore and experiment with various object characteristics by using the same movements over and over again, varying them little by little in an intentional manner. The child analyzes changes produced.

The Sixth Stage. The sixth stage begins at about eighteen months. During this stage the child develops new means through mental coordinations. Apparently the child is able to experiment mentally instead of physically trying out solutions. The child is able to represent objects through primitive symbols. Exemplifying these are such "symbolic schemata" as pretending to sleep (Piaget, 1950, p. 125).

The Period of Preoperational and Intuitive Thought

The first part of this period lasts from about two to four years of age, with the second part lasting until about six or seven. Behaviorally the period begins with the early stages in the systematic acquisition of language (Piaget, 1950, p. 123). This is the period of "preconcepts." These preconcepts are "notions which the child attaches to the first verbal signs he learns to use" (1950, p. 127). The signs are characterized by being between generalized concepts and the individual elements of which the generalized concept is composed. The child may report that several moons have been seen during the evening or that one snail was seen during a walk when in fact several have been seen. They are all "snail" or "moon." The child does not yet cope with general classes. A distant object, such as a mountain, is thought to have changed shape during a trip in which actually various views of the same mountain have been seen (1950, p. 128).

The latter part of this period is termed by Piaget as intuitive (1950, p. 129). It extends from about the fourth year to the seventh year. At this stage thoughts about object reality appear to be centered on one attribute while the child appears to ignore all the other possible attributes. This is called "centering" and it results in the child's lack of conservation of number, size, and volume. For example, two glasses of the same shape and size are filled by the child with equal numbers of beads. The experimenter then pours the beads from one glass into a thin taller glass. The child may then believe (1) that there are more beads in the taller glass if height is centered upon, or (2) fewer beads in the taller glass if thinness of the glass is centered upon. There are more beads "because it is taller" or less beads "because it is thinner." The child seems to remain perceptually bound (Piaget, 1952a, pp. 25-27). Yet toward the end of this period the child begins to be more flexible and begins to pay more attention to other characteristics—thus decentering and conservation begin to emerge.

The child at this stage remains egocentric in that he/she cannot take the role of another person or see his/her own viewpoint as one of many possible. The child does not justify his/her language or reasoning to another person.

This period of development is also characterized by the growth of quantitative thinking. Three major types of quantitative thinking are identified—gross, intensive, and extensive—developed in that order. These have been observed and investigated by Elkind (1961). Around age four the child is able to deal with *gross* quantity. This is the simplest form of perceived, uncoordinated quantity between two or more objects. In this type, A is recognized as longer than B. The facilitating behavior of *intensive* quantity relations at approximately age five is more complicated. At this point the child can perceive quantity relations taken two by two. For example, A is reported by the subject as being longer and wider than B. The most complex quantity relation type is *extensive*. The child recognizes unit relations between objects. For example, A can be seen to be one-half of B. These are logical constructs achieved through abstracts and reasoning. "Piaget assumes that once attained, the subject perceives them directly as perceptually given properties of the object" (Elkind, 1961, p. 38). Elkind found that his statistical testing of the repetition of Piaget's experiments supports the types and the ages of occurrence.

The Concrete Operations Period

This period may begin at approximately age seven and extend to age eleven, twelve, or beyond. The child is able at this point to achieve certain cognitive operations but these operations are bound by the concrete. Their "form is bound up with the concrete" (Inhelder & Piaget, 1964, p. 149). The child now is capable of increased conservation. In the case of the experiment previously cited in which the child is asked in which glass are there more beads after the experimenter shows two glasses containing an equal number of beads and then pours the beads of one into a taller, thinner glass; the child answers that they are the same and explains why.

The child has developed techniques of dealing with classes, relations, and numbers which enable the child to perform new cognitive operations. Several new processes emerge and three of these have to do with logical behavior. They are reversibility, inversion, and reciprocity (Inhelder & Piaget, 1958, p. 272). In concrete operational thought the three are existent in the thought process but they are not coordinated into a whole as they are in the subsequent period of formal operations. When the subject can reliably return to a beginning point in attempting a solution to a problem and begin new operations to replace ones already performed, reversibility is evident in that behavior. In the process of inversion, elements are added or subtracted in the construction of a class. The replacement of old operations with new ones may be an example of inversion. On the other hand, reciprocity is a process which has to do with relations rather than strictly class construction. For example, when in fact A=B and A implies B (A→ B), and B implies A (B→ A), then A ⇌ B—the process of reciprocity has occurred. The relations of reciprocity are symmetrical.

The term "grouping" is used by Piaget to describe the logic of the concrete operations period. "Groupings are systems of simple or multiple class inclusions or linkages, but they do not include a combinatorial system linking the various given elements n by n" (Inhelder & Piaget, 1958, p. 275). For example, an experiment was posed in which liquid substance g, when combined with substances from two of four beakers of liquid, will produce a yellow color. The child in concrete operations will set out to discover which combination will produce the color, but will not use a combining system which will result in systematically trying all possibilities in an orderly manner (Inhelder & Piaget, 1958, p. 109). The child will attempt various combinations (groupings) in an unsystematic manner—(g + 3 + 1), (g + 1 + 4), (g + 1 + 3), and so on; whereas the adolescent at formal operations will be systematic and nonrepetitious. This experiment is used as one test to determine if the person has attained formal operations.

Formal Operations Period

At about age eleven or twelve the child's grouping capacities become so sophisticated that further propositional or potential dimensions of the once naive and observationally bound schema can be seen. When this occurs the child has moved into the formal operations stage.

Formal operational thought enables the child to go beyond the actual and deal with the possible. The capacity of symbolic representation is refined a step further during this period. The adolescent hypothesizes about relations and classifications. When confronted with a problem, the adolescent constructs hypotheses about the solution. The adolescent uses permanent systematized, symbolic methods while developing these hypotheses. Formal operational thought goes beyond the symbolic propositional classes of the concrete operations period. The adolescent has the faculty of forming relational propositions about class propositions which identify commonalities in the object world. Hewson (1971) in studying university physics students' responses to Piagetian tasks concluded that a number of seventeen- and eighteen-year-olds do not seem to be able to use formal operations either when called upon to do so or in individual problem-solving tasks.

Piaget and Instruction

Ideas which may be generated from research and writings concerning the work of Piaget have implications for learning, instruction, and curriculum planning (Hooper, 1968, pp. 423-34). Piaget accentuates the importance of *action*. Action is essential to learning and involves behaviors which are really interactions with one's physical and social worlds. Piaget's views on action provide major support for the authors' view of the learner as an interactive, dynamic being.

Another important pair of ideas of Piaget with educational implications are the ideas of *matching* and *timing*. Instructional experiences may be matched with the cognitive developmental level of the student and timed to the rate of development. Failure to learn or resistance to learning might be attributed to a mismatch of instruction and developmental level.

The teacher may be assured that by the process of equilibration each student will be motivated to learn, even if the student does not seem to be actively disposed to learn exactly what the teacher plans. The teacher may need to individualize instruction to focus on the point of disequilibrium. The facilitation of equilibrium at times may only be done with tutoring type student-teacher interaction.

Summary of Major Dimensions of Cognitive Development

The foregoing discussion provides an overview of cognitive development, especially Piaget's work. By way of a brief summary there appear to be at least four dimensions of cognitive development during the first twelve or so years of life. The educator should consider these in terms of the mix of stages among the students in planning and conducting instruction.

- *Simple to Complex.* The tasks which may be dealt with most efficiently during problem-solving processing at early ages appear to be the more simple tasks. As age increases the individual appears to be able to deal with more complex types of tasks, if other variables are held more or less constant. Intelligence, socioeconomic class, and other experiential and organismic variables may enhance or inhibit the influence of age on this task variable. Simple tasks with concrete instances may be dealt with more effectively by the younger than the older individual.
- *Concrete to Abstract.* Problem-solving processes of younger children appear to operate more efficiently with concrete content than with abstract content. Problem solving by younger children frequently depends on whether the content is in a form which may be concretely manipulated.

- *Sensorimotor to Cognitive.* The problem solving of the younger child is sensorimotor bound. When language appears, the child has a new technique of manipulation, control, and representation. Language enables the child to abstract traits and attributes and to manipulate and categorize these traits in cognitive, symbolic ways instead of sensorimotor concrete ways.
- *Perceptual to Cognitive.* The younger child appears to be perceptually bound to the immediate presence of the content of the problems. As the child grows older perceptual immediacy requirements give way to capacities to deal with abstract possibility and potentiality.

Thought and the Nature of Stimuli

Stimuli may have an influence on thinking in at least two ways. First, various types of stimuli may influence the efficiency of thought. Secondly, different thought strategies may be used depending on the types of stimuli presented to the subject. Piaget's logical strategies; Miller, Galanter, and Pribram's (1960) TOTE units; Bruner's concept formation strategies (Bruner et al., 1956); and other strategies have been investigated through the presentation of different kinds of stimulation posed to the subject.

There are a number of ways to view the nature of stimuli. First, one could analyze stimuli according to representational mode (e.g., enactive, iconic, or symbolic [Bruner, 1964]), or the extent to which a stimulus is concrete or abstract. It may be that one mode is more conducive to efficiency, and that the mode may be dealt with more effectively by using one of a number of strategies to match the behavioral repertoire of the problem solver. Secondly, efficiency and strategy may be influenced by several factors such as (1) the amount of relevant and irrelevant information in the problem field, (2) whether bits of information are repeated, and (3) whether bits of information are contiguous (West & Loree, 1968). Finally, thinking may be influenced by the emotional connotations of the stimuli and whether or not the stimuli relate to some need or drive state of the organism.

Wohlwill (1962) treated *contiguity, redundancy,* and *selectivity* as three dimensions in the problem-solving process from perception to conception. In the case of *redundancy,* for example, as the problem-solving process moves from perception to conception, the amount of redundant information required is lessened. In the case of *contiguity,* the problem solver can tolerate greater distance between pieces of information as he nears conception. In the case of *selectivity,* the problem solver can tolerate greater amounts of irrelevant information as he nears conception (p. 98). These dimensions are characteristics of stimuli which appear to exert an influence on problem solving via the perceptual processes.

Gelfand (1958) investigated the effect of including irrelevant information into a problem-solving situation with college-age subjects. Performance was found to be in an inverse linear relationship with the amount of irrelevant information.

Mednick (1962) discussed ways in which contiguity of content aids the achievement of a creative solution of a problem. These are "methods of bringing the requisite associative elements together" (p. 274). The three methods are: *serendipity, similarity,* and *mediation*. *Serendipity* may be characterized as a situation in which a new and unexpected response emerges as a consequence of association with some combination of events (stimuli). Here stimuli appear contiguously with novel responses. *Similarity* is defined as the situation in which the stimuli, which elicit the associative elements, are similar. *Mediation* is defined as a situation in which common elements of the stimuli bring the associative elements together.

Johnson and Hall (1961) studied the influence of the amount of material on the problem-solving processes of college-age subjects. The experimenter posed both verbal and numerical type problems where an alternative was to be selected which met all of a varying number of specifications. The problem-solving period was divided into two phases—preparation and solution. During the preparation period subjects viewed the specification (criterial attributes of the solution). When ready, the subject turned a switch which exposed the solution alternatives. The switch could be turned back if the subject desired. An example of a verbal problem is given here (1961, p. 458):

Four Specifications	*Alternatives*
Flat	1. Map
Readable	2. Book
Descriptive	3. Label
Gummed	4. Paper
	5. Globe

Each specification (the number was varied) added a restriction on the solution. The experimenter found that when the number of specifications is decreased more time is spent on solution than on preparation. When the number of specifications is increased more time is spent on preparation than on solution.

Several additional studies indicate the influence of irrelevant dimensions on problem solving and concept formation. Lubker and Spiker (1966) report that the number of irrelevant dimensions adversely affects children's efficiency on cognitive tasks involving selecting blocks of an odd form. Suchman and Trabasso (1966) studied the influence of irrelevant dimensions on concept attainment.

When the subjects' preferred dimension is relevant, performance is aided. When the preferred dimension is irrelevant, performance is inhibited. Subjects were tested for preference but were assigned conditions randomly. Brown and Archer (1956) found that adding irrelevant dimensions in a concept formation task increases task difficulty. This supported earlier research of Archer et al. (1955).

One experiment helps explain a condition under which irrelevant information increases difficulty. Archer (1962) had subjects categorize patterns into four categories. The inclusion of irrelevant information increased the difficulty of concept identification. Obviousness of the dimension appeared to make a difference. Problem solving was more effective when the relevant dimensions were obvious and the irrelevant dimensions were not obvious. The optimum condition exists when the relevant dimensions were obvious and no irrelevant dimensions were included. The problems were most difficult when relevant dimensions were not obvious and the irrelevant dimensions were obvious. Thus, it appears that the degree of obviousness of irrelevant and relevant information makes a difference in the efficiency of problem solving. In educational practice, teachers can influence how obvious various relevant and irrelevant dimensions of a task are for students.

What makes the role of irrelevant information in human thought so important is that practically all problem situations consist of a plethora of information. One of the thinker's major tasks is to select the information which is relevant or pertinent to the problem and ignore the irrelevant. Dewey (1910) included this selection task in the third stage of problem solving. The research discussed previously lends credence to the importance of this variable. Teachers can provide opportunities for students to practice selecting relevant data from large data arrays.

Human Thought and the Frame of Reference

As has been mentioned, some types of content have relationships with a person's needs, values, and affect. The types of content also have been shown to influence human thought. These relationships and influences will be discussed in this section.

It should be remembered from chapter 3 that one's frame of reference—structures, concepts, affect, values, needs, attitudes, and interests—influences thinking. This influence on thinking occurs in a variety of ways such as:

1. *Stimulation.* Thought is influenced by the information on which it operates. The frame of reference components largely determine what information the mind manipulates (for example, through selective attention).

2. *Mediation.* The frame of reference components determine in one sense (and are equivalent to in another sense) the modes of thinking or the combining operations used in thought. The frame of reference includes structures, some of which are modes of thought and combining operations.
3. *Response.* Many of the responses of a person are information-seeking. The information is sought as a result of motivational aspects of the frame of reference. The information located and used thus influences thinking.

Now let us return to the influence of the affective aspects of the frame of reference on mediation. These affective aspects of the frame of reference operate as monitoring mechanisms over the logical combining operations of thought. A logical operation may result in behavioral mandates in one direction, but the affective monitoring mechanisms may override the logical behavioral mandate. This is the case where an individual thinks one action is appropriate but "feels" like doing another. The question may arise: Is it the *logical operations* or the *behaviors* that are monitored and modified? It could be that the logical operation is changed and then the behavior is changed. Or it could be that the logical mandate is ignored and the behavior simply is changed to match the intentional affective directions from the frame of reference. Or both could be influenced directly. It is difficult to answer this question. For practical purposes it may suffice to know that there may be modification by these aspects of the frame of reference and that behavior will be influenced accordingly. The question does illustrate the necessity of accounting for both rational and emotional "causes" of behavior.

Many psychologists have recognized the role of intention (Bourne et al., 1971, p. 6), theme (Bruner, Goodnow, & Austin, 1956, p. 35), or purpose in problem solving. Intention, theme, and purpose appear to be primary characteristics of human thought. Most persons of normal intelligence are capable of performing most logical operations correctly; but the affective aspects of the frame of reference also provide nonlogical dimensions to human thought which may override logic and reason. It seems that many thought distortions, biases, and errors are a result of different data and/or different behavioral outputs rather than merely logical malfunctions. Philosophers and psychologists still have work to do in specifying the linkage among thought, feeling, and action.

Guiding the Problem Solver

If more needs to be known about the psychology of human thought, then much more must be known about training for problem solving.

Guiding the Problem Solver

One training device is to help the students examine their own thought. The questions listed here may be used by the teacher to help the problem solver—either the solitary thinker or persons thinking in groups.

1. What is the problem?
2. What are my (our) motives, biases, feelings, prejudices, interests, or purposes about this problem? What emotional commitments do I (we) have?
    a) How might these interfere with my (our) gathering data about this?
    b) How might these interfere with my (our) logic?
    c) How might these interfere with my (our) responses regarding the solution?
3. What data do I (we) need to solve this problem? (A matter of transfer.)
    a) Once the data are collected and organized, are there more appropriate data in this situation?
4. What information do I (we) know which will help me (us) solve this problem? (A matter of transfer.)
5. How can I (we) represent the problem?
    a) Have I (we) stated the problem accurately?
    b) Should the problem be stated more concretely? Abstractly?
6. Is there another logical solution based on these data?
7. Is there another way to logically combine these data?
8. Is there another way to state the solution? More concretely? More abstractly?
9. What behaviors do the solutions logically suggest? Any other possibilities?
10. What additional problems may be raised?

These questions should help primarily with resolution of problems. Posing these questions individually or in groups to promote problem solving can be a worthwhile exercise. Such questions may also be used in connection with "brainstorming" exercises discussed further in the section on creativity.

Some of these questions should help the problem solver both to overcome *set* (a predisposition to perceive or behave in a certain way) when set is detrimental, and to use set positively when it is helpful. Perceptual sets and response sets are major factors in general problem solving and creativity, and students should be taught how to identify and analyze their own sets as well as the sets of others.

Thinking, Problem Solving, and Creativity

Related to helping people solve problems is the problem of judging logical content in written and spoken material. Students should learn to recognize illogical arguments. Some examples of typical argumental devices are included in table 5. An examination of these shows that the fallacy usually involves reference to peripheral "facts" which are more related to the "psychologic" of the persons involved than to the logic of the problem.

TABLE 5
Typical Illogical Devices Used in Arguments

The Complex Question
> *Example:* Why do educators behave so inhumanely toward students? A preliminary question should be: Do educators behave inhumanely?

Appeal to the Gallery
> *Example:* Everyone will agree . . . Informed people agree . . .

Glittering Generality
> *Example:* Not only is Mr. Smith a loving parent and upstanding citizen but . . .

Appeal to Force
> *Example:* You should support the findings of this committee. As you know, this is an important committee . . .

Arguments Directed to the Person
> *Example:* Ignore Miss Smith's appeal. Her ideas are always controversial and . . .

Appeal Based on Convention
> *Example:* For a long time many others have done this . . .

Appeal Based on Reasoning from the Particular to the General
> *Example:* It is always this way because once . . .

NOTE: Adapted from T. G. Aylesworth and G. M. Reagan, *Teaching for Thinking* (Garden City, New York: Doubleday, 1969), pp. 69-80.

Teaching Concepts

Helping students solve categorical problems (to form concepts) is largely a matter of carefully analyzing the attributes of the concept, analyzing the necessary associated concepts and their attributes, teaching those attributes and assorted concepts, and providing instances. Relevant attributes must be made obvious initially. Instances or examples should be familiar ones. It also helps if during the latter stages of concept learning, the student is shown some negative instance. For example, suppose the teacher wished to teach the concept *isosceles triangle*. Associated concepts are *isosceles* and *triangle*. The attributes of "three straight sides" or "three-cornered" would have to be learned. The attribute of "two equal sides" would also have to be learned. The teacher may also discover the learner is ignorant of associated concepts such as "angle" and thereby teach it. When all of this is accomplished the learner should be shown positive examples (e.g., triangles that are isosceles) and negative examples (e.g., triangles which are not isosceles).

Several steps are very important in concept learning. The teacher should

1. Be aware of related concepts and make certain that students know them
2. Define the concept, which includes discussion of salient attributes and instances
3. Relate the particular concept to a general principle or structure with which it is connected
4. Show and ask for some positive instances
5. Show and ask for some negative instances (usually later)
6. Provide student practice in the use of the concept in different contexts

Much of problem solving, concept learning, and creative behavior involves transfer of prior learnings. Therefore a teacher who wishes to promote concept learning and problem solving should be aware of teaching for transfer as discussed in chapter 5.

In this section you have read about teaching for better problem solving. It has been said that while education should stress problem-solving training, perhaps a greater puzzle involves helping people locate or identify problems. Brainstorming may be helpful in this phase of problem solving as well as use of aids such as questions 1, 4, and 8, in the list of questions on p. 159. At the time of this writing investigations of problem-finding skills are yet in their infancy.

Creativity

Basically creativity involves divergent, unique, or unusual responses to a problem or situation which suggests qualitatively different intellectual operations and processes. These processes or operations may be categorized (e.g., Guilford, 1967), together with other types of thinking in the larger category of intellectual operations. Creative operations also can be seen as being qualitatively different from the other cognitive processes which lead to convergent solutions. As was mentioned earlier in the chapter, creative operations may also be viewed as the *expression of possibilities*.

The accentuation on patterns of responses which suggest cognitive processes leads away from the view that creativity is some mysterious psychic ability present at birth which schools and society serve only to suppress. Research such as that of Mayer (1974) indicates clearly that creativity, like intelligence, is based on a rich, varied experiential background. It is remarkable how many people strongly believe that intelligence is primarily a function of environmental variables whereas creativity is genetic! Such bias is reflected in use of terms like "creative person" implying that creativity is a characteristic of only a few individuals. Simple substitution of the term "highly creative person" helps to illustrate that there are a range of creative behaviors even as "intelligent" behaviors occur over a wide range.

The view of creativity as (patterns of) unusual, unique, original responses allows one to accentuate the contribution of learning to creativity. As appears to be the case in intelligence, learning contributes to variations in creativity between individuals. Thus originality can be viewed in terms of one's learning to reorganize and transforms one's experiences in such a way as to produce novel behavior.

The Measurement of Creativity*

Before examining how learning makes a difference in creativity let us quickly review some of the ways of measuring creativity. Guilford (1962) conceived and measured creativity in terms of several dimensions: *fluency, flexibility, originality* (uncommonness of response), and *remoteness of association*. Some concern is often given to the practicality or usefulness of the response or solution as well.

Fluency is measured in terms of the quantity of ideas expressed in a given time period. For example, subjects are asked to list as many solids that float on water as they can, to list as many words as they can which have similar meaning to *calm,* or as many uses for some common object (such as a brick) as they can.

Flexibility has to do with the variety within the subject's classes of responses. The number of categories of responses is taken as an index of fluency.

Originality is computed by statistical infrequency of the responses given by the subject as compared to the occurrence of the response in a population.

In the case of uses for a brick, ten or more responses generated in one minute may be high fluency, but if they are all involved with building functions, the responses may be scored as low in flexibility. Much higher in flexibility, but lower in fluency than ten, would be five responses—a building block, a doorstop, an object of art, a pencil holder, and a weapon. The single response, "to clean a rug," given

---

*A critique of creativity measurement in terms of predictive validity is offered by Kogan and Pankove (1974).

Creativity

in one minute's time to the problem, "Write down as many uses as you can think of for a brick," would be low in fluency (number of responses) and flexibility (number of categories of response) but high in originality (that response is not commonly given).

Remote association involves finding a common word which encompasses two remotely associated words. For example, *rat* and *cottage* may be associated by the word *cheese*; *skull*, *pistol*, and *baseball* by the word *cap*; *fishing*, *movie*, and *dance* by the response *reel*.

Learning to Be Creative

Guilford (1967, p. 272) has discussed learning in connection with transformation of information. Interestingly, he also gives a discussion of the role of transformation in connection with divergent-production abilities (creativity), and particularly in terms of remote association responses. Thus he considers that creative production is, in fact, an instance of learning (1967, p. 279). It stands to reason, then, that differences which are observed among students or teachers in terms of creative behavior are the result of different learning experiences.

It is noted later that certain personality characteristics have been found to be associated with people exhibiting high levels of creativity. Since personality is regarded to be largely a learned phenomenon, it is plausible that certain aspects of one's personality and creative behavior are learned at the same time and by the same or similar means.

The fact that persons from different cultures perform differently on measures of creativity indicates that creativity is modifiable by culturally based learnings. Torrance (1970) has also shown how educational procedures make a difference in creativity. In his book, *Encouraging Creativity in the Classroom*, Torrance outlines procedures he uses with children from ages six through thirteen years. Through the use of devices or gimmicks such as the "magic net" (36" × 72" pieces of nylon net) as stimuli for imaginative play and drama in group settings, Torrance encouraged creative behavior. His work on creativity is also based on two principles: be respectful of unusual questions and ideas, and be respectful of imaginative ideas.

Saltz and Johnson (1974) used a treatment which they call thematic-fantasy in successfully promoting responses which are associated with creativity. Their approach is reminiscent of Torrance's work. The treatment consisted of fantasy stories read to students and then the students acted out roles in the story.

Other investigators have claimed success at the training of creativity with various techniques. As an example, Parnes (1971) describes a creative problem-solving course which results in increased expression of ideas. Students are taught to be sensitive to perceptual, emotional, and cultural blocks such as conformity, fear of mistakes, and reliance on authority. In another phase of the course students are taught to generate ideas first and judge later. This is done individually as well as in groups. Other techniques learned are looking at problems from a variety of viewpoints, comparing each idea generated on a problem with every other idea, and keeping records of procedures. Students who have taken the course produce more ideas than control subjects. This procedure may be applied to general problem solving. Courses or experiences such as these are frequently used to improve thinking as well as creative problem solving.

The principle of generating as many ideas as possible and looking at the problem from a variety of viewpoints has the effect of reducing the effects of perceptual and response sets when they are detrimental to creativity. It also enhances the influences of sets when they are helpful. This apparent contradiction requires some explanation. A set may aid the emergence of a different idea. Thus, usually, pooling of sets in a group is very productive, whereas the dominance of a single set may be detrimental. Frequently sets are most damaging when one is alone and seemingly unable to "break set" to solve a problem, or when a group of problem solvers persists in using a limited number of sets. Brainstorming is one way of using the different sets in a group.

Parnes and Meadow (1959) and Parnes (1961) have purported to demonstrate the creativity training value of the technique known as brainstorming. In brainstorming, groups of subjects are encouraged to express a large number of ideas as rapidly as possible. The purpose is to stimulate a pool of new solutions or ideas. Judgment of the quality of these ideas is delayed. Research in the 1950s indicated that such group techniques as brainstorming resulted in larger numbers of ideas and better solutions.(On the other hand, Meichenbaum [1975] has shown that individuals can learn to brainstorm alone.) More recent research results (e.g., Campbell, 1968) indicate that group problem solving may be no better than individual problem solving and under certain conditions may actually inhibit effective problem solving. Clearly brainstorming is no panacea in problem solving. It is sometimes an enjoyable experience with positive social by-products (e.g., aiding communication among co-workers).

In teaching for creativity, many of the ideas of reinforcement and imitation are as appropriate for creative behavior as any other type of behavior. One of the most important aspects of teaching for creativity is the establishing of an atmosphere in the classroom which stimulates flexible and unusual behaviors. The students must be made aware that these types of responses are encouraged, accepted, and expected. The teacher must then reinforce these responses when they occur. The teacher must also model these kinds of behavior.

It is likely that reinforcement and imitation account for the successes of brainstorming and "magic net-type" approaches. Students reinforce each other by accepting (which may be very reinforcing of itself) and reinforcing the creative responses of their peers. Students will also be modeling these behaviors for other students. A student viewing another student responding creatively and perhaps vicariously experiencing the reinforcement obtained may well imitate the flexibility and unusual responses.

Characteristics of Creative Personality

What personality variables coexist with creativity? A knowledge of these variables or characteristics may help us to understand some of the behavior we see in the schools. A word of warning, however, should be stated. Just because these characteristics tend to coexist with creativity does not mean that one could automatically shape these characteristics with the expectation that highly creative behavior will result. Should the educator wish to encourage creativity and plan instruction for it, it would be more effective to study the programs and experiments conducted on shaping creative behavior and applying these programs.* This is not to imply, on the other hand, that some personality traits are not amenable to modifications. Indeed a contemporary view of personality defines it as largely the product of learning.

One major source for the study of characteristics of highly creative persons is the Institute for Personality Assessment and Research of the University of California (Barron, 1968, pp. 220-13, 1971; MacKinnon, 1967). These investigators studied research scientists in industry, mathematicians, architects, and writers who had been rated as most creative in their respective fields by their fellows. Study of these persons yielded the following characteristics:

1. The highly creative describe themselves as inventive, determined, independent, and enthusiastic as opposed to reliable, dependable, tolerant, and understanding.

---

*One might ask if there are not already more persons reaching maturity exhibiting creativity than society and its institutions can tolerate. Schools might do severe disservice by shaping creativity purposefully. Certainly creative children sometimes drive parents and teachers "up the wall." Industrialists sometimes claim that they need more employee creativity. It is doubtful they would tolerate highly creative employees in large numbers if they could find them. Alternatively it could be argued that the serious problems society faces require novel solutions and creative approaches, and it is only through encouraging creativity that they can be solved.

2. Highly creative persons are independent in their own professional area. They accept their own experience and are also less subject to group pressures (Barron, 1968, p. 211).
3. The highly creative person is open to experience, generally preferring perception initially to rapid judgment. That is, some persons tend to judge situations rapidly; on the other hand, others tend to stress perception and delay judgments.
4. The highly creative personality tends towards richness, complexity, and lack of defensiveness.
5. Highly creative persons also prefer that which is complex and asymmetrical as opposed to the symmetrical and simple. They also experience more anxiety and tend toward introversion.

Conclusion

In this chapter, we have discussed topics related to thinking, problem solving, and creativity. We have attempted to discuss the primary psychological issues and principles as well as present some implications for educational practice. We have taken a position which accents the relationship between problem solving and creativity. Creativity is seen as a part of human thought and behavior.

This relationship emerges from the fact that the prosaic as well as original cognitive operations spring from richness of experiences or learning and "genetic endowments." Concepts and structures coordinated with the other aspects of the frame of reference generate in some instances the usual and the unusual forms of cognitive operations.

Discussion Questions

1. How can you determine when a student has actually learned a concept or merely learned a verbal statement of it by rote? Give examples.
2. What advantages do you see to "conceptualizing" the curriculum as opposed to teaching "facts"? Is there any place in school learning where rote learning is necessary or desirable?
3. What implications for teachers can be derived from Piaget's ideas of cognitive development? How might a teacher behave differently knowing the levels of development of students in his class? Give examples.
4. Can you distinguish between thinking and problem solving? To what extent is language involved in these operations?

5. How do you interpret Guilford's claim that all creativity involves problem solving—between spontaneous and adaptive types of tivity?
6. In terms of problem-solving skills in education, discuss Guilford's position that we need better balance of emphasis between divergent and convergent thinking in the schools.
7. Distinguish between fluency, flexibility, and originality in problem solving—between spontaneous and adaptive types of flexibility. Where in your intended teaching do you perceive opportunities for emphasizing these factors? Be specific!
8. Try brainstorming aloud with some friends—without regard for practicality or social desirability have everyone suggest ways to improve a "dribbling tea pot" or uses for a rubber band. Have someone keep track of the various solutions over a one minute period. Do you think there were more answers than if everyone had worked alone for a minute? What about originality? What about practicality?
9. What advantages do you see in teachers being receptive to unusual ideas of students? What advantages and disadvantages do you see to "set-breaking" in the classroom?
10. How do you distinguish between intelligence and creativity? What advantages and disadvantages do you see in trying to measure these two constructs for educational decision making?
11. How much creative thinking should be encouraged in schools? How much can society accommodate? Why do people say that creative teachers and children create problems?
12. Give some examples of how perceptual set helped you in solving a problem recently. Give some examples of how it delayed you recently in solving some problems.
13. Examine an editorial page or a "letter to the editor" column for examples of illogical argumental devices. What are some which are commonly used in discussion?

Recommended Readings

Aylesworth, T. G., and Reagan, G. M. *Teaching for thinking.* Garden City, N. Y.: Doubleday, 1969. A very good approach to teaching critical reading.

Barron, F. *Creativity and personal freedom.* Princeton, N. J.: D. Van Nostrand, 1968. Barron's research into highly creative persons.

Beadle, M. *A child's mind: How children learn during the critical years from birth to age five.* Garden City, N. Y.: Doubleday, 1971. A good overview of thinking and learning ages birth to five years.

Beard, R. M. *An outline of Piaget's developmental psychology for students and teachers.* New York: Basic Books, 1969. A good overview of Piaget's work.

Davis, G. A., and Scott, J. A. *Training creative thinking.* New York: Holt, Rinehart & Winston, 1971. Describes an effective method for creativity training.

Dienes, Z. P., and Jeeves, M. A. *Thinking in structures.* London: Hutchinson Educational Ltd., 1965. A description of research into some of Piaget's ideas.

Ginsburg, H., and Opper, S. *Piaget's theory of intellectual development: An introduction.* Englewood Cliffs, N. J.: Prentice Hall, 1969. Another overview of Piaget's work.

Piaget, J. *Six psychological studies.* New York: Random House, 1968. One of Piaget's most easily understood books.

Taylor, C. W. (Ed.) *Creativity: Progress and potential.* New York: McGraw-Hill, 1964. Some excellent original articles on creativity.

References

Adams, J. A., & Montague, W. E. Retroactive inhibition and natural language mediation. *Journal of Verbal Learning and Verbal Behavior,* 1967, *6,* 528-35.

Archer, E. J. Concept identification as a function of obviousness of relevant and irrelevant information. *Journal of Experimental Psychology,* 1962, *63,* 616-20.

Archer, E. J. et al. Concept identification as a function of irrelevant information and instruction. *Journal of Experimental Psychology,* 1955, *49,* 153-64.

Aylesworth, T. G., & Reagan, G. M. *Teaching for thinking.* Garden City, New York: Doubleday, 1969.

Bain, A. *The senses and the intellect.* London: Parker, 1855.

Barron, F. *Creativity and personal freedom.* Princeton, N. J.: D. Van Nostrand, 1968.

Barron, F. An eye more fantastical. In G. A. Davis & J. A. Scott (Eds.), *Training creative thinking.* New York: Holt, Rinehart & Winston, 1971.

Bourne, L. E., Ekstrand, B. R., & Dominowski, R. L. *The psychology of thinking.* Englewood Cliffs, N. J.: Prentice-Hall, 1971.

Brown, F. G., & Archer, E. J. Concept identification as a function of task complexity and distribution of practice. *Journal of Experimental Psychology,* 1956, *52,* 316-21.

References

Bruner, J. S. The course of cognitive growth. *American Psychologist,* 1964, *19,* 1-15.

Bruner, J. S., Goodnow, J. J., & Austin, G. A. *A study of thinking.* New York: Wiley, 1956.

Bruner, J. S. et al. *Studies in cognitive growth.* New York: Wiley, 1966.

Campbell, J. P. Individual versus group problem solving in an industrial sample. *Journal of Applied Psychology,* 1968, *52,* 205-10.

Denney, D. R. Relationship of three cognitive style dimensions to elementary reading abilities. *Journal of Educational Psychology,* 1974, *66,* 702-09.

Dewey, J. *How we think.* New York: D. C. Heath, 1910.

Duncker, K. On problem solving. *Psychological Monographs,* 1945, *58* (whole No. 270).

Ehri, L. C., & Muzio, I. M. Cognitive style and reasoning about speed. *Journal of Educational Psychology,* 1974, *66,* 569-71.

Elkind, D. *Children and adolescents.* New York: Oxford University Press, 1970.

Elkind, D. The development of quantitative thinking: a systematic replication of Piaget's studies. *Journal of Genetic Psychology,* 1961, *98,* 37-46.

Feigenbaum, E. A., & Feldman, J. *Computers and thought.* New York: McGraw-Hill, 1963.

Flavell, J. H. *The Developmental Psychology of Jean Piaget.* New York: D. Van Nostrand, 1963.

Furth, H. G. *Piaget and knowledge.* Englewood Cliffs, N. J.: Prentice-Hall, 1969.

Gelfand, S. Effects of prior associations and task complexity upon the identification of concepts. *Psychological Reports,* 1958, *4,* 568-74.

Guilford, J. P. Creativity: Its measurement and development. In S. J. Parnes & S. F. Harding (Eds.), *A source book for creative thinking.* New York: Scribner's Sons, 1962.

Guilford, J. P. *The nature of human intelligence.* New York: McGraw-Hill, 1967.

Hewson, M. G. A. A Piagetian analysis of intellectual performance on first-year university physics examinations. Unpublished master's thesis, The University of British Columbia, 1971.

Hooper, F. H. Piaget research and education. In I. E. Sigel & F. H. Hooper (Eds.), *Logical thinking in children.* New York: Holt, Rinehart & Winston, 1968.

Hovland, C. I. Computer simulation of thinking. *American Psychologist,* 1960, *15,* 687-93.

Hume, D. *An inquiry concerning human understanding.* Chicago: Open Court Publishing Co., 1912.

Inhelder, B., & Piaget, J. *The early growth of logic in the child.* London: Routledge & Kegan Paul, 1964.

Inhelder, B., & Piaget, J. *The growth of logical thinking from childhood to adolescence.* France: Basic Books, 1958.

James, W. *The principles of psychology.* Vol. 1. New York: Henry Holt & Co., 1918.

Johnson, D. M., & Hall, E. R. Organization of relevant and irrelevant words in the solution of verbal problems. *Journal of Psychology,* 1961, *52,* 99-104.

Judson, A. J., Cofer, C. N., & Gelfand, S. Reasoning as an associative process: II. "Direction" in problem solving as a function of prior reinforcement of relevant responses. *Psychological Reports,* 1956, *2,* 501-07.

Kagan, J. Reflection-impulsivity and reading ability in primary grade children. *Child Development,* 1965, *36,* 609-28.

Kaufmann, H., & Goldstein, S. The effects of emotional value of conclusions upon distortion in syllogistic reasoning. *Psychonomic Science,* 1967, *7,* 367-68.

Kogan, N., & Pankove, E. Long-term predictive validity of divergent-thinking tests: Some negative evidence. *Journal of Educational Psychology,* 1974, *66,* 802-10.

Köhler, W. *The mentality of apes.* New York: Harcourt, Brace, 1927.

Loree, M. R. Problem-solving techniques of children in grades four through nine. Cooperative Research Project No. 2608, U. S. H. E. W., 1965.

Lubker, B. J., & Spiker, C. C. The effects of irrelevant stimuli dimension on children's oddity-problem learning. *Journal of Experimental Child Psychology,* 1966, *3,* 207-15.

MacKinnon, D. W. The study of creative persons. In J. Kagan (Ed.), *Creativity and learning.* Boston: Houghton Mifflin, 1967.

Mayer, R. E. Acquisition processes and resilience under varying testing conditions for structurally different problem-solving procedures. *Journal of Educational Psychology,* 1974, *66,* 644-56.

Mednick, S. A. The associative basis of the creative process. *Psychological Review,* 1962, *69,* 220-32.

Meichenbaum, D. Enhancing creativity by modifying what subjects say to themselves. *American Educational Research Journal,* 1975, *12,* 129-45.

Mill, J. *Analysis of the phenomena of the human mind.* Vol. 1. London: Longmans, Green, Reader, & Dyer, 1878.

Miller, G. A., Galanter, E., & Pribram, K. H. *Plans and the structure of behavior.* New York: Holt, Rinehart & Winston, 1960.

Munn, N. L. *Introduction to psychology.* Boston: Houghton Mifflin, 1956.

References

Newell, A., & Simon, H. A. Computer simulation of human thinking. *Science,* 1961, *134,* 2011-17.

Ortony, A. Human associative memory—an essay review. *Journal of Educational Research,* 1975(a), *66,* 396-401.

Ortony, A. Opinions divided on whether artificial minds need matter. *The Times Higher Education Supplement,* March 14, 1975(b).

Ortony, A. TV "sees" for computers with steel fingers. *The Times Higher Education Supplement,* March 7, 1975(c).

Parnes, S. J. Can creativity be increased? In G. A. Davis & J. A. Scott (Eds.), *Training creative thinking.* New York: Holt, Rinehart & Winston, 1971.

Parnes, S. J. Effects of extended effort in creative problem solving. *Journal of Educational Psychology,* 1961, *52,* 117-22.

Parnes, S. J., & Meadow, A. Effects of "brainstorming" instructions on creative problem solving by trained and untrained subjects. *Journal of Educational Psychology,* 1959, *50,* 171-76.

Pavlov, I. P. *Conditioned reflexes.* London: Oxford University Press, 1927.

Piaget, J. *The psychology of intelligence.* London: Routledge & Kegan Paul, 1950.

Piaget, J. *The child's conception of number.* London: Humanities Press, 1952(a).

Piaget, J. *The child's conception of the world.* Paterson, N. J.: Littlefield, Adams & Co., 1963.

Piaget, J. *The origins of intelligence in children.* New York: International Universities Press, 1952(b).

Piaget, J. *Six psychological studies.* New York: Vintage Books, 1967.

Piaget, J., & Inhelder, B. *The psychology of the child.* New York: Basic Books, 1969.

Rankin, H. B. Language and thinking: Positive and negative effects of naming. *Science,* 1963, *141,* 48-50.

Reitman, W. R. *Cognition and thought.* New York: Wiley, 1965.

Robinson, J. E., & Gray, J. L. Cognitive style as a variable in school learning. *Journal of Educational Psychology,* 1974, *66,* 793-99.

Ross, W. D. (Ed.) *The student's Oxford Aristotle.* Vol. 3. New York: Oxford University Press, 1942.

Saltz, E., & Johnson, J. Training for thematic-fantasy play in culturally disadvantaged children. *Journal of Educational Psychology,* 1974, *66,* 623-30.

Sapir, E. *Selected writings of Edward Sapir.* D. G. Mandelbaum (Ed.) Berkeley: University of California Press, 1949.

Saporta, S. (Ed.) *Psycholinguistics.* New York: Holt, Rinehart & Winston, 1961.

Skinner, B. F. *Science and human behavior.* New York: Free Press, 1953.

Suchman, R. G., & Trabasso T. Stimulus preference and their function in young children's concept attainment. *Journal of Experimental Child Psychology,* 1966, *3,* 188-98.

Thorndike, E. L. *Human Learning.* London: The Century Co., 1931.

Torrance, E. P. *Encouraging creativity in the classroom.* Dubuque, Iowa: William C. Brown, 1970.

Vygotsky, L. S. *Thought and language.* Cambridge, Mass.: M.I.T. Press, 1962.

Wadsworth, B. J. *Piaget's theory of cognitive development.* New York: David McKay, 1971.

Wallach, M. A. Creativity and the expression of possibilities. In J. Kagan (Ed.), *Creativity and learning.* Boston: Houghton Mifflin, 1967, 36-57.

Wertheimer, M. *Productive thinking.* New York: Harper & Row, 1959.

West, C. K., & Loree, M. R. Selectivity, redundancy, and contiguity as factors which influence the difficulty of an achievement test. *Journal of Experimental Education,* 1968, *36,* 89-93.

Wiener, N. *The human use of human beings: Cybernetics and society.* Garden City, N.Y.: Doubleday, 1954.

Witkin, H. A., Dyk, R. B., Fattuson, H. F., Goodenough, D. R., & Karp, S. A. *Psychological differentiation.* New York: Wiley, 1962.

Wohlwill, J. F. From perception to inference: A dimension of cognitive development. *Monographs of the Society for Research in Child Development,* 1962, *27* (whole No. 83), 87-107.

Practical Organizer for Chapter 7

Teachers of grade seven classes which are not homogeneously grouped by ability may have students with reading levels at grades two through twelve. Homogeneous grouping typically will only reduce this range by one-half to one-third. In the high school grades, the range of differences will often be even greater. These and other related facts imply that instruction must become more individualized than it has been traditionally.

There are many methods of individualizing instruction. Oddly enough two approaches—mastery learning and programmed instruction—require more curriculum and content organization; whereas a third approach, open education, perhaps requires less of these kinds of organization and more teacher organization.

The serious instructor should consider carefully these three approaches to individual differences. Programmed instruction can be implemented without drastically changing a school situation. Mastery learning, on the other hand, requires at least in part the adoption of a new set of assumptions about learning. Open education will require school reorganization perhaps extending to modified school architecture as well as assumptions about learning.

There are other approaches to individual differences but these three seem to be more closely tied to one or another of the "schools" of psychology discussed in earlier chapters. They are also to be found currently in various stages of implementation in North American schools.

Educational Approaches to Individual Differences 7

This chapter contains a discussion of three systematic attempts to provide for student individual differences: mastery learning, programmed instruction, and open education. Think of these not as mutually exclusive alternatives, but in terms of which features of each approach seem to be most suggestive for your instructional planning. It is all too common an error to accept any one approach as a panacea and thereby reject others totally. Some recent developments in Canada, Great Britain, and the United States are also discussed.

From the preceding discussion as well as personal experience one can infer something of the range of individual differences among the pupils in any classroom or school situation. It has been part of the task of teachers to try to account for these differences when planning and carrying out learning activities. Among the individual differences commonly observed are variations in each aspect of the frame of reference discussed in chapter 3. Several attempts to systematize ways of meeting individual differences have been advanced. Each has generated controversy and acquired adherents and opponents. Three types of educational approaches to individual differences are discussed in the pages that follow: *mastery learning, programmed instruction,* and *open education*. These were selected for contemporary relevance and because preliminary evidence for each indicates some (at least partial) effectiveness in providing for learner individual differences. In addition each approach has psychological bases which have been identified in earlier chapters. The three approaches are presented here with a view to giving the reader a balanced perspective on what is known about the strengths and weaknesses of each. Some recent sources of additional information are also included for those who wish to pursue aspects of each approach further.

Mastery Learning

In 1926, Professor Henry C. Morrison at the University of Chicago proposed that secondary school teachers devise plans to provide for mastery of the subject matter by the majority of students. In 1968, again at Chicago, Benjamin S. Bloom described a model whereby upwards of 90 percent of students in any grade could be expected to master the content of that class. Typically however, schools still operate on the (usually explicit) assumption of the normal distribution of student achievement marks. Faculties of education still teach the "bell-shaped curve" as the "sanctioned" approach to school marking. Yet, as Bloom reminds us, one expects things which occur at random or by chance to be distributed normally as a bell-shaped curve. Considering the amounts of money, time, and effort put into the public schools by students, teachers, administrators, taxpayers, publishers, and curriculum directors (in no particular order), is it reasonable to expect student achievement to happen as if it were a random event, occurring by chance? Critics (e.g., Illich, 1971) might argue that traditional schooling may in fact have a deleterious effect upon pupil performance. We will attempt to provide evidence and argument to the effect that teachers do control vari-

Mastery Learning

ables which can encourage student mastery (or failure) as indexed by some reasonable criteria.

The notion of mastery, briefly stated, is that the attainment of a specified basic competency in any subject matter is within reach of virtually every student. And furthermore, it is the central responsibility of each teacher and student at any level to assure that mastery is attained by *every* student in the class. A rationale for this approach for college teaching as well has been worked out by Myers (1970).

Bloom bases his argument for mastery learning in the public schools on the suggestions of H. C. Morrison (1926) previously mentioned, and on details of J. B. Carroll's (1963) model for school learning. A brief description of Carroll's model and its implications for classroom learning is given here.

J. B. Carroll's Model of School Learning

Carroll has attempted to construct a model whereby the degree of learning of a school task is predicted from a combination of five variables. Three of the variables in Carroll's model are quantifiable in terms of time. His basic point is that any student can master any task provided he actually spends the amount of time he needs to master the task. This point is obvious, but the chief contribution of Professor Carroll's paper is the description and interrelation of those variables (typically measured by time) contributing to the amount of time any student needs to master the task and the time actually spent on the task. Like other models of human behavior, Carroll's oversimplifies the reality it purportedly describes, but also like other models its potential value lies in a better understanding of that reality. Moreover, the model provides a basis for planning a program of instruction.

As stated before, according to Carroll's model, the amount of student learning or degree of mastery of a task is a function of factors concerning the amount of time actually spent and time needed to accomplish the task.

The five variables in Carroll's model are *aptitude, perseverance, ability to understand instruction, quality of instruction,* and *opportunity for learning.* Together they can be organized so as to predict degrees of individual student learning for a specific learning task.

Aptitude and *ability* are individual difference variables having to do with the amount of time each learner needs for any task. Whereas aptitude refers to the amount of time any student requires to master a given task, ability is a more general concept referring to capability to perform classes of behaviors, like verbal or quantitative abilities.

Educational Approaches to Individual Differences

Perseverance and *opportunity* are variables which determine how much time a learner will spend and how much time the learner is permitted to spend on a task, respectively. Perseverance can be considered to be an operationalization of motivation inasmuch as any individual will persevere on a task to the extent that the individual is motivated to do so. There are both personal and environmental aspects to motivation: the personal aspect being central to the learner's frame of reference, and the environmental aspect involving incentives in the learner's environment. Opportunity refers to the amount of time allowed in the social-physical environment for the task. Some situations severely restrict opportunity either by design (e.g., school or teacher or curriculum allows only so much time) or by circumstance (e.g., noisy sibling or television programming interferes with study time).

Quality of instruction is related to the other variables in that it interacts with individual differences in aptitude, perseverance, and ability to determine levels of learning. For example, if the quality of instruction is low, only a few students—those high on the three "personal" variables—might master the task. Likewise, if the opportunity, or time allowed for learning, is restricted, only those who are high in aptitude and ability—those who work and understand rapidly—can be expected to achieve mastery.

Mayo (1970) has indicated that the mean achievement expected in a group will usually be about 60 percent accuracy in a traditional approach, about 77 percent for moderate mastery, and about 92 percent accuracy for thorough mastery.

In terms of Carroll's model, degree of mastery expressed as a percentage of items correct on an achievement test may be predicted for each individual for each task according to the following general equation:

$$\text{Degree of learning} = f \frac{\text{(time actually spent on task)}}{\text{(time needed for mastery)}}$$

$$= \frac{\text{(the lowest value of opportunity or perseverance or aptitude)}}{\text{(aptitude, as modified by ability and quality of instruction)}}$$

It can readily be seen that if the time a person requires to master a task is greater than the time he spends on it, the value of the fraction will be less than one and learning will thus be less than 100 percent (by definition, there cannot be more than 100 percent learning in this model).

For example, a student, Albert, by virtue of his aptitudes, or his general ability, may require two hours to master the tasks involved in doing the backstroke in swimming (mastery defined in terms of swimming four laps within a given time period). But he may in fact spend only half that time, because of his perseverance (perhaps he is willing to spend only an hour), or because of the opportunity provided (the swimming class might last only one hour). If learning were a linear function on time (which, of course, it is not!) one might expect Albert to perform near the 50 percent level, perhaps swimming only half as well in terms of style, or half as far (discounting fatigue and stamina factors for the time being). If, on the other hand, Albert were to spend the full two hours on the tasks, he would achieve mastery (i.e., attain criterion performance).

The general equation can be made specific by giving more careful definitions of the terms. Carroll (1963) tries to do this. The numerator of the fraction, the amount of the person's time actually spent on learning the task, is the smaller time value of perseverance, opportunity, or aptitude for the task as modified by ability to understand and quality of instruction. The denominator is the last of these, namely the sum of the person's aptitudes for aspects of the task, as modified by his ability to understand instruction and by variations in the quality of instruction. As aptitudes and ability for any task increase, a person will need less time to master that task. Quality of instruction is a modifier term, too, in that it must be considered in adjusting the denominator value up or down in terms of the time each person will need for mastery. It should be noted that the relationship between ability and achievement need not be great in mastery learning. If instruction is of high quality and sufficient opportunities are provided for learning, students of moderate to low ability should attain high achievement according to this approach.

Quality of instruction is perhaps the most difficult of the five variables to try to quantify. It involves the age-old question of "What is good teaching?" It is too simple to say that instructional quality must be high, obviously, it must be appropriate to the situation for each learner. It must somehow fit a student's ability, attitude, and motivation as well as the setting. Some correction must be applied to the denominator value (amount of time needed for mastery) to account for variations in instructional quality. Since different students do not benefit equally from the same instructional approach, the availability of a variety of instruction techniques and resources is indicated for high quality of instruction.

Formative Evaluation

Formative evaluation is a key part of mastery learning. This consists of periodic assessment of student progress for the purposes of giving student and teacher feedback for decision-making purposes. Is it time to go on to the next topic? Should another approach be tried for learning this topic? Should more or less time be allowed or spent on this task? All of these questions are approached through formative evaluation. Formative (progress) and summative (final) evaluation are discussed in more detail in chapter 9. (See also Bloom et al., 1971.)

Criticisms of the Mastery Learning Model

The notion of learning for mastery is certainly not without its critics. Some of the frequently encountered objections to mastery learning are summarized in table 6. In many cases it is not possible to cite published references for these as they have arisen in discussions with teachers and colleagues rather than in printed form. One published critique available at this time is that of Cronbach (1971). His main point is that the mastery learning notion is only clearly applicable at the "training" level of instruction and is not suited for education for maximum potential and creative self-direction. Cronbach's critique is reflected in the first response in table 6.

It may be correctly surmised from an inspection of table 6 that there are a variety of issues of educational philosophy and policy which underlie discussions of merits of mastery learning apart from psychological concerns. There are, of course, more points that advocates and opponents of mastery learning make. Suffice to say that mastery learning is a lively topic in educational circles today and is likely to be so for some time to come.

Strategies for Mastery

Bloom (1968) describes in detail one strategy for mastery learning in the classroom and suggests that teachers can develop "many alternative strategies." The five variables of aptitude, perseverance, ability to understand, quality of instruction, and opportunity for learning all play important roles in Bloom's strategy.

Basically, Bloom's strategy involves the supplementation of regular instruction with frequent formative evaluational procedures to find out where individual students are "at." It also involves a variety of alternative instructional methods and materials to try to bring as many students as possible up to predetermined standards of excellence. The model does not specify these standards but leaves that problem up to those involved (teachers, students, etc.).

A mastery strategy involves (1) deciding what constitutes mastery for a given course of study, (2) what procedures are appropriate to use to obtain mastery, and (3) what evidence is to be accepted that mastery has been attained. Stated another way, these three steps involve instructional objectives, instruction procedures, and evaluation of outcomes.

TABLE 6
Arguments For and Against Mastery Learning

Arguments For	Arguments Against
Mastery strategies can be worked out at virtually any level of schooling for any subject.	Mastery can be appropriate only for easily objectifiable technical skills and unsuited for most subjects where "education" rather than "training" is appropriate.
While admittedly oversimplified, the model explains the relationship between five important classroom learning variables and may help teachers develop instruction and evaluation strategies.	The model is drastically oversimplified; even though the variables are supposed to be quantifiable in terms of time, we have few good measures of many of them.
Upwards of 90 percent of students can and should master a course. It is the teacher's fundamental responsibility to seek pupil mastery.	It is unfair if most or all students receive the same mark since marks will become meaningless in terms of future opportunities.
Motivation, if increased beyond a certain level (see the discussion of the equation for predicting learning), will not result in greater learning.	Intuitively this does not make sense—as amount of motivation increases, degree of learning should increase accordingly.
Teachers can devise strategies for pupil mastery and put these into practice in their classrooms.	Most teachers are severely limited in their opportunity to devise and try out mastery strategies. The scarcity of reliable tests of the variables and unreliability of teacher-made tests are but two such limitations.
The goal of mastery learning is pupil success and excellence. Pupils can have a part in developing objectives.	Mastery learning is too teacher-centered and ignores credit for pupil effort which may not be reflected on summative tests.
Mastery learning can have important affective outcomes in terms of positive attitudes and self-concepts.	Too much emphasis on product, too little on process.
Mastery learning de-emphasizes competition and encourages cooperation.	Children need to experience failure in order to know how to deal with it when it comes (inevitably) later in life.

Step One: Course Content. The setting of the course content and objectives and standards of mastery is usually more difficult than it sounds at first. This is, however, an essential first step for informing both teacher and students what are the expected learning outcomes. Ideally, absolute standards of mastery should be worked out where teachers, individually or in groups organized by specialty, draw upon the resources available to them to decide upon course content, desired pupil outcomes, and levels of proficiency acceptable for mastery. At this point there are several good references available to teachers on setting instructional objectives. Among them are paperbacks by Gronlund (1970) and Kibler et al., (1970). These sources are recommended because they deal with learning objectives at levels of the three behavioral domains (cognitive, affective, and psychomotor). Both sources also give several sample objectives and lists of verb forms to use in writing objectives. In addition, Gronlund makes the very useful distinction between *general* and *specific* objectives. *General* objectives correspond to the overall course goals or lesson plans. *Specific objectives* refer to samples of student behavior which can be taken as evidence of attainment of the goals. These ideas are developed further in chapter 9.

Step Two: Procedures. The development and selection of a variety of instructional procedures should be geared to the objectives formulated in stage one. As Anderson (1959) has pointed out, it seems much too oversimplified to hold that there is one *a priori* teaching method that is superior to all others. The instructional methods should be geared not only to the objectives sought but to personal characteristics of the pupils and teachers involved (Thelen, 1967). Recent research into aptitude by treatment interactions (Berliner & Cahen, 1973; Hunt, 1975), while not as yet conclusive, highlights the issue of trying to optimize the "fit" between the learning styles of individual students and the differing instructional styles of teachers.

Step Three: Evaluation. Evaluation may be of two broad types: formative-diagnostic and summative-final. These ideas are also detailed in chapter 9. It should be noted that Cronbach (1971) has taken exception to this use of the term "formative" and has suggested the more descriptive phraseology of "monitoring evaluation" which suggests the checking or monitoring of pupil progress. We follow Bloom's terminology in our following discussion of this topic since all of the references cited with the exception of Cronbach's paper use the term "formative."

The summative evaluation in mastery learning should be based upon criterion-referenced tests (these are discussed in chapter 9) whereby the performance of learners is compared to predetermined standards. Achievement scores will be distributed as a mastery curve (as in Mayo, 1970) if the strategy has been successful. It should be noted that under traditional instruction there is a high correlation between student ability and student achievement, whereas under successful mastery conditions this correlation drops, that is, even learners of lower ability achieve satisfactorily. Figure 9 shows an expansion of the three stages already discussed into a schematic model for an instructional unit.

Planning and Instruction	*Formative (1b, 2b, 3b) and Summative (4b) Measurement and Evaluation*
1a. Select and compare course content and instructional objectives (consult pupils, fellow teachers, and curriculum resources).	1b. Assess the entering behaviors of pupils to determine ranges of interest, aptitude, and ability.
2a. Devise, select, and try out a variety of instructional procedures based upon appropriateness to 1a and 1b.	2b. Frequently sample pupil performance to determine effects and to revise procedures.
3a. Revise instruction procedures based upon feedback from 2b and continue to provide opportunities for learning.	3b. Identify pupils who have and have not achieved mastery. Try to assess what kinds of problems they are having.
4a. Set new objectives and procedures for those attaining mastery (including tutoring of other pupils); continue to try to facilitate learning.	4b. Assess degree of learning of pupils through sampling terminal behavior with reference to instructional objectives.

Figure 9. A Model for an instructional unit based upon Bloom's mastery strategy (1968)

Figure 10 is a flow chart, which illustrates a conception of a course of study composed of units organized around a mastery strategy. Figure 10 also shows an alternative instructional approach employing pretests which are used to assess the extent to which pupils have mastered skills prerequisite to the course or for purposes of placement in the available instructional alternatives or advanced placement in the course or in other related courses.

Summary and Evaluation of Mastery Learning

A number of questions remain to be investigated concerning mastery learning and its implications. Assumptions that most students are truly capable of mastery of most tasks and claims for the positive affective outcomes have yet to be thoroughly checked. There is some controversy also on what the student should study if that student fails to achieve mastery on any one test. Block and Tierney (1974) have indicated that it is better if a student is given new supplementary material than if the student is required to review the original material.

Finally, appropriate statistics to handle mastery score distributions need to be worked out. Most of the available test

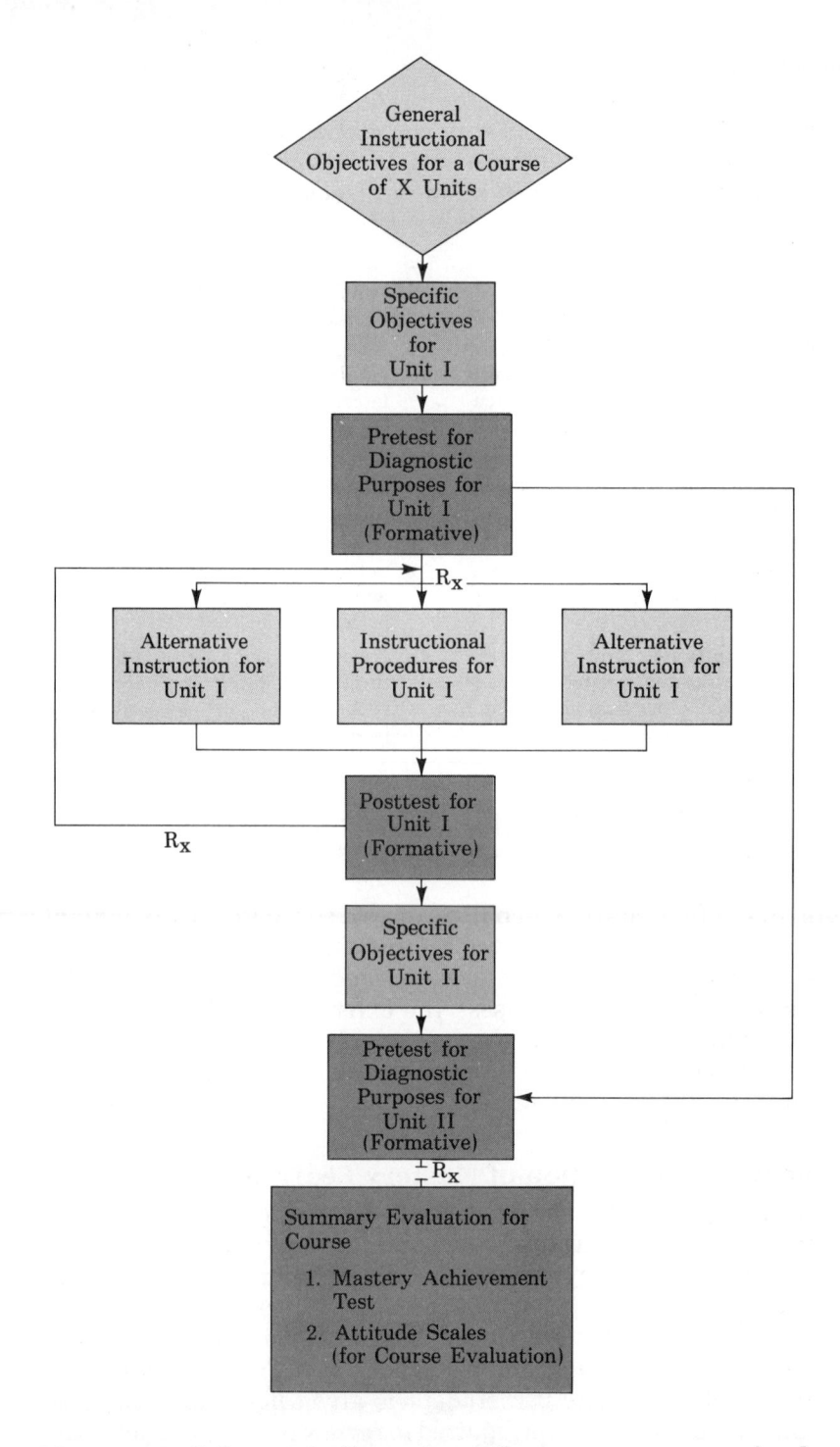

Figure 10. Schematic flow chart for a course organized according to a mastery learning strategy. R_x is prescription for alternative or supplementary instruction based on the results of formative testing.

Programmed Instruction

statistics are based on normal curve assumptions (see section on Testing For Mastery in chapter 9).

Results to date do suggest that mastery learning is a promising approach to individual differences in rate of learning.

Programmed Instruction

An approach to instructional problems associated with individual pupil differences has emerged from psychological theory and investigations of learning. It is programmed instruction—a way of organizing any subject-matter content to accomplish three goals: (1) to allow pupils to study individually (or in a small group) at their own rate of speed; (2) to provide frequent opportunities for pupils to actively respond to the subject matter; and (3) to provide feedback to each pupil as to the accuracy of responses. This feedback is to be provided almost immediately after a response is made. Additionally, many programs provide a record of pupil progress which is available to teachers for formative evaluation and educational decision-making purposes.

Description of Instructional Programs

Programmed instruction may take many forms. An instructional program may be in book or booklet form, may appear as a deck of cards, or may be in a simple machine or presented by a sophisticated electronic computer system. Essentially, a program is a sequence of bits of information called *frames* organized so that pupils frequently stop reading and respond to a question about the material. Typically the next frame following such a question begins by presenting feedback to the student in the form of correct "answers" which can be compared to the student's own responses. Occasionally, a student might be provided with remedial help or enriched information by means of a special sequence of frames known as a *branch*. Programs may be termed *linear* or *branched* depending on whether all students proceed through the same sequence (linear), or if special frames are available to some students (branched).

An example of a reasonably short branched program in paperback form is David Cram's (1961) *Explaining Teaching Machines and Programming,* which the authors recommend as an interesting introduction to the subject. Programmed instruction has been at the center of considerable controversy over the past two decades. Some enthusiasts and not a few opponents of the approach have claimed that teachers might be replaced by machines and that this was desirable—or horrendous—depending on one's view. In fact, programmed instruction is no more intended nor likely to make teachers obsolete than was the published textbook following the invention of the printing press, or the development of other media.

Programmed materials are perhaps best viewed then as tools, along with texts, tapes, films, television, and other media, for the teacher to evaluate as more or less appropriate and effective to promote student learning. To the extent that a well-written instructional program is available which appears to meet objectives of the class, a teacher might evaluate it for possible use the same as texts, films, or other instructional materials might be considered.

Some computerized instructional procedures have been influenced by the research in programmed instruction. Others have not. See Anderson et al. (1974) and Anderson et al. (1975) for descriptions of one computer managed instructional system. Computer assisted instruction (C.A.I.) has been to date more useful for instructional research than for widespread classroom use. With increased knowledge, lower costs, and the availability of electronic computing equipment in greater numbers of school systems the balance between research and application is likely to change.

Table 7 presents some of the arguments which have been advanced in favor of and against programmed instruction.

Despite these controversies, increasing numbers of publishers are producing programmed materials for school use. Educational and psychological research into learning variables and programmed instruction continue apace. It seems also to be the case that schools and industry are increasing their use of programmed training materials.

Basis for Programmed Instruction in Psychological Theory and Research

It was stated above that programmed instruction grew out of learning theory and research in psychology. In fact, programmed instruction may be considered as one of the most important contributions of learning psychologists to classroom practices to date.

Operant conditioning (discussed in chapter 2) formed the initial research base of programmed instruction; however, a variety of other theoretical orientations have made important contributions to the field. For example, some prominent former students of the contiguity theorist, Guthrie, have been active in programmed instruction research. Indeed, results of some studies in this area suggest that contiguity of stimulus (question frame) and response (pupil answer) may provide a satisfactory and parsimonious explanation of learning by programmed instruction (e.g., Anderson & Faust, 1967).

The operant conditioning analysis of learning by programmed instruction follows fairly closely the behavior shaping by the

Programmed Instruction

TABLE 7*
Arguments For and Against Programmed Instruction

Arguments For	Arguments Against
Programmed materials free a teacher's time for more creative work with individuals.	Teachers may find their positions are threatened by automation.
Well-written programs have the same "personal touch" as textbooks.	Programmed instruction is cold and dehumanizing.
Self-pacing individualizes instruction to the preferred rate of each learner.	Personal needs of students are sacrificed in favor of overall objectives for a group.
The basic learning ideas behind programmed instruction have been shown to apply to human learning.	Programmed instruction is based largely upon learning principles developed from animal studies.
When suited to a student's entering behavior, a well-written program is both fun and challenging.	There is much redundancy and potential for learning to become dreadfully boring.
It is another tool to be used for instruction, just as films, tapes, television, and books are tools. It frequently can be a good change of pace from other media.	Programmed instruction is just another educational fad that will be soon forgotten when it is found to be no panacea for learning problems.
In most cases studies have shown programs to be at least as effective as more traditional materials, and thus the technique can be regarded as "proven."	Research findings are spotty and frequently show that programmed materials are no better than the other approaches to instruction.
Self-pacing assures minimum student idleness when properly applied.	Programs, especially in book format, can encourage cheating and laziness.

*Adapted from R. H. Simpson, *Teacher Self-Evaluation*, New York: Macmillan, 1966. Used by permission.

successive approximations paradigm. Thus the teacher or programmer decides in advance what should be the terminal behavior of students and what sequence of intermediate specific responses are necessary to achieve it. Next the program is so constructed as to elicit from the student the first response in the chain by some means such as prompting. Then each student is guided through a linear sequence of frames calling for responses which lead up to the desired final terminal behavior. Along the way, the steps are kept small so that the error rate is low and so that most students experience success most of the time. This has the effect of preventing students from making and practicing "incorrect" responses. Two major emphases of the operant approach to programmed instruction are *active responding* by the student (usually a "constructed response"—one where the student writes out a key word or phrase) and *immediate reinforcement* (by knowledge of results feedback) at every response.

Research on student achievement in programmed instruction has centered on such issues as program versus alternative materials; overt versus covert response to programs; reinforcement of all, some, or none of the response frame types; effects of frame sequence; and attitudes toward programmed instruction.

It should be emphasized that there are a considerable number of ongoing investigations of aspects of programmed instruction and the "last word" is not yet in. In general, however, research results to date can be summarized as follows: programs, when well written, appear to aid student achievement about as well as well-prepared lectures, discussions, books, films, or other media. Programs do allow students to work at different speeds. The issue of whether the rate of speed a student adopts is always optimum or inefficient is as yet unresolved. Overt responding takes longer than covert responding and may not result in much improvement in learning and retention (Crist, 1966). Feedback does not appear to be very important to learning from programs when the step size is small; students are often correct and know answers without reinforcement in the form of explicit knowledge of results (Taber, Glaser, & Schaefer, 1965). Well-written frames (ones that call for key responses, not trivial responses; and ones that cause students to attend to and think about the material, not merely copy it) are more important than the careful sequencing of frames (Anderson & Faust, 1967). And it seems that attitudes toward programmed instruction vary widely among teachers and education students and tend to become more positive as a consequence of learning more about the topic (Foster, 1970).

Summary and Evaluation of Programmed Instruction

In summary, it may be said of programmed instruction that it provides student and teacher with another potential learning aid. It has obvious potential for remediation of deficiencies and deserves consideration as an alternate instructional method in a mastery strategy. In addition, programmed instruction also provides an opportunity to clarify one's objectives.

When evaluating the appropriateness of a published program one should look at what specific responses are required of the students. If, in a teacher's judgment, the responses required of the student are not trivial but represent desirable new behaviors and lead to terminal performance consistent with the aims and objectives of the course, the published programmed instruction is worth considering. An instructional program, unlike most textbooks, yields quantifiable data. Responsible publishers should make such data available to potential users. For example, in promoting a textbook, publishers can say that it is used in many schools, whereas in the case of an instructional program they ought to be able to say (1) how long it takes on the average to complete, (2) what is the range of completion time, (3) what is the error rate per frame for one hundred "typical" students, and (4) how well does a typical class score on given examination items after completion of the program. Of course, these are data a teacher can collect locally, but it would also be desirable to examine prior evidence of program effectiveness before committing funds and time to it.

Programmed instruction as a technique appears to be effective, however, just as there are well-written and poorly written textbooks, self-instructional programs vary widely in quality. Likewise, programs vary in terms of appropriateness to a given student or to the objectives of a course.

The same instructional model cited for a mastery strategy (see figure 10) can be proposed for effective programmed instruction. Namely, (1) devise objectives appropriate to students and the course, (2) develop procedures (one or more instructional programs) designed to enable students to accomplish the objectives, and (3) apply formative and summative evaluation procedures to assess the effectiveness of both student learning and instructional quality. While mastery learning seems to be more appropriate to group instruction and programmed instruction is a more individualized procedure, both are approaches to individual differences worth considering by the classroom teacher.

Programmed instruction also has demonstrated considerable value in research investigations into learning and various instructional variables, especially when the program is presented and the responses are recorded by an electronic computer.

Open Education

A third approach to individual differences is open education. Strictly speaking, this method of instruction may be no more responsive to individual differences than many of the so-called traditional forms of instruction, since by "open education" educators mean a wide variety of things from leaving one's classroom door open through forms of "institutional anarchy." Recently, open education has been highly touted so often as being responsive to individual differences and grounded in humanistic psychology, that a discussion of it is involved here. Open education has also been called "free schooling," "open-area education," "The British Infant School," and "informal schooling."

The open school idea in the United States has some consistency with the progressive education movement of the second, third, and fourth decades of this century (see Cremin, 1964, for an excellent discussion of the history of this movement). Open school ideas have gained momentum from this historical consistency as well as from *claims* that traditional Anglo-American public schools are, among other things, excessively bureaucratic, rigid, sexist, noncreative, feminine, racist, dehumanized, restrictive, and inefficient. Open education is touted as a way to rid the schools of these undesirable characteristics.

Instruction in the open school mainly involves moving away from large group-centered teaching to small group or individual conference-type teaching. Instruction has been characterized as informal and structured around the interests of the student. The ages of students in the class may vary by several years. Several small groups may be working at any one time. The room lends itself to different work arrangements and generally will contain much stimulating material. Interesting individual work areas and reading places may be contained in the room. The entire area is designed to stimulate interests and then to facilitate responding to those interests. That is, these interests become the bases of instruction through independent study, small group study, or total-class instruction; although the latter may be rare. Most of the time the students are free to move around and confer with each other or the teachers. The reader is referred to Engstrom (1970), Featherstone (1971), Gross and Gross (1970), Kohl (1969), Neill (1960), Silberman (1971), Sponberg (1969), and Stretch (1970) for descriptions of variations on open education and critiques of more traditionally organized schools.

Nongraded schools (Goodlad & Anderson, 1963) can be considered as a category of alternatives to traditionally organized schools. Again, there are many claims and counterclaims but little solid evidence concerning the comparative effectiveness of nongraded schools (Anderson, 1962). Hopkins, Oldridge, and Williamson (1965) report comparisons of reading and vocabulary comprehension scores of pupils in twenty ungraded and twenty-five graded primary classes in Los Angeles County. They also examined teacher's evaluations, sociometric patterns, and class attendance. No statistically significant differences or important trends were noted in these data.

Subsequently, Oldridge (1971) conduct a survey of parent, student, and staff evaluations of an open-area nongraded elementary school in British Columbia. Also investigated was whether the organization and function of the school fitted a conceptual model of a nongraded school according to a set of eleven propositions. These eleven propositions were originally developed by Purdom (1967) and are listed here.

PROPOSITIONS*

1. The school assists each learner in developing potentialities to the maximum.
2. The curriculum emphasizes the development of the broad structural concept and modes of inquiry of the disciplines.
3. Learning opportunities are provided on the basis of individual needs, interests, and abilities.
4. All phases of human growth are considered when making decisions about how to work effectively with a learner.
5. Learning opportunities are paced so that each child can progress in relation to the child's own rate of development in each area of the curriculum.
6. An evaluation of all phases of human growth is made for each individual.
7. Evaluation of each learner's progress is carried on almost constantly.
8. The adequacy of each child's progress is an individual matter determined by appraising the child's attainments in relation to estimates of the child's potential.
9. The school is organized to facilitate continuous and cumulative learning for each learner over the total years in school.
10. The school is so structured that there are alternate learning environments available to the individual, and opportunities within these environments to progress at different rates and work at different levels in each area of the curriculum.
11. Objectives are determined by the interests and needs of each learner.

Using from eight to twelve criteria for meeting each proposition, Oldridge found that the school evidenced notable strengths in propositions 5, 8, and 10 and weaknesses in 6, 7, and 11. He concluded, among other things, that it was possible to perform process evaluations of such schools, that open-area instructional space can provide an acceptable learning environment for children, that boys like open-area situations better than girls do, and that selection of staff is a crucial factor. He withheld a final analysis of academic achievement until the school could meet all of the criteria for nongraded schools.

At the present time there are not as many open education secondary classrooms as there are elementary. The approach is considered as being more appropriate for the earlier years, even in England. In England as in Canada and the United States, few secondary open schools exist. There is little reason to expect, however, that this approach would not be just as potentially effective at secondary levels as in elementary schools.

Many claims have been made for open education approaches. These claims are very broad and for the most part have not been checked

---

*Adapted from: A study of instructional innovation involving beginning teachers' attempting to nongrade an open-area school. (Report #9), Vancouver, B. C.: Educational Research Institute of B. C. by O. A. Oldridge. Used by permission.

empirically. These approaches may be in danger from the rhetoric of their own supporters. It has been claimed that students in open schools enjoy learning more, become more creative, develop better thinking abilities (Featherstone, 1971), have fewer inhibitions about sex, have increased self-confidence, appreciate freedom more, have better self-concepts (Neill, 1960), are more independent, more courageous, better prepared to cope with the modern world (Stretch, 1970), and are better able to express feelings and interests individually (Sponberg, 1969) when compared with students in more traditional settings.

Many of the supporters of open education see it as a panacea for all of our educational and social ills; or they see it as a philosopher's stone which will turn all the base educators and all their baser educational methods to a more noble (and "moral"?) hue. It is unfortunate that the claims have not been accompanied by closer empirical verification. It is possible that open education has certain advantages for teachers and students who have been selected according to personality characteristics for such an environment (Hunt, 1975). Table 8 lists some of the frequently voiced arguments for and against open education.

Research on Open Education

Some empirical comparisons have been made between the characteristics and performances of students in open and traditional settings. The claimed advantages for open education students in self-concept (Neill, 1960) was not supported by analyses made by Ruedi and West (1973). When achievement between "open" and "traditional" schools are compared the findings are inconclusive. *Good Housekeeping* (1971) reports that test averages of the open school students in North Bennington, Vermont, are above the national average. On the other hand, *Newsweek* (1971) reports test scores lower for the students in an open school than for students in a traditional school. Reports from Great Britain indicate slight advantages for traditional schools on conventional tests (Featherstone, 1967a, 1967b). No studies are known to the authors which compared achievement when intelligence, prior achievement, and social class were controlled.

It is likely that research comparing "open" and "traditional" schools will continue. For example, Wright (1975) found several interesting differences between these two educational approaches. "Traditional" schools were superior in terms of academic skills as measured by standardized achievement tests. Teachers in the "traditional" schools asked more direct questions of students, gave *fewer* directions, lectured more, and criticized students more as compared to "open" teachers. Teachers in the "open" schools asked

TABLE 8
Arguments For and Against Open Education

Arguments For	Arguments Against
Open education is more responsive to individual differences than are more traditional methods.	Open education does not place a proper emphasis on the basic skills.
British infant school methods can be modified to produce important results in any school system.	What works in England does not necessarily apply elsewhere, and there is some doubt how well it is working in England.
Traditional methods have elevated silence above worthwhile academic objectives.	Open education is noisy, inefficient, and tends to produce anarchy.
Learning groups should be flexible in size and age composition depending on the type of tasks involved.	There is little or no evidence that class size influences learning positively.
Students may progress at their own pace rather than being held back or advanced too soon by a school calendar.	The pace a student adopts may not be the most efficient for learning. Teachers are a better judge of pace.
Open education is the breakthrough which will humanize and deinstitutionalize schools.	Open education is just another fad representing "warmed over" progressivism from another generation.
Open education enhances self esteem and promotes positive student attitudes.	Evidence for purported positive effects is absent, scanty, or contrary to claims of advocates.
Schools should become more a microcosm of society than of prisons. Students can learn democracy by practicing and experiencing it.	Traditional methods have proven to be better for developing character and personal discipline, and such traits as honesty, citizenship, and fair play.

fewer questions, gave more directions, and participated in more student initiated exchanges than the "traditional" teachers.

Wright (1975) also tested students on six personality and cognitive variables: formal operations, locus of control, self-esteem, school anxiety, verbal creativity, and figural creativity. Only in school anxiety was there a significant difference. Children in the "open" school reported more school anxiety.

Walberg and Thomas (1972) compared United States and British open and traditional classes on eight themes suggested by previous literature on the topic. Among their findings was that differences between teachers who were identified as "open" or "traditional" were greater than were differences between schools in areas of higher or lower socioeconomic status, or than between schools in the United States and Great Britain. Open and traditional schools in both countries differed on all eight themes, which, it appears, correspond quite closely to the statements in the list of eleven propositions used by Oldridge.

The existing empirical evidence, then, is limited and neither supports nor invalidates all of the claims made by the advocates of open schooling. Certainly the many claims that open schooling produces higher self-concept have not been supported in two studies (Ruedi & West, 1973; Wright, 1975). Hopefully more research will be conducted on the influence of "open" schooling on achievement and student personality characteristics and on maximizing the "fit" between student, teacher, and learning environment. The importance of such research is briefly discussed by Friedlander (1975) and Hunt (1975).

A Concluding Note About the Three Approaches to Individual Differences

It must be apparent to the reader that the three approaches are based upon somewhat differing assumptions of the nature of learning and motivation, and the nature of the learner, not to mention different opinions on the purposes of education. Programmed instruction clearly has a basis in behavioristic learning theory, whereas open education appears to be based upon humanistic premises. Mastery learning purports to have a "foot in both camps," but is clearly more closely aligned with a systems approach, which emphasizes carefully specified curricula (as does programmed instruction), than it is with student freedom of choice (a characteristic of open education).

Advocates of open education would have one believe that many aspects of the learner's frame of reference are more readily accommodated by that type of approach than by traditional approaches. However, programmed instruction and mastery learning are not examples of strictly traditional approaches either. And claims can be advanced that these procedures can also account for such factors as learner affect, interests, etc. See, for example, Bloom's claims for the affective outcomes of mastery learning (1968, p. 11).

One recent approach which appears to combine some of the advantages of each of the three described above is reported by Hunt (1975). In York County, Ontario, Hunt and his co-workers have been implementing a "conceptual levels matching model" in selected elementary and public high schools. The basic idea is to group learners homogeneously by (conceptual) learning style and to tailor instruction accordingly (chapter 2 contains a brief introduction to Hunt's model). Teachers are trained and selected to organize learning activities to meet student needs for either greater or lesser structure.

While conclusive results are not yet available, this is the type of action research which is most clearly in the tradition of Kurt Lewin and the relativistic behavior model presented in chapter 3. Hunt presents a picture of some of the massive logistical as well as theoretical problems which are involved in restructuring education along these lines, concluding with the judgment that this is a difficult but highly important area for investigation and development in education. It should be noted that while programmed instruction is highly structured, and open education, typically, is not, Hunt's approach is to vary structure to suit learner needs.

Discussion Questions

1. Do you think that mastery learning and Carroll's model are too oversimplified and idealistic to be useful to teachers? Defend your answer against the opposite view.
2. Describe how mastery learning might work or fail in your (prospective) teaching situation.
3. What features of Carroll's model are most amenable to teacher influence? Which features are least amenable?
4. Have you tried programmed instruction as a student? What were your reactions to it? What variables may influence other people to react differently to it?
5. Does one have to accept an operant conditioning explanation of learning in order to accept the effectiveness of programmed instruction?
6. Have you seen one or more examples of open education? How would you compare these to traditional schooling—in terms of organization of instruction, student activities, and learning outcomes?
7. Does the literature on open education suggest ways in which traditional schools could respond to individual differences? What ways? Which approach seems better for gifted students? Why?
8. What kinds of differences between students appear to be met by the three approaches discussed above?
9. What important differences are suggested by your experience or by the frame of reference model which are not met by these three approaches?
10. Think about some courses you have taken. Would you have been helped by a mastery learning approach in any of them? Why or why not?
11. Would you be interested in trying a mastery approach for your teaching area and level? Why or why not?

Recommended Readings

Block, J. H. (Ed.) *Learning for mastery.* New York: Holt, Rinehart & Winston, 1971. Includes a compilation of recent research findings concerning the mastery variables.

Block, J. H. (Ed.) *Schools, society and mastery learning.* New York: Holt, Rinehart & Winston, 1974, 148 pp., paperback. A collection of essays by Bloom and others on applications and broader societal implications of mastery learning.

Calvin, A. D. (Ed.) *Programmed instruction—bold new venture.* Bloomington: Indiana University Press, 1969. Contains papers on teachers' role and the uses of programmed instruction in spelling, reading, social sciences, foreign languages, mathematics, adult education, and the nongraded school.

Hicks, B. L., & Hunka, S. *The teacher and the computer.* Philadelphia: W. B. Saunders, 1972. A clear statement on the aims and procedures of computer assisted instruction and the teachers' roles.

Holtzman, W. H. (Ed.) *Computer-assisted instruction, testing and guidance.* New York: Harper & Row, 1970. A collection of readings on contemporary uses and prospects of the computer in education.

Hunt, D. E., & Sullivan, E. V. *Between psychology and education.* Hinsdale, Illinois: Dryden Press, 1974, 312 pp. Contains detailed analysis of applications of psychological theory to educational practice in the traditions of Kurt Lewin's $B = f(P,E)$ and "The only good theory is a practical one" tradition.

Kohl, H. R. *The open classroom: A practical to a new way of teaching.* New York: Random House, 1969. This slim volume (116 pp.) offers some very practical advice to teachers concerning how to "open" their classrooms.

Nyquist, E. E., & Hawes, G. R. (Eds.) *Open education: A sourcebook for parents and teachers.* New York: Bantam Books, 1972. A set of readings which encompasses critiques and rationales for British and American open education attempts, examples of how open education functions and of its implementation and evaluation.

Silberman, C. E. *Crisis in the classroom.* New York: Random House, 1970. A critical analysis of traditional classroom practice and statement of the educational movement known as "open education."

References

Anderson, R. C. The case for nongraded homogeneous grouping. *Elementary School Journal,* 1962, *62,* 193-97.

Anderson, R. C. Learnings in discussion: a resume of the authoritarian-democratic studies. *Harvard Educational Review,* 1959, *29,* 201-15.

Anderson, R. C., & Faust, G. F. The effects of strong formal prompts in programmed instruction. *American Educational Research Journal,* 1967, *4,* 345-52.

Anderson, T. H., Anderson, R. C., Dalgaard, B. R., Paden, D. W., Biddle, W. B., Surber, J. R., & Alessi, S. M., An experimental evaluation of a computer based study management system. *Educational Psychologist,* 1975, *11,* 184-90.

Anderson, T. H., Anderson, R. C., Dalgaard, B. R., Wietecha, E. J., Biddle, W. B., Paden, D. W., Smock, H. R., Alessi, S. M., Surber, J. R., & Klemt, L. A computer based study management system. *Educational Psychologist,* 1974, *11,* 36-45.

Berliner, D. C., & Cahen, L. S. Trait-treatment interaction and learning. In F. N. Kerlinger (Ed.), *Review of research in education. Vol. I.* Itasca, Illinois: F. E. Peacock, 1973, 58-94.

Block, J. H., & Tierney, M. L. An exploration of two correction procedures used in mastery learning approaches to instruction. *Journal of Educational Psychology,* 1974, *66,* 962-67.

Bloom, B. S. Learning for mastery. *Evaluation/Comment,* 1968, *1.*

Bloom, B. S. Mastery learning and its implications for curriculum development. In E. W. Eisner (Ed.), *Confronting curriculum reform.* Boston: Little, Brown and Company, 1971, 17-48.

Bloom, B. S., Hastings, J. T., & Madaus, G. *Handbook on formative and summative evaluation of learning.* New York: McGraw-Hill, 1971.

Carroll, J. B. A model of school learning. *Teachers College Record,* 1963, *64,* 723-33.

Cram, D. *Explaining teaching machines and programming.* San Francisco: Fearon, 1961.

Cremin, L. A. *The transformation of the school: progressivism in American education 1876-1957.* New York: Vintage Books, 1964.

Crist, R. L. Overt versus covert responding and retention by sixth grade students. *Journal of Educational Psychology,* 1966, *57,* 99-101.

Cronbach, L. J. Comments on mastery learning and its implications for curriculum development. In E. W. Eisner (Ed.), *Confronting curriculum reform.* Boston: Little, Brown and Company, 1971, 49-55.

Engstrom, E. (Ed.) *Open education.* Washington, D. C.: National Association for the Education of Young Children, 1970.

Featherstone, J. Open Schools: The British and us; excerpts from booklets, informal schools in Britain today. *New Republic,* 1971, *165,* 20-25.

Featherstone, J. Schools for children: What's happening in British classrooms. *New Republic,* 1967a, *157,* 17-21.

Featherstone, J. Teaching children to think: Primary school reforms in Great Britain. *New Republic,* 1967b, *157,* 15-19.

Foster, S. F. A scale to measure attitudes toward programmed instruction and teaching machines. American Psychological Association, *Experimental Publication System,* 1970, *9,* Ms. No. 342-4.

Friedlander, B. Z. Some remarks on "open education." *American Educational Research Journal,* 1975, *12,* 465-68.

Good Housekeeping. School of your children's dreams; Prospect School, North Bennington, Vermont, 1971, *172,* 198.

Goodlad, J. I., & Anderson, R. H. *The nongraded elementary school.* (rev ed.) New York: Harcourt, Brace & World, 1963.

Gronlund, N. *Stating behavioral objectives for classroom instruction.* New York: Macmillan, 1970.

Gross, B., & Gross, R. A little bit of chaos. *Saturday Review,* 1970, *53,* 20.

Hopkins, K. D., Oldridge, O. A., & Williamson, M. L. An empirical comparison of pupil achievement and other variables in graded and ungraded classes. *American Educational Research Journal,* 1965, *2,* 207-15.

Hunt, D. E. Person-environment interaction: a challenge found wanting before it was tried. *Review of Educational Research,* 1975, *45,* 209-30.

Illich, I. *Deschooling society.* London: Caldar and Boyars, 1971.

Kibler, R. G., Barker, L. L., & Miles, D. T. *Behavioral objectives and instruction.* Boston: Allyn and Bacon, 1970.

Kohl, H. R. *The open classroom.* New York: Vintage Books, 1969.

Mayo, S. T. Mastery learning and mastery testing. NCME, *Measurement in Education,* 1970, 1.

Morrison, H. C. *The practice of teaching in the secondary school.* Chicago:University of Chicago Press, 1926.

Myers, E. C. The American school: Classroom or courtroom? Bureau of Institutional Research, University of Minnesota, 1970.

References

Neill, A. S. *Summerhill: A radical approach to child rearing.* New York: Hart, 1960.

Newsweek. Does school joy-learning? 1971, 77, 60.

Oldridge, O. A. *Overlander—A study of instructional innovation involving beginning teachers' attempting to nongrade an open-area elementary school.* (Report No. 9), Vancouver, B. C., Educational Research Institute of B. C., 1971.

Purdom, D. M. A conceptual model of the nongraded school. Unpublished doctoral dissertation. University of California at Los Angeles, 1967.

Ruedi, J., & West, C. K. Pupil self concept in an "open" and in a "traditional" school. *Psychology in the Schools,* January, 1973.

Silberman, C. E. *Crises in the classroom.* New York: Vintage, 1971.

Sponberg, R. A. New kind of school day. *Education Digest,* 1969, 34, 46-48.

Stretch, B. B. Rise of the free school. *Saturday Review,* 1970, 53, 76-79.

Taber, J. I., Glaser, R., & Schaefer, H. H. *Learning and programmed instruction.* Reading, Mass.: Addison-Wesley, 1965.

Thelen, H. A. *Classroom grouping for teachability.* New York: Wiley, 1967.

Walberg, H. J., & Thomas, S. C. Open education: an operational definition and validation in Great Britain and United States. *American Educational Research Journal,* 1972, 9, 197-208.

Wright, R. J. The affective and cognitive consequences of an open education elementary school. *American Educational Research Journal,* 1975, 12, 449-68.

Practical Organizer for Chapter 8

Attitudes are among the most important factors in school learning. A teacher must exert every effort to encourage positive attitudes toward learning in general as well as toward the content of the teacher's specialty. If the student forms negative attitudes toward the content, subsequent achievement will be more difficult. The student is also likely to avoid later study of that content area, and may come to dislike education generally.

To encourage learning of positive attitudes teachers must plan and provide pleasant learning atmospheres, enjoyable activities or experiences, and hold positive attitudes themselves toward the content area and toward education as well.

Even these approaches do not guarantee positive student attitudes. The teacher may wish to ascertain reasons why an individual student holds negative or undesirable attitudes. This may be accomplished by interviewing the individual student and discussing these undesirable attitudes. Some of the reasons may lead the teacher to discover ways of changing the attitudes.

Many negative attitudes about subject content have their beginning in the early stages of learning of that particular content. That is, the student finds it difficult and fails during early attempts to master the subject. Generally speaking the student will have positive attitudes toward material with which he or she is successful. This implies, of course, that teachers should attempt to assign beginning tasks which can be successfully accomplished, calibrating increased difficulty so that it is within the frustration tolerance of each student. Individualized instruction at some point is clearly called for if such attempts are to be successful.

Attitude Learning in the Schools

This chapter deals with the nature of attitudes and how they are learned and in turn how they influence the learning of other types of responses. Attitudes are dealt with here as learned evaluative responses—reactions which are learned the same way and at the same time as are facts, beliefs, and skills. In addition, attitudes are seen as mediating (i.e., serving to produce) other behaviors, especially in the areas of expressions of preference, choice, or persistence. Recent research and theory concerning moral attitudes, values, and self-regarding attitudes, attitudinal objectives, and the affective domain are also discussed in terms of educational practice.

The frame of reference, especially the aspects of interests, affect, values, and needs is interrelated with the psychology of attitudes. This is not to say that attitudes have nothing to do with knowledge, yet attitudes are strongly affective in nature and have a long-term influence on learning and behavior. Thus, the learning of attitudes is of increasing concern to educational psychologists.

This concern is a recognition of the fact that attitude learning is an integral part of school learning, whether or not attitudinal objectives are consciously introduced into the curriculum. It is impossible for one to learn anything even by rote, without forming accompanying attitudes.

The purpose of this chapter is to review selectively psychological theory and research as it applies to attitude learning in schools; and to make some tentative suggestions to educators about attitudinal objectives. A section on attitude measurement is included in chapter 9 on problems and issues in measurement and evaluation of learning.

Educators and psychologists traditionally have taken conflicting and equivocal positions concerning attitudes. In education, for example, teachers, administrators, and parents have long stated that the development of "good attitudes" was a chief goal of schooling. On the other hand, actual curricular planning and day-to-day operations of many schools frequently have neglected a consideration of attitude learning in any formal sense.

For their part, psychologists differ on what "attitude" means and how it can be studied. For example, Allport (1935) noted over one hundred definitions of the term "attitude" in his survey of the literature. Since then, a variety of theories of attitude learning and change have been advanced, but like the general learning theories discussed in chapter 2 none of these has been sufficient to account adequately for the range of observed attitudinal phenomena. Indeed, in contrast with cognitive achievement, psychologists have given little attention to problems of attitude learning in educational settings.

Despite this somewhat confused situation, recent research and theorizing on attitude learning and measurement as well as curriculum reform efforts among education faculties and public schools offer promise for near-term improvements.

Attitude Definitions—Distinctions

In various parts of this book there are statements about people's feelings or affective responses. Psychological conceptions of attitude have been constructed and operationally defined in attempts to account for such feelings. In 1931, L. L. Thurstone defined attitude as, "the amount of affect for or against a psychological object." Since that time numerous definitions of the term have been advanced, some fairly complex. Authors of recent texts in social and educational psychology conceptualize attitude as a multidimensional, often a three-part, construct consisting of cognitive, affective, and behavioral components (e.g., Krech, Crutchfield & Ballachey, 1962; Mouly, 1968).

The present authors, following Fishbein (1967c), prefer to assign the cognitive and behavioral functions to other concepts (beliefs and behaviors, respectively), reserving for attitude the unidimensional definition advanced by Thurstone. This approach is consistent with the way "attitude" is operationalized in the most frequently used measurement instruments.

Another way of approaching the same definition of attitude is through the work of Osgood and his associates (1957) on measuring the meanings of words and concepts. Osgood identified one important dimension of evaluative meaning of virtually any word, concept, or thing. This was characterized as *evaluative*. Every time a person learns beliefs about something, that person seems to acquire evaluations of it as well. Sometimes these are strong preferences or dislikes. At other times they are mild, almost neutral evaluations of the psychological object.

Osgood et al. (1957, pp. 190-91) defines "attitude" unidimensionally as an aspect of affect which can be called evaluative meaning. Thus, theoretical and practical issues important to psychologists and educators can be approached. For example, the problem of two persons having the same score on some measure of attitude, but exhibiting markedly differing behaviors toward the attitude object has long plagued researchers. In distinguishing between overt behavior and attitude, and defining attitude as one of the learned factors which may mediate behavior, researchers are provided with a rationale for more detailed attitude investigations. Likewise the distinction between cognitive learning (facts and beliefs) and affective learning (attitudes) allows for the separate measurement and study of these constructs.

Attitude learning theory

A plausible theoretical rationale for the relationship between beliefs and attitudes and between attitudes and behavior has been worked out by Fishbein (1967a, b, c). Briefly, attitudes are described as affective components of beliefs. Therefore, as a person learns individual beliefs (about an object), that person simultaneously acquires attitudes made up of the affective ("evaluative," in Osgood's terms) aspects of those beliefs. A set of closely related beliefs can be called a *belief system* and the corresponding evaluations of these beliefs collectively is termed an *attitude system*. Changing attitudes, then, requires one of three things to happen: the learning of new beliefs, the reevalution of old ones, or the unlearning (forgetting) of beliefs. These three are stated in the order in which one might expect to find increasing difficulty in obtaining change. Since overlearning of attitudes and beliefs would, theoretically, tend to make them resistant to extinction this is taken to be more difficult than reevaluation involving the change of an already learned response, or the easiest (comparatively), learning a new belief.

Of the concepts from learning theories outlined in chapter 2, several can be employed to explain the available evidence about attitudes. Fishbein (1967b) has critically evaluated these concepts. Briefly, psychological experimentation has demonstrated acquisition of attitudes toward some specific object by classical conditioning (e.g., Staats & Staats, 1958) and by operant conditioning with mediation (Lott, 1955). Cases also have been made for acquisition of attitudes by social learning (Bandura, 1969) and a concept formation process (Rhine, 1958). Although this latter formulation is not without some criticism (see for example, Fishbein, 1967a).

In addition to classical and operant conditioning explanations, Fishbein (1967b) used Hull's habit family hierarchy concept (chapter 2) in building his attitude learning theory. Thus, a person's belief system is considered to be organized according to a hierarchy of salient beliefs, in terms of the probability of association between any object of awareness and the person's beliefs about that object. The position of a belief in a hierarchy is dependent upon such factors as overlearning, past and perceived future reinforcement values of holding such a belief, and is modified by interference or forgetting variables. As affective components of beliefs, attitudes occupy like positions in the belief hierarchy.

From the point of view of learning psychology, then, an attitude can be defined as a learned evaluative (affective) response for or against some object as perceived. Attitude learning takes place simultaneously and according to the same principles (e.g., conditioning) as the learning of beliefs, facts, skills, concepts, etc.

Advantages of a learning theory approach to attitudes as taken by Fishbein lie in parsimony (unidimensional definition), researchability (hypotheses concerning attitude learning can be more readily derived and tested), and applicability to education settings. Employing a learning theory interpretation of attitudes should make it possible to formulate affective objectives and to measure whether or not the specified attitudes have been acquired or changed in desired directions.

Ways in Which Students Learn School Attitudes

As noted before, pupils are likely to learn attitudes through the classical and operant conditioning and concept formation processes described in chapters 2 and 3. There is also the likelihood that school-related attitudes are acquired through the social learning processes of imitation and modeling (Bandura & Walters, 1963). The following paragraphs are hypothetical classroom examples of some of these approaches to attitude learning in the classroom. The reader is invited to consider personal learning experiences and those personal classroom observations to see how well these interpretations fit.

School Attitude Learning—Conditioning Paradigm

An instance of attitude learning in the classroom interpreted according to a classical conditioning approach would be the generalization of positive or negative affect already learned toward some object to a new object through the contiguous association in space and time of the two. For example, consider a youngster in primary grades who has learned to take great pleasure in hiking, fishing, and other outdoor recreations, but is indifferent to school-related learning. The youngster may have learned to dislike reading ("reading is girls' stuff"). One time-honored tactic a reading teacher might take would be to select, adapt, or create some primary level reading materials about things the pupil likes. At this point the distinction between classical and operant conditioning blurs somewhat. It would appear that the pupil may come to like reading more because it is associated (by contiguity) with something he/she likes, namely recreation. Actual reading responses may be said to be learned operantly when they lead to positive consequences. That is, finding out about sports, through reading, rewards attempts to read. Perhaps both will take place in an instance such as this. Hopefully, it will be the case that the student will in the future find out about many more things that the student likes and dislikes through use of personal reading skills.

The classical conditioning paradigm may be redrawn to include this attitude learning and also to show overt responses on an attitude scale. See figure 11 for this schematic representation of attitude learning in a mode analogous to classical conditioning. The initial element is labeled (U)CS because although it operates like the UCS of Pavlovian conditioning, it is in reality a CS condition at an earlier time.

Early (1968) performed an experiment in attitude learning by classical conditioning using sixty fourth- and fifth-grade students.

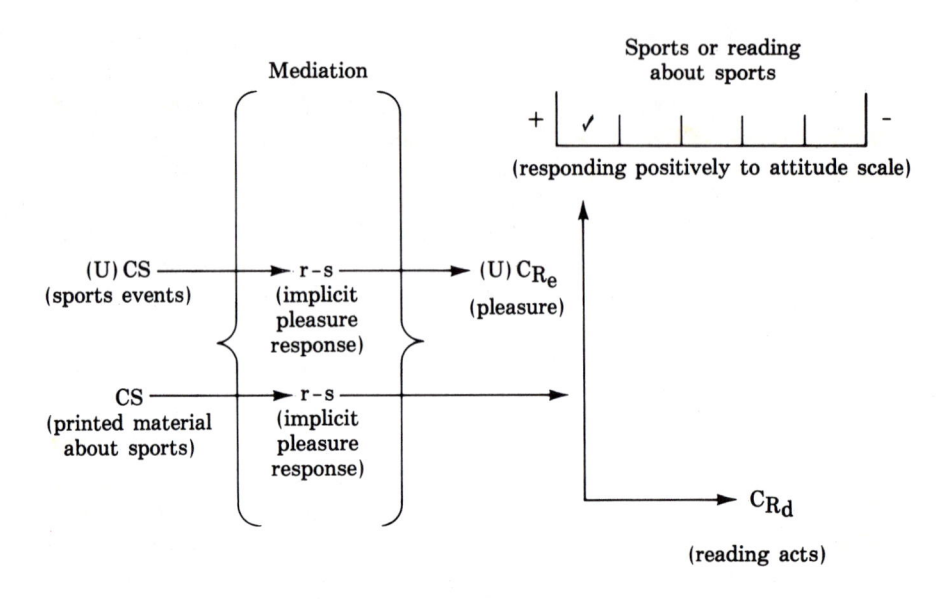

NOTE: (U)CS operates like an "unconditioned" stimulus in classical conditioning—regularly eliciting r
    CS   Conditioned stimulus—new reading materials
    r   Implicit pleasure response
    s   Internal stimulus produced by r
    (U)CR   Unconditioned overt pleasure responses
    CR   Conditioned responses of seeking, choosing sports-related or reading activities. Responding to attitude scales.

Figure 11. Positive attitude learning by classical conditioning paradigm

Using sociometric techniques (chapter 9 briefly describes sociometry) she identified social "isolates"—those children receiving one or no choices when each pupil listed on sheets of paper the names of classmates they liked. The unconditioned stimuli (UCS) in this study were words that the children had previously identified as positive (e.g., good, kind, friendly) or neutral (and, table, chair).

    The children were told they were in a study of memory and that they had to remember a list of thirty-two word pairs. These pairs consisted of names of their classmates plus one of the positive or neutral words. For one group the isolates were consistently identified with positive words, an example of association by contiguity. The other group memorized lists where names of isolates were associated with neutral words.

Two dependent variable measures were employed—observations of pupils' play behavior and a posttest sociogram. Statistically significant differences were noted in posttest play behavior, for the isolates whose names had been paired with positive words were approached more than they were previously and more than the nonidentified control isolates. Sociogram reports likewise showed evidences of conditioning but mainly in responses of children who had originally been identified as very popular.

School Attitude Learning—Operant Conditioning Paradigm

An operant conditioning approach to attitude learning assumes that attitudes which result in positive consequences will tend to be learned. Since an attitude has been defined as a covert positive or negative evaluative response it is difficult to see how attitudes can be directly reinforced. In practice it is the attitude mediated overt behaviors that are reinforced by some positive consequences in the environment. Whichever attitudes mediated the overt behaviors are thus presumed to be reinforced.

A classroom example of this approach to the operant conditioning of educational attitudes might be constructed from a variety of school experiences. Consider a high school student who elects to take a course in industrial education such as electronics. His choice is manifested in the overt "approach" behaviors of signing up for that course instead of some other and may be mediated by a variety of motives, beliefs, and attitudes. Among these might be a faintly positive liking for tinkering with radios. The student takes the course and does well, learning aspects of electronics theory about why circuits work, as well as having an opportunity to work with radio components. These positive consequences of this chosen behavior also serve to reinforce (strengthen) the student's attitudes (and any other mediating responses). In short the student has learned some new beliefs and changed some former ones in terms of coming to evaluate them more positively.

It is possible to diagram schematically this instance of attitude learning by operant conditioning with mediation as well. Figure 12 shows the learning events just described. This is an overly simplified presentation since in any real life situation there are a variety of attitude objects, mediations, beliefs, attitudes, and overt responses which can form quite a complex network.

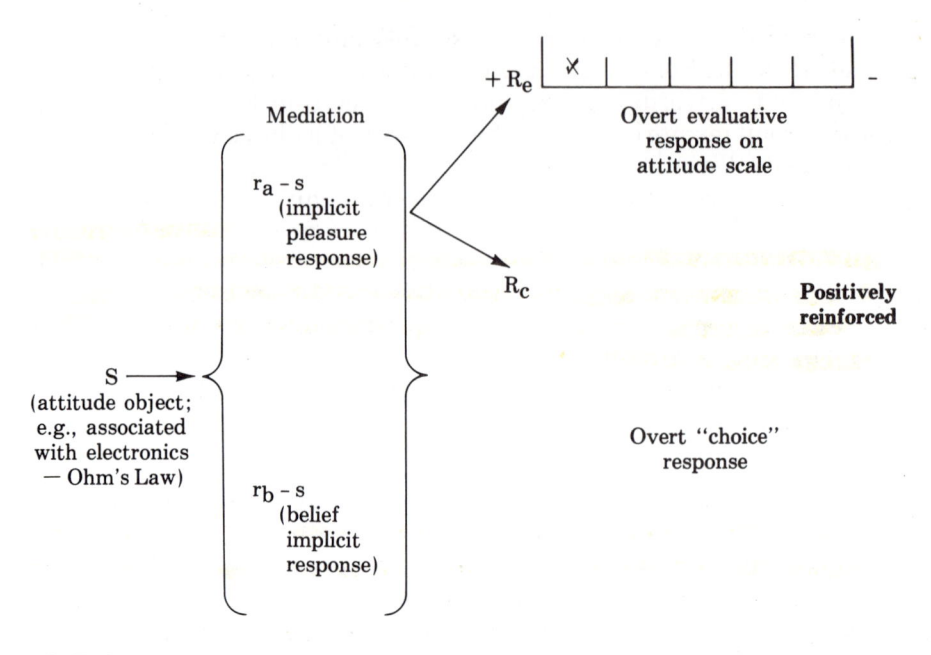

NOTE: S = stimulus event which can be called the "attitude object"
r_a-s = stimulus producing implicit affective response
r_b-s = stimulus producing implicit belief response
[ ] = summation of mediation for any S-R connection learned through earlier classical or operant conditioning
R_c = overt "choice" response
R = overt evaluative response on an attitude scale which becomes conditioned to s and thus S through reinforcement

Figure 12. Positive attitude learning by operant conditioning

School Attitude Learning—Concept Formation

Some attitudes and their associated attitude objects are complex. School-related attitudes are likely to be derived from combinations of beliefs about objects relating to school (including teachers, subject matter, course materials, and self as student). To try to index a student's school attitudes in one questionnaire or in some global assessment probably oversimplifies the situation. School-related attitudes can be said to coalesce to form evaluative concepts. Rhine (1958) describes attitude formation as occurring after the learning of specific facts, and being a kind of abstracted synthesis of the persons' evaluations of those facts. In criticizing Rhine's position, Fishbein (1967b) emphasizes the simultaneous learning of the attitudes and facts. Despite this point, the subsequent "conceptualization" of

Ways in Which Students Learn School Attitudes

attitudes toward a common domain of objects may well occur, just as the realization of an interrelationship or commonality among facts or the formation of a concept may follow the learning of the individual facts. Attitudinal concept learning is thus part of concept learning as described in chapter 6.

McKie and Foster (1972) have described an approach to the multidimensional measurement of attitudes as evaluations of individual beliefs and as evaluative clusters (attitudinal concepts). Diagramming attitude learning by concept formation is difficult because of the many facets to be considered. Figure 13 shows a simplified diagram of attitude learning by concept formation. See Fishbein (1967b, pp. 390-91) for additional examples of diagrams of attitudinal concepts.

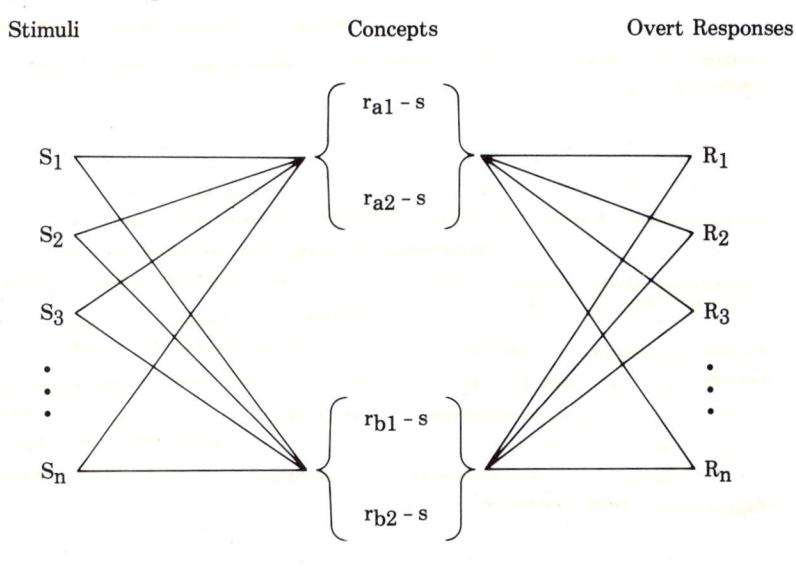

Stimuli	Concepts	Overt Responses
S_1	$r_{a1}-s$	R_1
S_2	$r_{a2}-s$	R_2
S_3		R_3
⋮	$r_{b1}-s$	⋮
S_n	$r_{b2}-s$	R_n

(Stimuli, e.g., related to study arithmetic in Johnny's grade six class)

(Concept clusters of attitudinal (r_a) and belief responses (r_b) associated with aspects of the class)

(Overt responses mediated by the attitudinal concept)

NOTE: S_{1-n} = stimuli in context of one's learning environment
  $r\ a$ = implicit affective responses
  $r\ b$ = implicit belief responses
  [ ] = summation of mediation, e.g., concepts
  R = overt responses mediated by attitudinal and belief concepts

Figure 13. Diagram of attitude learning by concept formation

School Attitude Learning—Social Learning Theory

In a social learning interpretation of attitude acquisition, the teacher would exhibit, perhaps without conscious awareness, positive or negative attitudes producing corresponding approach or avoidance responses toward (aspects of) a subject matter; and pupils would acquire, again perhaps without conscious awareness, those evaluative responses. Of course the same processes can work in terms of parent and peer influences.

Consider for example a teacher in grade six who hates and fears arithmetic and mathematics. Yet that teacher's job is to teach the subject, so the teacher perseveres and teaches mathematics. But by a variety of subtle cues negative attitudes are betrayed and many students learn to hate and fear mathematics at the same time as they learn to do mathematics. That is, they imitate the behaviors modeled for them by their teacher. Positive attitudes can be learned by the same process. If a teacher is very enthusiastic and positive about the subject matter, students may also learn to view positively the topics and things related to it.

There are five factors which would operate to modify the degree of attitude learning for each student in the previous situation, however. Among these are: (1) the degree to which the teacher is regarded as a "significant other" or someone who is a high status communicator of attitudinal information; (2) the degree of reinforcement value (as perceived by the student) in holding various attitudes; (3) prior learning and overlearning of attitudes in relation to the attitude object; (4) the degree of exposure to the teacher-model as compared to other sources of beliefs; and (5) evaluations of the object (in the example noted before—things related to the study of mathematics in the sixth grade).

Because of these factors and their differential application to various students, a considerable number of individual differences in school-related attitudes can be observed. Like differences in ability and achievement, individual differences in attitude learning need to be taken into account by teachers in planning for effective instruction.

A study by Litcher and Johnson (1969) demonstrates the incidental learning of racial attitudes from curriculum materials. Two groups of thirty-four middle-class, white second graders in a predominantly white, upper-midwest U.S. city were in reading classes for a four-month period, one group using the Scott-Foresman regular (all-white) reader, the other group using a multiethnic edition of the same reader. The two curricula were the same except for the pictures and names which featured some of the characters in the multiethnic reader as nonwhite and having ethnic names. Individual interviews were conducted of each child before and after the study, as well as the gathering of four specific dependent variable measures, to try to assess racial attitudes and preferences.

On pretest, the experimental and control groups were markedly similar in their racial perceptions. On posttest, however, the pupils in the multiethnic reader group made statistically more favorable scores on attitudes toward blacks for all four dependent variables. Second graders who had learned to read using the multiethnic reader were more likely to select a brown-colored doll to play with, less likely to exclude a picture of a child on the basis of race, and less likely to attribute negative traits to blacks and exclusively positive characteristics to whites than were the control pupils.

The investigators concluded that the results of this study yielded evidence for an analysis of attitude conditioning (Bandura & Walters, 1963) wherein the stimuli associated with "black" are reportedly paired (by contiguity) with others which already elicit a positive response, for example related to "middle class" on "like me" characteristics. The investigators also recommended greater visibility of ethnic minorities out of stereotypical roles in school curriculum materials to promote the learning of equalitarian racial attitudes.

Other Theories of Attitude Change

Consistency Theories

Besides learning analyses such as those noted above, other theories have been proposed to account for attitude change. A prominent group of approaches to attitudes could be called consistency theories (McGuire, 1966). Typically these posit a motivation to reduce perceived discrepancies between two or more beliefs or between one's beliefs and one's actions. This pressure toward consistency or "cognitive balance" could be considered as a psychological counterpart to the construct of homeostasis in physiology, the term applied to the processes within the organism which tend to regulate characteristics such as body temperature.

While the consistency theories provide a challenging explanation of how attitudes change, they lack precision in predicting exactly what will change and how much. A person experiencing dissonance between conflicting beliefs can change one or the other or both beliefs, or the salience (importance) of one or the other belief may change, or the person may rationalize the conflict away ("I just don't believe it" or "Well, that doesn't apply to me"). An impressive array of studies, nonetheless, has appeared in the social psychology research literature, dealing with aspects of the various consistency theories.

A possible educational use of one of these consistency approaches, cognitive dissonance theory (Festinger, 1957), which does not yet appear to have been systematically explored, has been alluded to by Loree (1971, p. 114). This would involve teaching students by inducing dissonance (conflicting beliefs and perceptions), and structuring the situation so that the most probable change would be learning behaviors which are consistent with course objectives. In science classes, for example, observing some effect contrary to a pupil's expectations could lead to a desire to find out why (and thereby reduce dissonance). For example, finding out that hot water freezes more rapidly than cold water might induce enough dissonance to motivate students to perform additional studies in heat and related physics problems (see *The Christian Science Monitor*, July 8, 1971, p. 1). It is conceivable that discovery learning techniques (e.g., Suchman, 1960) implicitly involve dissonance induction as a goal of channeling the resultant motivation toward desired learning objectives. This possibility requires additional analysis and research investigation.

Achievement and Attitudes

Investigations into relationships between school achievement and school-related attitudes suggest that attitude measures explain or account for at least 10 percent of achievement scores (and considerably more when measurement methods are improved). Such findings suggest that as mediators of achievement-related behaviors, school attitudes can, for some pupils, make the difference between mastery and nonmastery of course content. Other behaviors related to the attitude objects may also be modified in attitude learning (cf. Mager, 1968). In academic matters, such future behaviors may include choosing or avoiding advanced study in given areas, and persisting to mastery or nonmastery in the related subjects.

It must be stressed that changing a person's attitudes (covert behavior) does not imply a change in overt behavior and *vice versa*. There are factors besides attitudes which mediate behavior, and clearly the way one responds in a questionnaire situation (taken as an index of one's attitudes) may be quite different from the way one reacts in another setting.

Should Schools Teach Attitudes?

A contradiction in formal education which, for many, remains unresolved concerns the teacher's role in relation to student attitudes. Educators have long claimed for schools the inculcation of attitudes especially those relating to citizenship, democracy, and patriotism; often also leadership, brotherhood, fair play; and even occasionally, scholarship, intellectualism, and personal integrity. (Note:

Other Theories of Attitude Change

these high-sounding terms are usually left undefined.) In actual practice, however, teachers are frequently encouraged to concentrate on pupil achievement (in achievement-oriented areas) or pupil social development at best (at worst on an unquestioned obedience to higher authority), and generally to neglect other affective learnings. Teachers who have attempted to involve their students in discussions of opinions and feelings have often been "rare" among the faculty, if sometimes exceedingly popular among students. Too often the "game" seems to be: if it is sanctioned in society's mores and is not too controversial (e.g., love of country), then proceed, but if the attitudes concern any controversial issue (e.g., discrimination by sex or race), it is best to drop it. Those who take the position that a teacher should present alternative sides of an issue find even "love for one's country" becomes a very controversial matter.

Some would argue of course that attitudes are not interesting, almost by definition, unless they are controversial. Noncontroversial affect approaches triviality. Take student attitudes toward Warren G. Harding's untimely death in a San Francisco hotel for example. Consider an American history teacher in school and three students, Allen, Bonnie, and Gamaliel. Allen may say, "Warren G. Harding, who's that?" and with his lack of information (few beliefs) have essentially trivial attitudes. The attitudes may be only slightly positive in that he asked "who's that?" instead of merely shrugging (but that is an inference which could be checked, perhaps empirically). Bonnie, on the other hand, might say, "Ugh, old, dead American presidents, who needs them?" and in so doing express the negative evaluation of the few beliefs she has acquired about Harding. Gamaliel, as you might expect, is exuberantly positive about Harding and about learning more of him. "Why his middle name was the same as my given name and my grandmother's maiden name, do you think we could be related?" "Grandma was from Ohio, too, I think." The teacher has to deal somehow with these differences in entering attitudes of students, and of course the teacher has more than three students, and each may have previously acquired more than one attitude pertinent to the material.

Perhaps accounting for entering attitudes seems a more formidable task than coping with individual differences in entering achievement and variations in abilities. But attitude scores are of a different order than grades for achievement since attitude measurement and marks formally based on attitudes are foreign to most school classrooms, as well they should be. Pupil attitude learning may be considered to be one basis for teacher evaluation—the awarding of marks to teachers.

Why then consider attitudinal objectives and some assessment of entering and terminal pupil attitudes? Not as a means to award marks, the authors believe, but to recognize attitude learning as being concurrent with and mediating achievement, and thus important in its own right. Attitudes are far from perfectly correlated with overt behavior, but typically they *are* positively correlated with it (Fishbein, 1967a). And the evidence indicates that school attitudes do mediate along with other variables, school achievement, and possibly subsequent achievement and choices of activities (cf. Mager, 1968).

Bereiter (1970) has identified the teacher's dilemma in pointing out that we think we can teach attitudes but perhaps we should not. The danger of some evil authority dictating how students should feel as well as what they should study lurks behind this idea. But what about teachers who find their students learning to hate and fear mathematics, swimming, literature, or music? Not everyone should or could have identical attitudes about these things, but when schools are at least partly responsible for such learnings do they not have commensurate responsibility to encourage what could be called more positive attitudes? Who should be responsible for determining what attitudes are formally dealt with? In this policy area school officials will have to decide. The authors would venture that the relevant authorities in most cases are the classroom teacher and that teacher's students.

Moral Attitudes and Values

Issues concerning morality have probably concerned educators since the first schools. In a pluralistic society, questions arise as to what should be the nature and scope of the public school involvement in this area. In the context of these philosophical issues, psychologists have examined various dynamics of moral behavior.

There has been a renewed interest in what has been called "moral education" in recent years (Wilson, Williams & Sugarman, 1967). We say "renewed" since psychologists, notably G. Stanley Hall (1911), were very interested in this area during the early decades of this century. Other concerns such as new mathematics and science curricula have occupied the attention of educators more recently.

Moral attitudes can be defined as evaluative aspects of beliefs about the "goodness" or "badness" of certain acts with respect to the rights of others. *Moral values* may be thought of as the internalization of those beliefs and attitudes about the goodness or badness of acts to the point where one's behavior is guided and judged by those standards. Values are thus considered to be broader and more enduring than attitudes, and operate like conceptualized attitudes.

Recent research in this area has focused on the following topics: resistance to temptation and cheating; altruism and helping;

Moral Attitudes and Values

conscience and guilt; and factors affecting development and change in different kinds of moral judgments. (See Hoffman, 1970, for a comprehensive review of psychological research in these areas.)

Much of the recent experimentation in these topics has been in the framework of one of two kinds of theories, a *cognitive-development view* of moral behavior (Piaget, 1965; Kohlberg, 1963), and the *social learning theory* of Bandura and Walters (1963), which has been mentioned before. A short statement of how these theories are purported to account for moral attitudes is included here.

The Cognitive-Development Theory

Briefly, the cognitive developmental theories explain moral judgment as developing through an invariant sequence of stages. These stages result from the interaction of hereditary tendencies with environmental experiences. Piaget's theory of moral development involves two broad stages. In the first, the young child's view of morality is governed by respect for and submission to an outside authority (parent, teacher, priest, etc.). Justice is retributive in the second, more advanced stage; the child has shifted to self-control and relies on his/her own internalized values as guidelines for behavior. Punishment is seen as fitting the crime. The first stage has been characterized as *heteronomous*, the second as *cooperative*.

Kohlberg's theory is similar to that of Piaget but the developmental sequence is broken down into three levels comprising a total of six separate stages, each successive one characterized by less reliance on external authority and a greater degree of individuality. Research evidence (e.g., Turiel, 1966) suggests that the overall sequences suggested by the theories may be sound but that at any given age there is considerable variability among children as to their level of operation. As such it is inappropriate to speak of the developmental stages as characterized by exact chronological ages. Kohlberg's three levels of moral development comprised of six stages (see Turiel, 1973) are outlined here:

Level One—Preconventional morality

Stage one is called the punishment and obedience orientation. At this stage an act is considered good if the act is not punished.

Stage two is the stage in which an action is considered right or good if it meets the child's own needs.

Level Two—Conventional morality

Stage three is the good-boy, nice-girl orientation. At this stage right behavior is that which pleases others.

Stage four is the legalistic orientation in which rightness is obedience to the law. If an action is legal it is considered moral.

Level Three—Postconventional morality

Stage five is the social contract orientation in which right actions are those which are legal, but the laws are not viewed as immutable. They are changeable if they are not consistent with the agreed upon principles of the society.

Stage six is termed the principled level. At this stage moral actions are those which are consistent with a universal principle such as a "golden rule". The principle must include elements which recognize equality of human rights and respect for the dignity of persons, such as a principle of universal justice.

To the teacher, the theory and evidence on moral development suggest that adult standards of moral judgment may be not only inappropriate to children in a given situation, but that in any classroom there are likely to be pupils at a variety of different developmental stages. Moreover, one goal of schooling might be to facilitate moral development so that pupils are exposed to standards at their own level and the one immediately beyond. Indeed Turiel (1966) found that seventh graders who were exposed to moral arguments at one and two stages beyond their own level of moral reasoning were more likely to accept the former (i.e., the argument nearest to their own stage) than the most advanced judgments. These "highest" judgments would be those most closely approximating adult positions on the issues. Moral judgments and not overt behavior are the focus of developmental theories and the linkage between the two remains problematical.

Social Learning Theory

Social learning theory has been proposed to account for the actual mechanisms by which both moral judgments and overt behaviors are acquired and modified. The illustration given of social learning of attitudes by modeling and imitation characterizes an implication of this approach for education. One means by which children learn more sophisticated moral attitudes seems to be through imitation of the behaviors of esteemed parents, teachers, or peer models.

A study of Bandura and Mischel (1965) illustrates social learning influences in postponement of gratification decisions of fourth and fifth graders. Exposure to an adult model who expressed preference for either immediate or delayed gratification significantly influenced pupils' choices on a similar task. The effect, though not as pronounced, appeared to hold up on a delayed posttest conducted four to five weeks later. Although this and similar studies are not without criticism (cf. Hoffman, 1970), the social learning approach seems to be of value in explaining the acquisition and modification of moral judgments (cf. Bandura, 1969). Dorner (1976) found significant correlations between parents' and their adolescent's moral stage of development (as defined by Kohlberg). The correlations suggest that modeling between parents and children does occur in regard to moral development.

Recent studies by Rosenkoetter (1971) demonstrated the effects of modeling influences on both the *inhibition* and *disinhibition* (encouragement) of responses of deviation from explicit instructions among school children. The experimental situation was one where students were told to remain at a task and not leave it. However, in staying at the task, students would be unable to see a lively cartoon film being shown across the room. Exposure to deviating models greatly increased the likelihood of deviation (leaving the task to watch the cartoon), whereas exposure to conscientious models depressed disobedience to a rate of occurrence which was below that of a no-model control group of youngsters.

Recommendations for Teachers' Education

Research in moral education has received renewed attention in Canada (Association for Values Education and Research [A.V.E.R.], 1972, 1975) and in England (Kay, 1975) as well as in the United States. In British Columbia, the A.V.E.R. group found that teachers tend to avoid value discussions and change the subject of discourse to factual claims when value issues arise in the classroom. However, teachers can profitably learn techniques for promoting student growth in clear thinking and reasoning about values (e.g., distinguishing between factual and value claims in advertising, role playing a conflict in viewpoints, discussing moral dilemmas, and devising simulations of real events). Among the recommendations which can be drawn from the findings of this ongoing project are that teacher education programs should include value and attitude learning and moral development issues, and that there are few if any areas of the curriculum where teachers and students cannot profitably deal with attitudes and values.

The Teachers' Attitudes Toward Pupils—Teacher Expectancy

One area of interest to teachers involves the study of teachers' own attitudes toward students. Research has been conducted in recent years on an issue related to teacher attitude—teacher expectancy. Teacher expectancies are those teacher beliefs about how well or how poorly individual students should perform academically.

In 1968, Rosenthal and Jacobson published a highly controversial book entitled *Pygmalion in the Classroom*. This book described research in which it was claimed that teachers' expectations that students should do well caused substantial gains in students' measured intelligence over several months.

Rosenthal and Jacobson pretested students in grades one through six with an intelligence test. They randomly selected some students and placed those students' names in a letter to appropriate teachers indicating that those selected students should be expected to do well. Only the youngest groups showed significant I.Q. gains.

Numerous critiques of this study have been published (Snow, 1969; Thorndike, 1968; and Elashoff & Snow, 1971) indicating faulty design and inappropriate statistical treatment of the data. Dozens of replications have been conducted. Many other studies have attempted to explicate some of the related issues.

One of the basic issues which Rosenthal and Jacobson (1968) did not approach was the possibility that teachers' expectations of students may be rooted in knowledge about the students' ability or achievement rather than students' achievement really being a function of the teachers' expectations.

West and Anderson (1976) reviewed in excess of thirty studies in the expectancy area. These reviewers found more support for the hypothesis that teacher expectations are based on the achievement of students as opposed to the hypothesis that teacher expectations influence students' achievement.

These same reviewers also reanalyzed data collected by Williams (1972). Williams gathered data on approximately 3,000 high school students at the first year, second year, and fourth year levels. The data included teacher expectations and student achievement. Regression coefficients were computed for both expectancy and achievement. The regression weight (an indication of predictive value) for achievement at the first year on achievement at the second year was .57. The comparable weight for expectancy on achievement for the same years was .12. For the prediction of expectancy at the second year the weight for expectancy at the first year was .20 and the weight for achievement on expectancy was .37. Thus, not only is achievement a much better predictor than expectancy for subsequent achievement; achievement also predicts expectancy better than previous expectancy.

It would appear, then, that teacher expectancy does not influence achievement to any great extent. Expectancy does not seem to influence later expectancy to a great extent either, when compared to the weights of achievement on expectancy.

One cannot help but wonder at such an oversimplification that a teacher's attitudes would have so much influence when it is known that the factors which promote academic achievement are so numerous and complex.

Thus teachers can be skeptical about claims that merely their expectations about students have direct influence on achievement.

Self-Regarding Attitudes

Another area of theory and research in attitudes which has implications for classroom learning is self-regarding attitudes, how positively or negatively a person evaluates beliefs about self. A considerable body of research has been amassed concerning the self-concept (Wylie, 1961; Hamachek, 1971), and as in the case of "attitude" different researchers do not always agree on the definition of this construct. One way of considering self-concept is as a sum of self-regarding attitudes.

Of course, a complex concept like "the self" can be broken down into simpler attitude clusters and individual attitudes. For example, Brookover et al. (1967) have considered "self-concept of academic ability" to be more pertinent than a global self-concept in studies of predictions of pupil achievement. Likewise self-concept of teaching ability—the evaluations one has of beliefs about his ability to teach, is probably a more useful consideration for teacher education purposes than a global self-concept. Levels of specificity from global to specific in dealing with self-attitudes are important and should depend on the kind of problem being faced at the time.

Self-attitudes are social phenomena in that evaluations of self appear to be a consequence of one's perceptions of the reactions others have to one's self. Thus the origins of the belief-attitude, "I am a competent person in mathematics, and that's good" may be in the perception that another important person regards you as competent in mathematics, and the prior learning that competence is a positive virtue. With reference to the behavior frame of reference model described in chapter 3, the prior learning of competence as being "good" (likely established early by classical conditioning and overlearning through the years) is one of the attitudes in a person's behavioral capacity. A desire to be competent in mathematics is an example of "Sip" or internal motivation to do something well and "Sie" or reaction to incentives from the environment to do well in mathematics. The reader may review the roles of Sip and Sie in behavior in chapter 3.

Of course the perception that another person believes one to be competent must be tempered by that person's credibility in terms of status as a "significant other" in one's life and the credibility of the message in the context of other events (e.g., failing a math exam). The message can come to introduce and reinforce specific self-attitudes as well as whatever overt behavior was present at the time of the message or subsequent rehearsals of it. Foster (1970) found that expressed acceptance of self was much more positively related to at least two measures of student teaching success than was university grade-point average. In fact, student teachers judged to be most and least successful by either the criteria of supervisor's ratings or self-evaluation had virtually identical grades in their college classes; whereas they differed considerably as successful student teachers scored significantly higher on expressed acceptance of self. Purkey (1970) has summarized research relating pupil self-concept and school achievement. He concludes that, "... there is a persistent and significant relationship between the self-concept and academic achievement at each grade level and that change in one seems to be associated with change in the other" [p. 27].

Several recent studies have attempted to aid achievement by enhancing the students' self-concept. The expectation being that achievement would improve if the self-concept became more positive (Thomas et al., 1969; Carlton & Moore, 1966). In general these attempts have been successful at improving the self-concept, but gains in achievement have not followed. Calsyn (1973) using cross-lagged panel analysis has found that gains in achievement appear to precede gains in *academic self-concept* (but not the other way—gains in *academic self-concept* do not precede gains in achievement). No such pattern in either direction emerged in Calsyn's study for *general self-concept* and achievement. Nonetheless there is a significant relationship between self-concept of ability and school achievement.

Self-attitudes form one important area of affective learning influenced by school activities. Moreover, self-attitudes are related to other school variables, including course achievement. Brookover et al. (1967) believe that the student's self-concept of ability sets the upper limit on achievement and that the self-concept of academic ability is established through interaction with significant others as the student perceives others' evaluation of the students' ability.

Two assumptions underlie Brookover's ideas. One assumption is that the social and personal processes for learning attitudes are the same as those for learning school achievement behaviors. A second assumption is that a student learns to behave in the classroom in ways which are consistent with that student's self-perceptions, beliefs, and attitudes. Inconsistency between overt behavior and self-attitudes results in pressure to change one or both toward some consistency. Thus when a pupil has a highly positive self-concept of science ability and does poorly in a science course, that pupil will be motivated to do better next time, to come to evaluate self less positively, or both in some combination. Consistency theories of attitudes (cf. McGuire, 1966) typically fail to predict exactly which will change. It is at this point that a learning analysis is helpful.

Negative attitudes which have been learned toward studying self as student or toward the subject matter can be the source of resistance to learning. Attitude change may therefore be a necessary prerequisite to performance change. Because of the covert nature of attitude learning it is not always clear to either teacher or student why there is any difficulty. It is a reciprocal problem since skill improvement may provide for learning more positive attitudes as well. The skillful teacher attempts to ascertain the most viable approach to overcome resistance.

One determinant of resistance to change is overlearning. In other words, with practice beyond the amount necessary to acquire the response, the strength or resistance to extinction of that response increases. Other things being equal, greater change might be expected in the less-overlearned behavior. Other variables affecting retention of learning and resistance to extinction (e.g., overlearning, distributed or spaced practice, and past or perceived future reinforcement value of alternative behaviors) can be used in explaining resistance to attitude change.

Educational Attitudinal Objectives

As mentioned before, this is a controversial area of discourse. However, this did not stop Krathwohl et al. (1964) from developing the *Taxonomy of Educational Objectives, Handbook II—The Affective Domain,* a key purpose of which was to help teachers to classify, select, and construct outcomes for their pupils—including those for attitudinal outcomes.

> The affective Taxonomy arranges objectives along a hierarchical continuum. At the lowest point on this continuum, the subject is merely aware of a phenomenon, simply able to perceive it. At the next level he is willing to attend to the phenomenon. The next step finds him responding to the phenomenon with feeling. At the next point the subject goes out of his way to respond to the phenomenon. Next he conceptualizes his behavior and feelings and organizes these into a structure. The subject reaches the highest point in the hierarchy when the structure becomes his life outlook.

The authors of the Taxonomy describe this continuum as one of internalization, in which the affective component passes from a level of bare awareness to a position of some power and then to control of a person's behavior. The five categories on internalization, arranged in order of degree, are these (as adapted from Krathwohl et al., 1964):

> 1.0 Receiving (attending). The first category is defined as sensitivity to the existence of certain phenomena and stimuli, that is, the willingness to receive

or attend to them. A typical objective at this level would be: "The student develops a tolerance for a variety of types of music."

2.0 Responding. "Responding" refers to a behavior which goes beyond merely attending to the phenomena; it implies active attending, doing something with or about the phenomena, and not merely perceiving them. Here a typical objective would be: "The student voluntarily reads magazines and newspapers designed for young children."

3.0 Valuing. Behavior which belongs to this level of the taxonomy goes beyond merely doing something with or about certain phenomena. It implies perceiving them as having worth and consequently revealing consistency in behavior related to these phenomena. A typical objective at this level would be: "Writes letters to the press on issues he feels strongly about."

4.0 Organization. Organization is defined as the conceptualization of values and the employment of these concepts for determining the interrelationship among values. Here a typical objective might be: "Begins to form judgments as to the major directions in which American society should move."

5.0 Characterization. The organization of values, beliefs, ideas, and attitudes into an internally consistent system is called "characterization." This goes beyond merely determining interrelationships among various values; it implies their organization into a total philosophy or world view. Here a typical objective would include: "Develops a consistent philosophy of life" [Krathwohl et al., 1964, pp. 176-85].*

Attitudes, as defined here, would appear to fit best under Category 3, Valuing. From this standpoint the teacher's task concerning attitudinal objectives is to decide what things the students should learn to value as a consequence of the class, and how positively.

In the area of academic self-attitudes, or what Brookover et al. (1967) have called self-concept of academic ability, teachers may want students to have realistic evaluations of themselves as students of a given subject matter. And, to the extent that pupils and teachers succeed in a course of study so that mastery levels of achievement result, then a positive self-concept of academic ability becomes "realistic" and should be sought. Even the student who has not yet mastered a subject matter should be learning positive evaluations about it and self in relation to the subject matter as these are likely to mediate the maintenance of the student's interest and willingness to continue to spend time on the task of learning it. In this discourse a criticism of a strict hierarchical arrangement of the taxonomy of affective objectives is implicit in that it would appear that while initial willingness to attend (1.0) precedes valuing (3.0), subsequently valuing may also be necessary to ensure future willingness to attend (motivation). The social psychologist Rokeach (1971) has presented

---

*From D. R. Krathwohl, B. S. Bloom, and B. B. Masia, *Taxonomy of Educational Objectives, Handbook II—Affective Domain.* Copyright © 1964 by David McKay Company, Inc. New York. Reprinted by permission of the publisher.

evidence which suggests that a change in one's values may be a necessary prerequisite for some important attitude changes.

Mager (1968) describes students' educational attitudes in terms of approach toward and avoidance of certain activities or objects. For example, one could judge that a person had positive attitudes toward rock music if that person was observed to listen frequently to rock records and to often read articles about rock music (approach behaviors). And likewise one might judge from observing the avoidance responses of someone spending as little time as possible with baroque music that that person held negative attitudes toward that attitude object. Indeed approach and avoidance behaviors can be considered to be mediated by corresponding positive and negative attitudes in the absence of force or other compelling reasons to behave contrary to one's attitudes. Thus, the relative frequency of a certain behavior can be used as an index of attitudes towards such acts, other things being equal.

Another educational use of pupil attitude data is in the area of teacher self-evaluation (cf. Simpson, 1966). In addition to gains in achievement, one important way in which a teacher can judge instructional effectiveness is in terms of attitudinal outcomes in that teacher's class. If, for example, a teacher had certain attitudinal objectives for the class or for certain members of the class, the teacher may attempt to measure or estimate the degree to which these objectives have been met by students and take that as feedback as to success or failure in teaching. Pupil achievement data may of course also be taken as evidence of teacher success.

Obviously, there are many reasons why grades ought not to be awarded on the basis of pupil attitudes or attitude change, not the least of which is the susceptibility of most attitude measures to faking or distortion of responses in order to appear in favorable light. Rapport and anonymity are useful in obtaining honest expressions of attitude whether by paper-and-pencil scales or through observation of behavior in some situation. Unobtrusive measures of attitude (Webb et al., 1966) may be employed where social desirability or faking may be a problem. Rokeach (1971) describes a clever example of an unobtrusive measure of attitudes toward civil rights activities, wherein subjects in his study were subsequently solicited by the local NAACP chapter to find out if they would return a stamped envelope to receive free information about civil rights. A positive relationship existed between responding and prior indications of attitude.

Should all students be expected to learn equally positive attitudes toward all subject matters and aspects of school? Obviously not! It is plausible however, to believe that at the same time as pupils are learning any subject matter, they are learning relevant attitudes toward aspects of school, and that teachers have control over variables which influence attitude learning.

Attitudes and values which are learned at school may mediate future learning and performance (and vocational choices) throughout a person's entire life. Whereas several specific skills taught in school may be later forgotten, attitudinal concepts are often overlearned through practice, and thus form a major enduring outcome of schooling. In view of this, the ordering of values in many of today's schools which emphasizes cognition and skill learning, while nearly ignoring affective and attitude learning, needs to be seriously questioned. Emphasis on cognition to the exclusion of affect is incomplete in that the two cannot be separated in a person's life—they are dynamically intertwined.

Suggestions on the application of theory and research in attitude learning are incorporated in chapter 10 on teacher-controlled and influenced variables.

Specific issues in measurement of school attitudes will be dealt with in chapter 9 concerning the measurement and evaluation of learning outcomes.

In addition to the references noted herein, some recent works on attitudes and closely related topics are listed under Recommended Readings. The reader will find these short paperbacks deal in greater detail with some of the issues raised above.

Discussion Questions

1. Should teachers concern themselves with attitude learning? Explain and justify your answer.
2. What about controversial conceptualized attitudes such as political values and moral values—should these be dealt with in schools? How can a teacher handle such topics?
3. Give examples from your experience of relationships between self-concept, attitudes, and learning.
4. How could cognitive dissonance be used by teachers to achieve learning goals?
5. The authors state that there are many reasons why grades ought not to be awarded on the basis of student attitudes or attitude change. What are some of these? Do you agree or disagree with this point?
6. When there is a technical controversy in psychology, for example between attitude learning theory and cognitive dissonance or between moral development and social learning, what immediate concern is it to teachers?

7. Give examples where a teacher might inadvertently encourage undesirable attitudes through conditioning, concept learning, and social learning. Give positive examples of each.
8. Describe a situation in school where attitude learning appears to be necessary before skill learning can take place. What is the teacher's role?
9. List some positive and negative attitudes that may be acquired in school and explain how they can relate to future vocational and educational choices.
10. Where do value issues fit into studying mathematics, science subjects, French?

Recommended Readings

Backman, C. W., & Secord, P. F. *A social psychological view of education.* New York: Harcourt, Brace & World, 1968, 152 pp.

Bem, D. J. *Beliefs, attitudes and human affairs.* Belmont, Calif.: Brooks-Cole, 1970, 114 pp. See, for example, the chapter for the attitudinal bases of women's liberation.

Bloom, B. S. Affective consequences of school achievement. In J. H. Block (Ed.), *Mastery learning: Theory and practice.* New York: Holt, Rinehart & Winston, 1971.

Brookover, W. B., & Erickson, E. L. *Society, schools and learning.* Boston: Allyn & Bacon, 1969, 149 pp. In this context, see especially chapter 5 on self-concept and self-concept of ability.

La Benne, W. D., & Green, B. I. *Educational implications of self-concept theory.* Pacific Palisades, Calif.: Goodyear, 1969, 134 pp.

Lee, B. N., & Merrill, M. D. *Writing complete affective objectives: A short course.* Belmont, Calif.: Wadsworth, 1972, 110 pp. This brief paperback is actually a self-instructional program of writing affective objectives.

Triandis, H. C. *Attitude and attitude change.* New York: Wiley, 1971, 232 pp. Contains useful discussions on attitude measurement, theory, and research with special projects for advanced students.

Zimbardo, P., & Ebbesen, E. B. *Influencing attitudes and changing behavior.* Reading, Mass.: Addison-Wesley, 1969, 148 pp. A well-written manual which provides basic information about attitude change and measurement.

References

Allport, G. W. Attitudes. In G. Murchison (Ed.), *A handbook of social psychology.* Worcester, Mass.: Clark University Press, 1935, pp. 789-844.

A.V.E.R. Fellows of the Association for Values Education and Research. *Final report on an experiment in moral education at Surrey, B.C.* Report No. 6, Faculty of Education, U.B.C., Vancouver, 1975.

A.V.E.R. Fellows of the Association for Values Education and Research. *A study of the characteristics of moral discussions in Vancouver elementary schools.* Report No. 1, U.B.C., Vancouver, 1972.

Bandura, A. *Principles of behavior modification.* New York: Holt, Rinehart & Winston, 1969.

Bandura, A., & Mischel, W. Modification and self-imposed delay of reward through exposure to live and symbolic models. *Journal of Personality and Social Psychology,* 1965, *2,* 698-705.

Bandura, A., & Walters, R. H. *Social learning and personality development.* New York: Holt, Rinehart & Winston, 1963.

Bereiter, C. *Teaching what is teachable.* Invited address division C, American Educational Research Association, Annual Meeting, Minneapolis, 1970.

Brookover, W. B., Erickson, E. L., & Joiner, L. M. *Self-concept of ability and school achievement,* III. Final report on Cooperative Research Project Number 2831, U.S.O.E., H.E.W., 1967.

Calsyn, R. *The causal relation between self-esteem, locus of control, and achievement: cross-lagged panel analysis.* Unpublished doctoral dissertation, Northwestern University, 1973.

Carlton, L., & Moore, R. H. The effects of self-directive dramatization on reading achievement and self-concept of culturally disadvantaged children. *Reading Teacher,* 1966, *20,* 125-30.

Dorner, P. Relationships between parent's and adolescent's moral development and moral attitudes. Unpublished doctoral thesis, University of Illinois, Urbana, 1976.

Early, C. J. Attitude learning in children. *Journal of Educational Psychology,* 1968, *59,* 176-80.

Elashoff, J., & Snow, R. E. *Pygmalion reconsidered.* Worthington, Ohio: Charles A. Jones Publishing Co., 1971.

Festinger, L. *A theory of cognitive dissonance.* Evanston, Illinois: Row & Peterson, 1957.

Fishbein, M. F. Attitude and the prediction of behavior. In M. F. Fishbein (Ed.), *Readings in attitude theory and measurement.* New York: Wiley, 1967a, pp. 477-92.

References

Fishbein, M. F. A behavior theory approach to the relations between beliefs about an object and the attitude toward the object. In M. F. Fishbein (Ed.), *Readings in attitude theory and measurement.* New York: Wiley, 1967b, pp. 389-400.

Fishbein, M. F. A consideration of beliefs, and their role in attitude measurement. In M. F. Fishbein (Ed.), *Readings in attitude theory and measurement.* New York: Wiley, 1967c, pp. 257-66.

Foster, S. F. Self-acceptance and two criteria of elementary student teaching effectiveness. Paper read at American Educational Research Association Annual Meeting, Minneapolis, 1970.

Hall, G. S. *Educational problems Vol. 1.* New York: 1911, pp. 627ff.

Hamachek, D. E. *Encounters with the self* New York: Holt, Rinehart & Winston, 1971.

Hoffman, M. L. Moral development. In P. Mussen (Ed.), *Carmichael's manual of child psychology* (3rd ed.) Vol. 1. New York: Wiley, 1970.

Kay, W. *Moral education.* London: Allen & Unwin, 1975.

Kohlberg, L. Moral development and identification. In H. W. Stevenson (Ed.), *Child Psychology—62nd Yearbook of N.S.S.E.* Chicago: University of Chicago Press, 1963, pp. 277-332.

Krathwohl, D. R., Bloom, B. S., & Masia, B. B. *Taxonomy of educational objectives, handbook II—Affective domain.* New York: McKay, 1964.

Krech, D., Crutchfield, R. S., & Ballachey, E. L. *Individual in society.* New York: McGraw-Hill, 1962.

Litcher, J. H., & Johnson, D. W. Changes in attitudes toward Negroes of white elementary school students after use of multiethnic readers. *Journal of Educational Psychology,* 1969, *60,* 148-52.

Loree, M. R. Shaping teachers' attitudes. In B. O. Smith (Ed.), *Research in teacher education.* Englewood Cliffs: Prentice-Hall, Inc., 1971.

Lott, B. E. Attitude formations: The development of a color-preference response through mediated generalization. *Journal of Abnormal and Social Psychology,* 1955, *50,* 321-26.

McGuire, W. J. The current status of cognitive consistency theories. In S. Feldman (Ed.), *Cognitive consistency.* New York: Academic Press, 1966, pp. 1-46.

McKie, D., & Foster, S. F. A general model for the multidimensional analysis of semantic differential attitude data. Paper presented at the American Psychological Association, Honolulu, 1972.

Mager, R. F. *Developing attitude toward learning.* Palo Alto: Fearon, 1968.

Mouly, G. *Psychology for effective teaching* (2nd ed.). New York: Holt, Rinehart & Winston, 1968.

Osgood, C. E., Suci, G., & Tannenbaum, P. H. *The measurement of meaning.* Urbana: University of Illinois Press, 1957.

Osgood, C. E., & Tannenbaum, P. H. The principle of congruity in the prediction of attitude change. *Psychological Review,* 1955, *62,* 42-55.

Piaget, J. *The moral judgment of the child.* (Translated by M. Gabain), New York: Free Press, 1965 (orig. 1932).

Purkey, W. W. *Self-concept and school achievement.* Englewood Cliffs: Prentice-Hall, Inc., 1970.

Rhine, R. J. A concept-formation approach to attitude acquisition. *Psychological Review,* 1958, *65,* 362-70.

Rokeach, M. Long range experimental modification of values, attitudes and behavior. *American Psychologist,* 1971, *26,* 453-59.

Rosenkoetter, L. I. Resistance to temptation: inhibitory and disinhibitory effects of models. Unpublished doctoral dissertation, University of Illinois, Urbana, 1971.

Rosenthal, R., & Jacobson, E. *Pygmalion in the classroom.* New York: Holt, Rinehart, & Winston, 1968.

Simpson, R. H. *Teacher self-evaluation.* New York: Macmillan, 1966.

Snow, R. E. Unfinished Pygmalion. *Contemporary Psychology,* 1969, *14,* 197-200.

Staats, A. W., & Staats, C. K. Attitudes established by classical conditioning. *Journal of Abnormal and Social Psychology,* 1958, *57,* 37-40.

Suchman, J. R. Inquiry training in the elementary school. *Science Teacher,* 1960, *27,* 42-45.

Thomas, S., Brookover, W. B., La Pere, J. M. et al. An experiment to modify self-concept and school performance. *Sociological Focus on Education,* 1969, *3,* 55-67.

Thorndike, R. L. Review of R. Rosenthal & L. Jacobson, *Pygmalion in the Classroom. American Educational Research Journal,* 1968, *5,* 708-11.

Thurstone, L. L. The measurement of social attitudes. *Journal of Abnormal and Social Psychology,* 1931, *26,* 249-69.

Turiel, E. An experimental test of the sequentiality of developmental stages in the child's moral judgments. *Journal of Personality and Social Psychology,* 1966, *3,* 611-18.

Turiel, E. Stage transition in moral development. In R. M. W. Travers (Ed.), *Second handbook of research on teaching.* Chicago: Rand McNally & Co., 1973, 732-58.

References

Webb, E. J., Campbell, D. T., Schwartz, R. D., & Sechrest, L. *Unobtrusive measures-nonreactive research in the social sciences.* Chicago: Rand McNally, 1966.

West, C. K., & Anderson, T. H. The question of preponderant causation in teacher expectancy research. *Review of Educational Research.* In press, 1976.

Williams, T. Students, teachers, and educational expectations: Reciprocal effects at three points in time. (Unpublished manuscript.) Ontario Institute for Studies in Education, April 1972.

Wilson, J., Williams, N., & Sugarman, B. *Introduction to moral education.* Baltimore: Penguin Books, 1967.

Wylie, R. *The self-concept—a critical survey of pertinent research literature.* Lincoln, Nebraska: University of Nebraska Press, 1961.

Practical Organizer for Chapter 9

Few areas are more important to the educational practitioner than knowledge of the basic concepts and principles involved in knowing when learning takes place and how much learning has taken place.

In this chapter we discuss many concepts and principles which should alert you to problems of measurement and evaluation of learning.

Effective teachers know that the evaluation of learning is an intrinsic part of instruction and that it should be considered at each stage in planning for and carrying out instruction. The teacher should also be sensitive to techniques and problems associated with measurement. Some of these problems have to do with the extent to which tests measure what they are designed to measure and the extent to which tests are consistent in what they measure.

Many of the current issues which teachers must face involve measurement and evaluation. Some issues involve assessment of social interaction in the classroom, attitude measurement, and testing for mastery, as well as the more traditional issues concerning achievement testing and standardized tests.

Measurement and Evaluation of Learning   9

As examination of any list of courses offered by a school of education will reveal, each of the topics discussed so far can be the subject of an entire course of study. This is especially so with the areas of measurement and evaluation of learning. Our purpose here, as elsewhere, is not to provide a methods course or a manual on "How to do it." Rather we have tried to acquaint you with concepts and issues which are appropriate to the thoughtful use of measurement and evaluation methods when you are trying to determine if learning has taken place, and if so, what and how much was learned, and by whom. Some details concerning attitude measurement are included since these are often omitted in measurement and evaluation sources. Methods are detailed in several of the recommended readings listed at the close of this chapter.

Instruction with integrated evaluation—as conceptualized in figure 1—is a corrective operation. Instructional plans with integrated evaluation should result in greater teaching effectiveness and a more permanent and profound impact on the student, in each aspect of the frame of reference.

Students and teachers alike find that some of their most serious academic problems are associated with measurement and evaluation. Yet, both may gain considerably from a clear understanding and wise use of the principles and concepts associated with these topics. This is not a chapter on how to make and use classroom tests; there are already several good sources on that topic. Rather, it is a discussion of some of the aspects and issues which are central to effective measurement and evaluation in education. "Classical" topics such as test reliability and validity are discussed along with some contemporary issues such as mastery testing and the "behavioral objectives controversy." Also included are some specific details concerning attitude measurement in the classroom since this topic is not usually handled in texts for teachers on test construction. Throughout the discussion, the reader should keep in mind that promotion of effective student learning is the main point of educational measurement and evaluation.

An important distinction can be made between the measurement and the evaluation of learning. *Measurement* involves *procedures* to determine what and how much learning has taken place. *Evaluation* involves judgments of the extent to which the learning (as measured) actually fulfilled certain instructional objectives. Measurement and evaluation procedures both are useful in trying to improve learning outcomes through the assessment and judgment, respectively, of the relative merits of instructional procedures and materials. Hence, a test might sample student A's performance on some tasks and *measure* (with some degree of error) that six out of ten problems have been solved correctly, after a given instructional unit. The *evaluation* procedures would involve the judgment that, for example, a score of 60 percent on that test fails to reach mastery, and therefore...(among possible options for the teacher might be: the awarding of less than a top mark, or reteaching of the material subject to subsequent measurement and reevaluation of learning).

We will consider the concepts of measurement and evaluation of learning as separate but closely related clusters of topics. Some key distinctions will be drawn between ideas associated with the two concepts. Finally, we will make specific recommendations to teachers about further resources and educational practices.

The overall purpose of educational measurement and evaluation, as stated earlier, is to facilitate learning. Failure to recognize and attain this goal—improved learning—constitutes one of the persisting problems for many teachers. As indicated in the discussion of instructional models presented earlier, measurement and evaluation can occur at the beginning, throughout, and at the end of instruction to enable both teacher and student to judge their success to that point, and to make decisions on what to do next.

Other uses of measurement and evaluation in education focus on the improvement of student learning. These include the assessment of curriculum (e.g., evaluating instructional objectives and materials); assistance in pupil counseling and guidance (e.g., course selection); and research into problems of learning and instruction (e.g., assessing and evaluating the learning outcomes of different instructional procedures).

Measurement and Evaluation of Student Achievement—Some Issues and Points of View

Two basic questions that arise in teaching are: How does one know when learning has taken place? and What (or how much) learning has taken place? The distinction between *learning* and *performance* as drawn in chapter 2 (discussed in Tolman's learning theory) is important here. One infers that learning has taken place after observing changes in performance following some experience, such as studying or participating in a discussion or lecture. Since learning can be considered *processes* involving acquisition of facts, skills, beliefs, concepts, attitudes, etc., one infers that these processes have taken place by noting what are assumed to be *products* or outcomes of learning, namely performance, in some setting, often a test situation. Since learning may be defined in terms of changes internal to the person, one may only *infer* that learning has taken place by observing external changes in behavior.

The measurement of learning outcomes may be accomplished *informally* by observation of pupil activity in some situation, or *formally* by tallying scores on some form of achievement test—teacher-made or standardized. In general, formal methods have been recommended as being less likely to be influenced by errors of measurement. Of course, errors are present in all measurement activities. While attempts to minimize errors are important, teachers should avoid being lulled into a false sense of security by the claims which are advanced for any test or battery of tests. The most highly reputable published test is vulnerable to misuse and misinterpretation of results. Carefully constructed, administered, and interpreted teacher-made tests can likewise yield valuable information about student performace. Of course, the converse of these two statements is also true. Thus it behooves educators to consider in detail the purposes and conditions of test use, whether the instruments are teacher-made or published tests.

In any event, what one does in trying to measure or sample the results of learning can be fraught with difficulties. It is important to recognize these problems in dealing with measurement issues as they may arise in the practice of education. Likewise, it is important not to take an oversimplified position nor to reject educational testing out of hand because of such problems. Advocating the abolition of educational testing because of abuses and misuses of tests is somewhat analogous to proposing the banning of knives because people can and often do cut themselves. The handling of testing procedures and test results must be done with care to avoid mistakes in judgment and possible damage to the people who are involved.

Testing—the sampling of pupil performance on a given set of tasks under some specified conditions—is commonly done in the measurement of school learning outcomes. The idea of a *sample of behavior* is important since it is virtually impossible to assess, for any student, all outcomes even of relatively simple learning experiences. Thus, the behavior sample must be representative. And indeed, a common complaint of students is that a test is unfair because it does not *adequately* reflect what *they* got out of a course. Obtaining a fairly representative sample of learned behavior is a major task for the test-maker and test-user.

One key problem in educational measurement concerning sampling of behavior involves the different levels of competencies which may be tapped by test items. It is comparatively easy to write test items at low levels of competency. Such items would call for the recall or recognition of labels or for simple associations. However, teachers need to develop skills in selecting and writing items which assess the comprehension of and ability to use concepts and principles in problem solving. Among other sources, the Educational Testing Service (E.T.S., 1963) and Jenkins and Deno (1971) have given examples of test items to assess these "higher levels" of performance. The reader who believes that multiple choice items cannot be written to tap higher levels of competence may be surprised and enlightened by some of the examples cited in the 1963 E.T.S. pamphlet.

In achievement testing the necessity of obtaining a representative sample of pupil behavior, bearing in mind that it is only a sample, is a basic concern of teachers. This consideration leads to sources and types of errors in measurement—problems in reliability and validity of tests—which are briefly discussed here. More detailed and technical discussions of these topics can be found in standard references on tests and measurements such as Cronbach (1970) and Helmstadter (1964).

Errors of Measurement—Reliability

Reliability refers to consistency in measurement. The extent to which a test is consistent in measuring something is the extent to which it is reliable. Less than perfect consistency implies some degree of measurement errors. The reliability of any set of measurements can be estimated by a variety of procedures according to the requirements of the situation. While it is desirable to have measurements be as reliable as possible, test users should be aware that errors in measurement always exist, and it is thus necessary to try to account for them in the interpretation of test results. Some approaches to the determination of test reliability are discussed in the following paragraphs.

Standard Error of Measurement. The reliability of a single test score can be determined through calculating, or estimating, a statistic known as the *standard error of measurement*. This statistic indicates the probable amount of error affecting a score on a given test. This error would tend to reduce or inflate the value of an obtained score from that of a "true" score (one free of error). In other words, repeated measurement on the same task might yield different results for an individual. The degree of difference among such repeated scores can be taken as an index of consistency or reliability of measurement. Thus the standard error of measurement provides a range around an obtained score within which a hypothetical "true score" (free of measurement errors) might be expected to occur. The standard error of measurement can be considered to be the average of the degree to which obtained scores deviate from the assumed true score. Gronlund (1968) offers an easy way to estimate standard error of measurement from the number of items in a test (pp. 10-11) and to compute its value when some other test statistics are known (p. 97). The absolute value of the standard error of measurement increases as a test is lengthened (i.e., more items are added), but relative to the length of the test the amount of error decreases. For example, doubling the number of items on a test from twenty-five to fifty results in an increase in standard error of about one point, from 2.0 to 3.0. Therefore, increasing the length of a test has the result of tending to reduce relative error and thus increasing reliability.

Internal Consistency. Another approach to reliability relates to a *set* of scores obtained from a group of persons on some test or measure. This is termed *internal consistency*—the extent to which a set of items is homogeneous or can be said to measure one thing. If a test is supposed to be internally consistent, that is, if all items are supposed to measure the same thing or construct, then a calculation or an estimate of internal consistency should be obtained in order to check that supposition. A common way to do this is to correlate the results a group of persons made on half of the items of the test with their results on the other half of the items. Usually the results on the odd-numbered items are correlated with those of the even items since it is often the case that the second half of a test is more difficult or somewhat different than the first half. If different things were being measured by the items, a low coefficient of correlation might result. However, if the test were internally consistent (homogeneous), then a high correlation (approaching a value of 1.00) would be expected. Various formulas are available for the calculation of internal consistency reliability. Gronlund (1968, pp. 95-96) gives handy procedures for teachers to use in estimating the internal consistency reliability of their test scores.

Stability. *Stability* is another type of reliability, or consistency, in measurement. A stability coefficient indicates the degree to which the test scores of a group are similar to those obtained upon retesting. If whatever is being measured is not supposed to change between one testing and another, that is, if the characteristic being measured is expected to remain stable, a reliable test should result in highly similar scores for the same people on the two testing sessions. A low coefficient of correlation between the scores made on the same or parallel tests by the same persons at two different testing times would indicate either instability of the measure, or changes in the thing being measured, or both. If the characteristic being measured was presumed to be stable, one would suspect that the test was unstable. Of course, there are matters such as reminiscence effects and test-taker's learning items from the first test, which affect retest scores. Parallel forms, two tests of different items of about equal difficulty which are supposed to assess the same thing, can be developed to accommodate this problem. Correlation between scores of a group of persons on parallel forms of a test provides an index of this type of reliability.

As noted, test reliability generally increases as the number of items in the test increases. This is one argument in favor of lengthening tests. Reliability may also be increased by improving the quality of each item—for example, reducing ambiguity in wording of items and instructions and reducing subjectivity in scoring. Three approaches to test reliability have been discussed: standard error of measurement, internal consistency, and stability. Each of these types of reliability involves a way of expressing the degree to which measurement errors affect the consistency of a test score or set of scores.

Measurement and Evaluation of Student Achievement

Errors of Measurement—Validity

Reliability is a necessary but not sufficient condition for the usefulness of educational tests. A test may be highly reliable (consistent) in measuring something, but it may in fact measure the wrong thing in terms of what the user intended. Such a test would be invalid. Thus, considerations of test *validity*—the degree to which a test measures what it is purported to measure—are also important in using tests and their results.

A test constructed to measure a certain thing should, in fact, measure that thing and not something else. A certain amount of measurement error including items tapping things other than what they were composed to is present in virtually all measurement. A test is thus said to be valid to the extent its scores reflect what it is supposed to measure. Tests which are valid to measure one thing are likely to be invalid for other purposes, even if these are closely related to the original purpose. Moreover, tests which are valid for measuring one part of a range of values may be invalid for measuring another part of that range. For example, an ordinary household thermometer would be invalid for measuring temperatures in the oven or sauna-bath because it does not cover a sufficient range of "scores." Likewise, a postal scale usually would be an invalid instrument for weighing persons. Before using a test it is wise to investigate evidence of validity for one's intended purpose. In trying to interpret test scores, validity data also should be considered. Several types of test validity have been identified and three are described below. These classifications may be used in deciding what evidence to seek or accept in assessing the validity for either published or teacher-made tests.

Content Validity. Content validity involves the extent to which the items or individual parts of the test *appear* to be an adequate and representative sample of what is purportedly being tested. Sometimes test items will actually require behaviors other than those the test was designed to measure. In such cases, test scores will reflect this. Likewise, if tests or scores on tests are used for purposes other than those for which the items were developed and, presumably, validated, invalidity may be a serious problem. For example, test items which are composed so as to discriminate among individuals on the basis of anxiety, may turn out to be measures of verbal ability in test-taking. Thus, discrimination among persons on the basis of anxiety is maximally valid only among persons of approximately equal verbal ability. As persons who take this hypothetical test differ in verbal ability, differences in their scores may reflect less well their differences in anxiety.

237

There is no statistical procedure for determining content validity. A logical or conceptual analysis of the test items is required. One useful approach to the problem of content validity is the *Table of Specifications* (cf. Gronlund, 1968, pp. 19-23) wherein the numbers of test items in each topic area can be listed for each level of the learning outcomes (using the six levels of the cognitive domain of the *Taxonomy of Educational Objectives*). A table of specifications makes it possible to plan the content structure of a test as well as to make judgments about its content validity. A table of specifications for an examination over a unit from an educational psychology course with numbers of test items in each content category and performance level is shown in table 9.

TABLE 9
Specifications for an 80-Item Multiple-Choice Examination in Educational Psychology

Topic Content	Knowledge	Understanding	Application	Total Number
Conditions of Learning	3	3	5	11
Motivation	2	6	5	13
Planning for Instruction	-	5	1	6
Attitudes & Values	5	8	5	18
Cognitive Processes	1	3	2	6
Transfer & Memory	-	4	3	7
Creativity & Self-direction	1	1	1	3
Individual Differences	5	7	4	16
Total Number of Items	17	37	26	80

Criterion-Related Validity. Criterion-related validity is important in making predictions to some other performance situation either in the future or concurrently with the test in question. Sets of test scores should show high correlations with those of other tests which purport to measure the same thing. Likewise, in attempting to predict nontest behavior (e.g., course grades or job success), criterion-related validity is evidenced by the degree of successful prediction of these criteria from test scores.

Authors of new tests often support test validity claims by offering the evidence of positive correlations between the scores made by a group of persons on the new test and scores obtained by the group on some older, established, and widely regarded instrument. Since the original instrument itself had less than perfect validity, such correlations must be carefully considered and interpreted.

Whenever tests are used for placement or prediction purposes, it is wise to have acceptable evidence of criterion-related validity. This is so because considerable time and money, not to mention personal inconvenience, may be involved if the test scores make no improvement over another form of prediction, or over chance.

Construct Validity. Construct validity has to do with inference of the presence of a psychological trait or hypothetical construct from test scores. "Intelligence," "ability," "anxiety," "aptitude," "achievement," and "creativity" are all examples of hypothetical constructs or concepts which are created in the attempt to understand human behavior. These constructs, like "learning," typically are inferred from test performance rather than being directly validated in experience. Tests, of course, need not always be of a paper-and-pencil nature. Situational tests or simulations of actual "life" situations may be used to obtain appropriate samples of behavior. Validity and reliability are as important as considerations in situational tests as they are in paper-and-pencil tests.

The procedures of construct validation involve attempts to assess the extent to which a construct, purportedly measured by a test, is actually represented in persons' scores on that test. There are several ways to establish construct validity. For example, one might check to see if a test of some construct successfully discriminates between two groups of persons, one group which is known to be high and the other group to be low in that quality. A test of anxiety, for example, ought to identify persons who have been clinically judged as anxious. Likewise, if a construct is supposed to be amenable to change, test scores should vary in accordance with theoretical expectations. Consider the following points in the case of pupil achievement. Achievement test scores should distinguish between high and low achievers. If instruction has been successful, final test scores should reflect improvement (learning) over initial performance. On the other hand, constructs which are assumed to be stable should be reflected in little or no change in test scores over time. An example of this would be the construct *intelligence* which can be considered to be a trait or group of traits which, according to some theories, is not amenable to alteration by any specific experiences. Intelligence test scores should thus be stable over time.

In practice, the influences of more than one construct including a variety of sources of error determine obtained test scores. Many times, experimental procedures are necessary to determine the degree of influence of each of several factors. Such procedures might involve systematic alteration of one condition, assumed to represent a given construct, while holding others constant. Then one might predict changes in test scores. Cronbach and Meehl (1955) have provided the most definitive explanation of this difficult idea—construct validation.

Correlation

Evidence concerning test reliability and validity is often expressed in terms of a statistic known as the *correlation coefficient* (r). Correlation is widely used in educational measurement, but it is also frequently misunderstood. Statistical correlation is a statistical technique for the assessment of the relationship between two sets of scores—the extent to which scores of one set vary together with scores of the other; and thus, the extent to which it is possible to predict from one set of scores to the other. While the degree of relationship is indexed by correlation, the type of relationship is not. Thus it is fallacious to assume that because a positive correlation exists between test scores indexing two phenomena, that one has caused the other, even when the one is known to have preceded the other in time. It is often the case that a third factor (or some combination of factors) has caused the two sets of scores to vary together.

Correlation coefficients may have values between -1.00 and +1.00, thus correlation values look like a positive or negative decimal expression of a percentage (e.g., r = +.20, or r = -.50). But, in fact, correlation is not a percentage, and in order to make a statement about percentage of relationship it is necessary to square the coefficient (r^2) so that the above parenthetical instances would represent a 4 percent and 25 percent relationship, respectively (.20 × .20 = .04 or 4%; .50 × .50 = .25 or 25%).

Commonly used approaches to reliability and validity have been discussed. In conclusion, it should be pointed out that while these concepts have to do with measurement problems they have important implications for evaluation of learning. This is so because judgments which are based upon invalid or unreliable test data are obviously biased and may even be worse than the decisions which would be made in the absence of such data. Many popular criticisms of educational measurement seem to be based more on instances of misuse rather than on the informed applications of measurement principles and techniques.

Formative and Summative Evaluation of Learning

This section includes a discussion of the ideas of formative and summative evaluation of student learning and some of the implications of mastery learning, as discussed in chapter 7, for classroom testing.

Formative Evaluation. Scriven (1967) has drawn attention to the distinction between *formative* and *summative* evaluation, a distinction which classroom teachers have for years known intuitively. Formative evaluation is not the basis for grades but is for diagnostic and prescriptive purposes. Formative evaluation has to do with procedures whereby teacher and pupil alike come to know where pupil performance is in relation to the level of task mastery described by instructional objectives. Formative or "monitoring" evaluation occurs at stages 2, 3, and 4 of the instructional model shown in figure 1. It takes place with a view toward deciding if further instruction is necessary, and if so, in what areas. If a course is broken down into smaller units of learning, such as topics or textbook chapters, formative evaluation may be based on the results of short quizzes. Bloom (1968) has called such quizzes "brief diagnostic-process tests." Formative evaluation may take place at the outset of a course to determine the entering behaviors of the students. It may also occur at intervals, say within each unit, to check pupil progress. Recently, Cronbach (1971) has proposed use of "monitoring evaluation" in order to more clearly describe what occurs in such progress testing.

Summative Evaluation. Summative evaluation has the purpose of making a final statement of course performance for each student in terms of his mastery or nonmastery of the course objectives. Likewise, the course itself may be evaluated by determining the proportion of students attaining mastery. The teacher then may judge his own degree of teaching success. Summative evaluation is an expression of the results of a completed course on terms of student achievement. It is "for the record."

Bloom, Hastings, and Madaus have drawn together current thinking on these subjects in their *Handbook on Formative and Summative Evaluation of Student Learning* (1971) which contains chapters written by experts in the fields of preschool education, language arts, social studies, art education, science, mathematics, literature, writing, second language, and industrial education about the evaluation of learning in these areas. The reader interested in educational evaluation, especially in these content areas, is encouraged to consult this handbook.

The separate purposes of formative and summative evaluation of learning should not be confused either by teachers or students. The common goal—that of promoting pupil learning—also needs to be kept in mind. Too often, approaches to the evaluation of learning in schools have emphasized aversive or punishing aspects of testing. Persistent misuse of educational measurement and evaluation techniques probably is a major source of negative attitudes toward school and learning among both pupils and teachers.

Testing for Mastery. Whereas traditional educational measurement procedures incorporate a concern for maximum discrimination between individuals in terms of achievement, the *mastery learning* point of view as discussed in chapter 7 entails a somewhat different set of assumptions. The desired discrimination in *formative mastery* testing involves diagnosis of exactly what aspects of the subject matter or skills were and were not learned and by whom so that appropriate remedial steps such as reteaching can be determined. In *summative* mastery testing, the important discrimination sought is between the group of pupils attaining mastery and those, hopefully few, not attaining mastery. Rank ordering of students within the mastery and nonmastery categories is of much less importance in the mastery model than in traditional approaches. Discrimination among scores of those who fail to attain mastery may be useful to teachers in making educational decisions concerning further instruction and testing, but this is essentially a formative function. Any strategy for mastery learning should involve a clear set of instructional objectives or criteria by which to judge when student performance meets mastery levels.

One approach to criterion referenced assessment involves "contract" grading. In this procedure teachers enter into agreements (often written) with individual students concerning the type, amount, and quality of work which is appropriate for the awarding of certain marks. Contracts can be very specific as to the conditions under which the desired performance may take place and the standards by which it will be judged.

In contract grading, students and teachers become very clear on the objectives of the course of study and on the outcomes which indicate satisfactory completion of those objectives. Some students may elect to contract for something less than the top mark possible. Others may wish to "renegotiate" some of the terms of the agreement under certain conditions. Provision for alternate marks (higher or lower than the one initially agreed upon) may be made for work which fails to attain or exceeds the specified standards. Contracts for top marks may contain a clause requiring the student to tutor others in the subject matter, helping "slower" students to attain better task mastery.

Instructional Objectives and the Evaluation of Learning

Gronlund (1970) draws the important distinction between *general* and *specific instructional objectives*. It may be considered possible for any teacher to come close to having a set of general objectives to cover comprehensively a course of instruction. However, it is practically impossible to do more than have pools of specific objectives from which samples may be drawn to tap the domains of possible learning outcomes of any course.

It is usually recommended that instructional objectives be written in terms of student behavior—hence the term "behavioral objectives." The objectives specify what the student will learn to do as a consequence of the course (formal learning experience). General objectives are statements of broad classes of learning outcomes such as, "Students shall learn to read French" or "Students shall learn to do the breaststroke"; whereas the specific objectives are statements of samples of student behavior which can be considered to be evidence that a more general objective has been met. An example of a specific objective which is related to sampling the general objective for language learning would be "The student will be able to translate a 600-word French passage in three hours with 80 percent accuracy, using a dictionary."

Mager (1962) has suggested that specific objectives should include: a statement of desired student behavior, the conditions under which that behavior is to be demonstrated, and a standard of acceptable performance (how well a student must do the thing to evidence mastery). Thus the specific counterpart to the general objective about swimming would be a statement such as, "A student shall be able to perform the breaststroke for two consecutive laps of an Olympic-sized pool in under x minutes."

In practice, specific instructional objectives have a one-to-one correspondence with test items, where both specific objectives and test items represent samples of a class of student behaviors as described in the general objectives. It might be considered desirable for committees of teachers and students to meet to develop pools of specific objectives and (related) test items for each of the general objectives they can identify for their subject matter. Thus, general objectives should be stated so as to allow the student and teacher freedom to select which specific objectives are appropriate to individual learning situations. Specific objectives can then be considered to be samples of pupil behavior which may be considered as evidence that the general objective has been met. An example of a general objective with some parallel abbreviated samples of specific objectives at both recognition and recall levels of performance is:

General objective —Student understands basic physics principles.
Specific objectives —Recognition level of memory:
  1. Identifies correctly ten physics principles from a list
  2. Distinguishes correct and incorrect applications of principles
—Recall level of memory:
  1. States ten physics principles
  2. Makes correct application of physics principles

As stated before, sources of objectives vary. Educational philosophers, committees of educators, and curriculum developers have all worked at developing instructional objectives for classroom use. In day-to-day school practice each teacher has considerable freedom to control the specific objectives that apply in his classroom. Thus, teachers should be aware of the availability of objectives and how to select and originate them. The Instructional Objectives Exchange at P.O. Box 24075, Los Angeles, California 90024, is one source of instructional objectives for a variety of subject matter areas.

The Behavioral Objectives Controversy.

In recent years a controversy has arisen in education circles between those advocating specific behavioral objectives across the board (e.g., Mager, 1962; and Popham, 1970) and those advising caution and pointing out the limitations in trying to objectify all school learning (e.g., Atkin, 1968).

There are several reasons why specific objectives cannot or should not be advocated for comprehensive coverage of a course of study. For one, how can a teacher objectify or plan for serendipity? One can provide for the unexpected, but to do this is to avoid having all of the time for instruction taken up by activities which are oriented toward the attainment of specific behavioral objectives. Furthermore, one may seriously question whether teacher unfamiliarity with an issue is sufficient reason for exclusion of that topic from class attention. The authors would support a contrary position that no item be excluded solely by reason of the teacher being unacquainted with the topic.

One of the authors had this point brought home to him quite clearly in the classroom recently. Early in an undergraduate educational psychology course, two students who were majoring in music education asked if they could prepare a report on music therapy. The instructor was almost totally unfamiliar with this topic. He said that he did not know if it had relevance to the course but that the students should conduct a preliminary survey to determine the nature and scope of the topic. The result was an annotated bibliography of books, journals, and articles about music therapy, a class presentation, and the identification of a music therapy research project which, it turned out, was located in a nearby school district. How can an instructor, in advance, devise specific objectives about something such as this, a quite legitimate topic with which the instructor has little prior acquaintance? Student participation in the setting of objectives as well as provision for unexpected but valuable events is clearly called for in most classroom situations.

The previous question also spotlights one of the important advantages to using instructional objectives, namely the clarification of a teacher's thinking about the specific skills which are to be learned by the students. This clarification of intent may well be the most valuable contribution made by having clear-cut instructional objectives for teachers and pupils alike. An in-class discussion of "what you would like to get out of this course" is often the most lively session of the early meetings of the author's courses. Follow-up incorporation of student ideas into the activities rarely fails to improve upon the objectives originally planned by the instructor.

Another advantage in the use of specific instructional objectives has been mentioned before—that is, in matching test items to clearly stated objectives and to specific instructional procedures. This goes a long way toward ensuring what one of our students has termed an "honest test," that is, items which are pertinent to the purposes of the course and that which actually transpired within it.

A potential disadvantage to an overemphasis on specific objectives concerns the fact that it seems comparatively easier to write objectives about student behaviors at low levels than at high levels of the taxonomies (e.g., "Students will correctly label instances of centrifugal and centripetal force," as compared to "Students will be able to explain the interrelations between two force concepts"). A teacher with a large number of objectives at the "knowledge of facts" level might be lulled into a false sense of security. The preparation of a table of specifications for objectives and test items, as mentioned in connection with the discussion of content validity, should tend to alleviate this problem. A table of specifications would allow a teacher to determine the proportions of specific objectives and test items at different taxonomic levels. It would make it easier to detect an imbalance favoring lower levels of learning (e.g., rote recall of facts).

The position which is taken here on the functions of instructional objectives in teaching is summarized in table 10. It can readily be seen that the three stages shown in table 10 correspond quite closely to the three phases of Bloom's suggested strategy for mastery learning (discussed in chapter 7): *preconditions, operating procedures,* and *outcomes.*

TABLE 10
Functions of Instructional Objectives
Before, During, and After Instruction

1. Before	2. During	3. After
General objectives and related *samples* of specific behaviors are stated.	Instruction is geared toward the general objectives. Formative evaluation samples of specific behaviors are used.	Test items are used which correspond with samples of specific behaviors, for summative evaluation.

It should be emphasized that there can be many specific samples of behavior for any one general objective. Obtaining *representative* samples of specific objectives and corresponding items is an important task in test development. Because of special circumstances, some specific objectives may be more appropriate for certain pupils than for others. Teachers of similar courses can cooperate in selecting and writing objectives and pools of items. These objectives and items can be organized under general objectives during course planning and test construction activities. Attitudinal objectives in education are discussed in chapter 8. The notion is advanced there that evaluation of attitudinal outcomes of instruction properly belongs in the area of course evaluation rather than for marking purposes.

In assessing retention of learning in terms of performance on a task or set of tasks, two general approaches are typically taken. These may be termed *recognition* and *recall.* In recognition the task involves identifying a response as either a correct or incorrect solution to a question or problem. Examples of recognition tasks are multiple-choice, matching, and true/false items. Recall tasks are generally more difficult in that the person taking the test must supply the correct response. Examples of recall tasks include fill-in completion, short answer, and essay items.

Instructional Objectives and the Evaluation of Learning

In composing test items, the choice of item types depends upon the instructional objectives. Some objectives seem to be more appropriate to recognition items as they call for the learner to make discriminations among alternatives. Other objectives may be better suited to recall and learner-produced responses. It is a stark oversimplification to say that recognition items are appropriate only at the "factual" levels of learning and recall items are useful solely for assessing "higher level" concept learning and problem-solving skills. In fact it is considerably easier to compose items which tap simple recall or recognition of facts than some of the higher order functioning. However, multiple-choice items can be constructed to tap recognition skills at all levels of the cognitive taxonomy. Recognition of appropriate applications, analyses, and syntheses, especially with respect to unfamiliar (but meaningful) materials, are clearly appropriate learning outcomes for many courses of study. It is true, of course, that production of applications, analyses, and syntheses, as may be tapped by short answer and essay (or oral examination) items, allows for a wider range of student expression. Nevertheless, a mix of item types, a possibility often overlooked by teachers, should certainly be considered when it is desired to sample a broad range of learning outcomes.

Item Analysis

There are different kinds of conceptual analyses of test items and their corresponding learning objectives which can be recommended to teachers using or constructing classroom tests. The table of specifications (cf. figure 8) is one approach to assigning items to taxonomic levels and subject-topic categories. As mentioned before such analyses can be undertaken to ensure content validity and representativeness of test items.

In addition to a logical or conceptual analysis of test items, there are simple numerical procedures which can be performed on test data to identify which items are performing well and which require rewriting or replacing. Item *difficulty* and *discrimination* among high and low total scorers are two functions which can be determined from test results.

Item difficulty is simply assessed by determining the proportion of those attempting an item who gave correct answers to that item. Teacher-made tests should usually contain items at various levels of difficulty (or easiness) to provide sufficient "ceiling" and "floor" so that students have an opportunity to demonstrate how much or how little they have learned.

247

Item discrimination involves determining the extent to which each item contributes to the discriminating power of the total test. In other words, if a test is supposed to identify those who attained all or most of the objectives from those who achieved far less well over a large group of students, the subgroup reflecting the highest total test scores might be expected to perform better on each item than the group having the lowest total scores.

Additionally, in the case of multiple-choice items, responses should be inspected to determine if each distractor (incorrect alternative) is plausible. No distractors should be so implausible as to fail to draw responses from test-takers who have not learned the task being assessed by the item.

Although large-scale item analyses can be efficiently performed by computers, simple methods are available for classroom use. These and specific details of item writing techniques can be found in several sources including Gronlund (1968).

Table 11 illustrates some item analysis results for five multiple-choice items with one correct response and three distractors apiece. Study table 11 and see if you can answer these questions:

1. Can you identify examples of each of the following:
    a) a very easy item
    b) the most favorable item all around
    c) the most difficult item of the five
    d) two items that discriminate well
    e) two items that should be rewritten, rekeyed, or thrown out
    f) some extremely ineffective distractors
    g) a reverse discriminating item
    h) a reverse discriminating distractor

2. What can a teacher do with data like these for the teacher's own test items?

3. How can data like these be gathered with a simple show-of-hands procedure in the classroom?

The Measurement and Evaluation of Pupil Attitudes

In chapter 8, attitude toward any psychological object was defined in terms of (a compound of) learned evaluations of beliefs about that object. An appropriate way to obtain a measure of attitudes, then, is to have people evaluate beliefs about some attitude object, and to try to quantify these evaluations in some appropriate way. This is, in fact, what is done in the most commonly used techniques for measuring attitudes, namely, a set of belief statements is provided for persons to

TABLE 11
Item Analysis Results for Five Multiple-Choice Items

Items		A	B	C	D	omit	Easiness	Discrimination
		\	\	(Circled Choice Is Correct Response)				
Item 1	Highs	2	14	©3	3	0	50%	+6
	Lows	4	8	5	5	0		
Item 10	Highs	9	5	©7	0	1	29%	0
	Lows	8	4	7	0	3		
Item 20	Highs	Ⓐ8	7	4	3	0	50%	-7
	Lows	14	5	2	1	0		
Item 25	Highs	Ⓐ8	2	4	8	0	23%	+6
	Lows	2	8	7	2	3		
Item 30	Highs	Ⓐ22	0	0	0	0	98%	+1
	Lows	21	0	1	0	0		

Note: The item analysis results show numbers of persons omitting or selecting each alternative, easiness index, and the discrimination between high and low scorers on the test (median split of a class of 44 students, 22 "highs" and 22 "lows").

evaluate. One's attitude is indexed by the sum or average of values assigned to such evaluations.

Reliability and validity are important issues in the measurement of attitudes as they are in achievement testing. Evidence of these characteristics should be sought for any attitude scale which one proposes to use. Item analysis techniques should be employed when developing one's own attitude items to ensure having items which contribute to the validity and reliability of the total scores. Item analysis procedures typically include a determination of the proportion of persons omitting and choosing each alternative for an item, and the degree to which each item contributes to the total score. That is, the item provides for discrimination between high and low scorers overall.

Social psychologists have developed several techniques for attitude measurement. Among the more prominent of these is Thurstone's method of "equal-appearing intervals," Guttman's "scalogram analysis," Likert's technique of "summated ratings," and Osgood's "semantic differential." The latter two techniques are currently more widely used for the measurement of educational attitudes and are described later. A brief comparison of all four approaches can be found in Zimbardo and Ebbesen (1969, pp. 123-28). Each of these techniques yields a single score for each person for each attitude object. In practice, these scores are highly intercorrelated between different techniques when attitudes toward the same object are measured. Thus it can be said empirically that these four techniques when properly applied appear to measure the same construct—attitude.

Semantic Differential Scales

Where facilities for computer analyses are available and when more than one attitude object is involved, the authors recommend the semantic differential technique as an approach to the measurement of educational attitudes (cf. McKie & Foster, 1972). This technique allows one to determine empirically what items (scales) are "evaluative" for given persons and attitude objects, and it also allows for the empirical clustering or grouping of the attitude objects. Moreover, it is possible to develop attitude profiles for individual students who may have similar total global scores.

Semantic differential scales were originally developed by Osgood et al. (1957) in attempting to measure the meanings of words and concepts. As noted in chapter 8, it was found that one consistent and strong component of meaning for most any word could be characterized as *evaluative*. Because of high correlations with other types of attitude scales, and for theoretical reasons, this evaluative

The Measurement and Evaluation of Pupil Attitudes

dimension came to be regarded as an index of attitudes, and the evaluative scales of the semantic differential are now widely used in attitude measurement.

Semantic differential data are comprised of scores which represent the positions of check marks that persons place between bipolar adjective pairs (the attitude scales) in describing a word or thing (the attitude object). "Bipolar" refers to the fact that the adjective pairs are antonyms. For any attitude object, the determination of evaluative scales is done by analyzing semantic differential data by using a set of statistical techniques—an extension of statistical correlation known as factor analysis. This is best accomplished with the aid of electronic computers since the calculations would be extremely tedious to perform manually.

Semantic differential scales are bipolar adjective pairs placed immediately below a description of the object to be evaluated. The task is to "describe" or "rate" the object (word or concept) in terms of each of the scales. Figure 14 shows a sample of semantic differential scales used to assess attitudes toward arithmetic.

Directions: Place a check mark on a space (✓) between each adjective pair to best describe the concept.

Arithmetic

good	___ ___ ___ ___ ___ ___ ___	bad
positive	___ ___ ___ ___ ___ ___ ___	negative
happy	___ ___ ___ ___ ___ ___ ___	sad
nice	___ ___ ___ ___ ___ ___ ___	awful
useful	___ ___ ___ ___ ___ ___ ___	useless

NOTE: Scoring each scale space 7, 6, 5, 4, 3, 2, 1 or +3, +2, +1, 0, -1, -2, -3 are typical procedures.

Figure 14. A sample of semantic differential scales used to assess attitudes toward arithmetic

Scoring of the semantic differential involves assigning each blank between adjective pairs a numerical value (often 1 to 7, or -3 to +3) and either summing or averaging the values for each set of scales according to a scheme so that the highest positive numbers reflect positive evaluations of the object. Each scale (adjective pair) should contribute to the discrimination between high and low scorers on the total set of scales in order to be considered "evaluative." Interscale correlation, and then factor analysis, of the results is done to determine the degree to which each scale does contribute to an evaluative dimension or factor.

The Likert Technique

In the absence of electronic computers, there are other methods which are appropriate for the measurement of educational attitudes. Consistent with the definition of attitude noted before and in chapter 8, Likert's technique involves asking persons to evaluate a set of belief statements about an attitude object. Evaluations are usually on a five-point scale using categories such as: (1) strongly agree, (2) agree, (3) undecided, (4) disagree, and (5) strongly disagree. The response choices then are assigned values in terms of whether the statement was positive or negative toward the object. A person's attitudes can then be indexed by summing the values assigned to the positions of that person's responses to the set of belief statements.

The belief statements used in the Likert method can be drawn from a large pool of opinions given, often anonymously, about the object in question by persons who are similar to those whose attitudes eventually will be measured. This approach is taken in order to assure content validity of the scales. Shaw and Wright (1967) describe this procedure in somewhat greater detail and give several examples of Likert scales that have been used to assess attitudes toward a wide variety of attitude objects.

After a set of belief statements about the attitude object has been drawn up, a decision is made as to which represent positive and which negative statements about the object. For the purposes of item analysis and further scale development, a trial group of individuals is then asked to evaluate the belief statements along an agree/disagree continuum like the one shown in figure 15. On the basis of total scores (summing the values of each person's responses on overall items) the most and least favorable 25 percent of the group of persons are selected. Then, for each item, the responses of these polar attitude groups are compared. If an item is useful, it will discriminate well between these two groups. Statistical tests such as item-total biserial correlations may be used instead of the hand tally item analysis procedures if more precision is desired in arriving at the final attitude scale items. Item data should also be inspected to check the effectiveness of alternative response choices. Some statements may be so extreme in wording as to provide for little or no strong agreement or disagreement. The item analysis information given by Gronlund (1968, chapter 6) is useful in these operations.

The final instrument contains instructions on how to evaluate the items (usually along a strongly agree/strongly disagree dimension) and the set of belief statements (attitude items) to be evaluated. Assessment of educational attitudes is often made anonymously because the purpose of such measurement is usually to evaluate the degree and range of positive and negative attitudes of a class or group of persons and not to identify the attitudes of any specific individual within the group. Rapport with the respondents is necessary because responses to attitude items can easily be "faked." Items are usually worded such as to provide for a wide range of evaluations and not to be so exclusively extreme as to have most persons agreeing or disagreeing. The discriminative purpose of an attitude item or scale is, of course, to identify among persons having different evaluations of the attitude object. Figure 15 shows four illustrative Likert items from a twenty item set of belief statements designed to assess attitudes toward programmed instruction and teaching machines. Further discussion of attitudinal objectives for classroom learning is included in chapter 8.

Directions: For each item, mark your answer sheet according to the choice which best indicates your views according to the following key:
A=strongly agree, B=agree, C=undecided, D=disagree, E=strongly disagree

---

Item

* 1. Programmed instruction does not work in some subjects.
 6. Any subject, if properly organized, is good material for programmed instruction.
*14. Teaching machines remove an essential element from education—humanity.
 17. Teaching machines are no more cold or impersonal than are textbooks.

---

*Negative items scored A=1, B=2, C=3, D=4, E=5, other items are positive A=5, E=1.

From S. F. Foster, A scale to measure attitudes toward programmed instruction and teaching machines, Experimental publication system, A.P.A., 1970, 9, Ms. No. 342-4.

Figure 15. Sample Likert items 1 and 14 are negative; 6 and 17 are positive.

Sociometry

The assessment of interpersonal attitudes may be performed by using a technique known as *sociometry* (Gronlund, 1959). Typically, this method involves asking pupils to list first, second, and third choices among their peers in connection with a question such as: With whom would you like to work? or Whom would you invite to a party? Questions also are worded to identify individuals who would be excluded from such choices as well. It is possible then to chart such student acceptance and rejection data onto diagrams called sociograms using squares and circles for boys and girls respectively, and arrows to indicate choices with double arrows indicating reciprocal choices. In this way interpersonal evaluations can be studied as the diagram will identify cliques, "stars," "isolates," "two-person dyads," and "rejectees" among the students. Teachers can use such data to organize classroom activities in an attempt to improve the social position of isolates and rejectees, for example, or to identify potential peer allies in the social planning of learning situations. Sociograms can be taken before and after certain group experiences to assess changes in the "social structure" of a class.

Summary

In this chapter, we have attempted to focus upon some of the key issues facing teachers concerning measurement and evaluation of student learning. First, the concepts of *measurement* and *evaluation* were characterized and distinguished. Then a brief introduction to classroom testing was given, followed by a discussion of the measurement topics of types of *reliability* and *validity* and *statistical correlation*.

Formative and *summative* evaluations of learning were introduced and their uses distinguished. A section on testing for mastery followed in which some of the implications for classroom testing of the learning for mastery model which was developed earlier in chapter 7 were sketched out.

Finally, some commonly employed approaches to attitude and sociometric measurement were discussed.

Discussion Questions

1. Distinguish between measurement and evaluation. Why is this distinction important?
2. Distinguish between reliability and validity in educational testing? Which one refers to accuracy in measurement?
3. Why are reliability and validity discussed in terms of errors in measurement?
4. When might one be more interested in stability reliability than in internal consistency?
5. When might one desire a test to have low face validity?
6. Can you think of a rare instance when the validity of a test might be greater than its stability reliability?
7. Distinguish between formative and summative evaluation. Which is most often done formally? Which informally? During what stages of instruction do these most realistically occur?

8. Can attitudes really be measured? Can and should teachers get involved in this?
9. Which technique of attitude measurement involves the lowest face validity—Semantic Differential or Likert Items? Why?
10. How could you use sociometry? What decisions might be aided with the availability of sociometric data?

Recommended Readings

Ahmann, J. S., & Glock, M. D. *Evaluating pupil growth: Principles of tests and measurements.* (4th ed.) Boston: Allyn and Bacon, 1971, 621 pp. An up-to-date edition of one of the most comprehensive standard texts on the topic for educators.

Educational Testing Service: *Tests and measurement kit.* Princeton, N. J., 1973. Contains material on aspects of educational tests and measurements. Includes information on teacher-made tests, published tests, and short-cut statistics for teachers.

Evans, K. M. *Sociometry in education.* London: Routledge & Kegan Paul, 1962. A British text on the uses of sociometry.

Gorman, A. H. *Teachers and learners—the interactive process of education.* Boston: Allyn and Bacon, 1969. In this text, see especially chapter 5 on reaction and evaluation instruments to assess classroom "process."

Gronlund, N. E. *Measurement and evaluation in teaching.* (2nd ed.) New York: Macmillan, 1971. A recent revision of a standard text for teachers on measurement and evaluation.

Gronlund, N. E. *Readings in measurement and evaluation.* New York: Macmillan, 1968. A collection of original articles which discuss details of tests, measurement, and evaluation.

Knapp, T. R. *Statistics for educational measurement.* Scranton, Pa.: Intext, 1971. Explains and illustrates the statistical techniques associated with test development, use, and analysis.

Lyman, H. B. *Test scores and what they mean.* (2nd ed.) Englewood Cliffs, N. J.: Prentice-Hall, Inc., 1971, 200 pp. A helpful guide to the interpretation of test scores and use of tests. Contains, among others, a section on testing and social responsibility and a chapter on how to interpret test manuals.

Tyler, L. E. *Tests and measurements.* (2nd ed.) Englewood Cliffs, N. J.: Prentice-Hall, Inc., 1971, 99 pp. Oriented toward an understanding of psychological tests. Contains sections on intelligence tests, tests of special ability and personality measurement.

Wardrop, J. L. *Standardized testing in the schools: Uses and roles.* Monterey, Calif.: Brooks/Cole, 1976. An up-to-date discussion of the uses of standardized tests and the interpretation of them.

References

Atkin, J. M. Behavioral objectives in curriculum design: A cautionary note. *The Science Teacher,* 1968, 27-30.

Bloom, B. S. Learning for mastery. *Evaluation Comment,* 1968, *1,* (2).

Bloom, B. S. et al. *Taxonomy of educational objectives, handbook I: Cognitive domain.* New York: McKay, 1956.

Bloom, B. S., Hastings, J. T., & Madaus, G. F. *Handbook on formative and summative evaluation of student learning.* New York: McGraw-Hill, 1971.

Cronbach, L. J. Comments on mastery learning and its implications for curriculum development. In E. W. Eisner (Ed.), *Confronting curriculum reform.* Boston: Little, Brown and Co., 1971, 49-55.

Cronbach, L. J. *Essentials of psychological testing.* (3rd ed.) New York: Harper & Row, 1970.

Cronbach, L. J., & Meehl, P. Construct validity. *Psychological Bulletin,* 1955, *52,* 231-302.

Educational Testing Service pamphlet. *Making the classroom test: A guide for teachers.* (2nd ed.) Princeton, N. J., 1961.

Educational Testing Service pamphlet. *Multiple-choice questions: A close look.* Princeton, N. J., 1963.

Foster, S. F. A scale to measure attitudes toward programmed instruction and teaching machines. *Experimental Publication System,* A.P.A., 1970, *9,* Ms. No. 342-44.

Gronlund, N. E. *Constructing achievement tests.* Englewood Cliffs, N. J.: Prentice-Hall, 1968.

Gronlund, N. E. *Sociometry in the classroom.* New York: Harper & Row, 1959.

Gronlund, N. E. *Stating behavioral objectives for classroom instruction.* New York: Macmillan, 1970.

Helmstadter, G. C. *Principles of psychological measurement.* New York: Appleton-Century-Crofts, 1964.

Jenkins, J. R., & Deno, S. L. Assessing knowledge of concepts and principles. *Journal of Educational Meaurement,* 1971, *8,* 95-101.

McKie, T. D. M., & Foster, S. F. A general model for the multidimensional analysis of semantic differential attitude data. Paper presented at the American Psychological Association Annual Meeting, Honolulu, 1972.

Mager, R. *Preparing instructional objectives.* Palo Alto, Calif.: Fearon Publishers, 1962.

Mayo, S.T. Mastery learning and mastery testing. *NCME Measurement in Education,* 1970, *1.*

References

Osgood, C. E., Suci, G., & Tannenbaum, P. H. *The measurement of meaning.* Urbana: University of Illinois Press, 1957.

Popham, W. J., & Baker, E. L. *Systematic instruction.* Englewood Cliffs, N. J.: Prentice-Hall, 1970.

Scriven, M. The methodology of evaluation. In R. Stake (Ed.), *Perspectives of curriculum evaluation.* Chicago: Rand McNally, 1967.

Shaw, M. E., & Wright, J. M. Scales for the measurement of attitudes. New York: McGraw-Hill, 1967.

Zimbardo, P., & Ebbesen, E. B. *Influencing attitudes and changing behavior.* Reading, Mass.: Addison-Wesley, 1969.

Teacher-Influenced Learning Variables and Implications for Teaching

10

In the preceding chapters facts, concepts, and findings of psychological theory and research concerning human learning and instruction have been presented. In many cases tentative implications for teaching have emerged in the course of discussion. The purpose of this chapter is to summarize these implications in concise form. In most cases the recommendations listed herein will be best understood as a result of knowledge about the theory and research cited in previous chapters and knowledge about learners' frames of reference and the stages of planning for instruction.

Psychological theory and research have identified a variety of factors which can, singly or in combinations, affect school learning. Among these are some over which a teacher may have no actual control, such as heredity, early child rearing practices, prior school learnings, and out-of-school learning experiences. Other factors, such as physical health or emotional problems, are indirectly amenable to teacher influence since it is often the teacher who makes decisions regarding professional referrals. Of course, teachers can and should take cognizance of such circumstances and try to make wise use of such knowledge in coming to such decisions.

There are as well a number of variables affecting pupil learning which can be under the partial or direct control of teachers. The purpose of this chapter is to identify psychological principles associated with some of these teacher-influenced learning variables with a view toward encouraging the reader to draw specific implications for teaching.

It is hoped that the discussion which follows aids in the development of a rationale for certain actions which the teacher otherwise might take or possibly reject in many cases solely on an intuitive basis. Educational psychology is often criticized as composed largely of "common sense" notions. Often what is overlooked in making such a statement is that a key purpose of research activity is to put "common sense" to the test and try to determine the extent to which it is confirmed, denied, or modified by actual data. Also, one person's "common sense" is another person's "common nonsense." Thus it behooves one to take a careful look at human behavior by testing intuition and hunches with systematic theory and data evidence whenever possible. In all fairness to educational research, that which is labeled as "common sense" is often after-the-fact labeling. The person learns of the findings of the theory or research and only then terms the knowledge "common sense."

In this context, it should be emphasized that all data on the recommendations listed are "not in." These suggestions represent, then, a highly tentative set of statements reflecting the authors' interpretations of the current status of psychological work in terms of implications for educators. These principles and suggestions are grouped according to the outline of the five stages of planning instruction presented in chapter 1. The reader should recall that these stages are not mutually exclusive nor are they always distinct in actual practice. Rather, they represent one way to promote discussion, analysis, and interpretation of classroom teacher-learning processes.

Stage 1: Establishing Goals and Objectives

Unlike previous chapters of this book there are few references cited in this chapter for three reasons. First, the statements herein are likely to reflect the authors' biases as noted in the Preface and chapter 1 more directly than the details in the other eight chapters. Secondly, the key reference is this volume itself because, for each statement made herein, the research base (where such exists) for the principles and recommendations to follow has been discussed, or at least noted, in the body of the previous nine chapters. And finally the work of other authors (Bugelski, 1964; Hilgard & Bower, 1975; Klausmeier & Ripple, 1971; Seagoe, 1970; Stone, 1969; and Travers, 1972) in the areas of listing "what teachers can or should do in view of the findings of psychological theory and research" was also consulted in the preparation of this chapter. This is not to say that we either totally agree or disagree with these sources. In most cases we have modified, deleted, or added to their prescriptions from the point of view of our biases and our interpretations of the available data. However, we heartily encourage the reader to consult these other sources, as we have done, in an attempt to ascertain suggestions for more direct applications of the psychology of learning to teaching. It should be noted that at least one of these authors has suggested that subsequent authors try to do what we have attempted here, namely to modify and extend the guidelines.

The remarks and suggestions which follow should be read critically with the reader always asking: "What research or theory base would support opposing or conflicting viewpoints?" and "Does *my experience* tend to confirm or deny the statement?"

Stage 1: Establishing Goals and Objectives

In recent years much has been written on the subject of instructional objectives. As stated in chapter 9, probably the main advantage to objectives involves teachers and pupils clarifying their intentions for their course in terms of fairly specific learning outcomes.

There are potentially important motivational advantages to recognizing and incorporating pupil needs and interests into objectives. Likewise, encouraging students to set their own standards cooperatively with their teacher ensures that the objectives are well understood by teacher and pupils alike.

There are potential affective consequences of honest pupil-teacher participation which should not be overlooked in planning instructional activities. Perhaps, the learning of self-confidence and self-respect and the transfer of such aspects of pupil self-concept to other situations, academic and out-of-school, are chief among such affective potentials.

Suggestions for Stage 1

In advance of "planned" learning experiences, teachers should:

1. Clarify the content of the course, unit, or topic in terms of categories of learning outcomes (general instructional objectives) within cognitive, affective, and, when appropriate, psychomotor domains of behavior. Descriptions of pupil-entering behaviors assist in defining appropriate learning outcomes (see stage 2). In other words, select and originate general instructional objectives which are appropriate to the pupils and the course of study involved, and provide for clear communication of the general objectives to all concerned. These general objectives should be stated in terms of classes of pupil behaviors (e.g., students will understand and apply principles in physics [such as Boyle's laws]).
2. Samples of outcomes (specific learning objectives and final test items), to be taken as evidence for the mastery of the general objectives in each of the performance domains which are identified under number 1, should be selected and devised in terms of:
   a) What can be determined about existing pupil abilities, needs, and interests (see stage 2 suggestions).
   b) The nature of potential transfer tasks in other courses and out-of-class activities.
   c) Opportunities for pupil participation in the determination of objectives and standards of mastery of such objectives.
3. Be prepared to modify instructional objectives when necessary and to allow for opportunities for serendipity to occur.
4. Look at these specific objectives (and test items) in terms of a table of specifications (using categories such as in Bloom's taxonomy) to ensure content validity with respect to the intentions of pupils, teachers, and school.
5. Evaluate general objectives for comprehensiveness, and evaluate specific objectives (and related test items) for fairness and representativeness. Is there the desired balance between lower and higher levels of learning? Have affective outcomes and psychomotor skills objectives received due consideration?

Stage 2: Assessing Pupil-Entering Behaviors and Resistance to Change

In light of the comments under stage 1 and the discussions in earlier chapters, the following guidelines are suggested. In advance of formal learning experiences, teachers should:

Stage 2: Assessing Pupil-Entering Behaviors and Resistance to Change

1. Assess pupil-entering behaviors. The assessment may be formal or informal, but assessment should be geared to ascertaining frame of reference details in what have been called the cognitive, affective, and, when appropriate, psychomotor domains of behavior.
   a) This may be so formal as to involve initial screening tests of prior achievement or may merely be an inspection of the objectives and course materials of prior courses of study and discussion with the teachers of the prior courses.
   b) Appraisal of pupil attitudes and interests toward (especially controversial) aspects of the subject matter may be involved here. Positive affect may enhance desired learnings whereas prior negative feelings may induce resistance to change.
2. Review possible learning activities and media, including audio visual and programmed aids, to determine the way in which different pupils may likely react and adapt to variations in these "environmental" aspects. Look for data on the effectiveness of published instructional programs and the degree to which they appear to meet the objectives which were selected and written in the stage 1 activity.
3. Using the instructional objectives at hand, plan and prepare the physical learning environment with a view to the possible effects on pupil performance of lighting, temperature, noise levels, and equipment needed.
4. Plan to carry out small systematic investigations on the effects of variations in environment and resources, factors on pupil learning and performance—in short, plan to collect comparative data for future decision making—through in-class research. Seek advice and cooperation from colleagues including those in nearby schools, colleges, and universities.
5. For future use in setting up behavioral contingencies, ask each student to list those privileges or activities the student regards as desirable and worth trying to get. Add to this list those things that you observe have "reinforcement value" for each student (teacher attention, peer approval, etc.).
6. Discipline. Classroom discipline problems have been dealt with from a learning psychology point of view (see Clarizio, 1971). Briefly, this approach advocates the following:
   a) For each student, clarify desirable behaviors (preferably ones which are incompatible with those identified under "b") which are "do-able" and desirable in the same settings as the undesirable behaviors listed under "b."

    b) For each individual student, identify those behaviors and classes of behaviors which are clearly undesirable and need to be extinguished.
    c) Over a period of time, record the "baseline" instances (by frequency, duration, or both) of the behaviors listed under "a" and "b" above to determine their relative degree of occurrence in the setting in question.
    d) Apply conditions whereby outcomes deemed desirable by the individual students in question are immediately contingent upon doing "a" behaviors but not "b" behaviors. This may involve "contracting" with individual students on a "for value received" basis.
    e) Recheck the relative frequency and duration of "a" and "b" behaviors after the "d" conditions have been applied for varying lengths of time.
    f) Revise the conditions as appropriate to changes in what individual students regard as desirable outcomes, and in view of changes (or lack thereof) in behaviors as a result of applying the discipline conditions.

7. Punishment effects have been extensively studied by psychologists. In general, punishment is not effective in controlling behavior over a long term. Punishment, or the threat of it, may serve temporarily to prevent some behaviors from occurring. In any situation consider what are the nonaversive alternatives to punishment.

8. Since punishment evokes negative affective responses, a danger to its use is that negative attitudes may become conditioned to aspects of the setting wherein the punishment takes place. Such attitude conditioning and generalization takes place without the awareness or intention of the participants, and may serve to mediate other undesirable behaviors.

9. Punishment, if used at all, must be carefully dealt with and it should be very clear to the participants that it is a *specific bevavior* that is being punished.

10. The social learning implications of punishment should be considered. Is the net effect to increase the status of the transgressor or the transgression among the students? Does the person doing the punishment become more feared than respected thereby? Are the transgression and punishment so separated in space and time that the connection is unclear to the participants? And finally, does the institutionalization of punishment thereby sanction interpersonal violence and even teach students techniques of violence?

Stage 3: Selecting and Organizing Learning Experiences

In light of the activities of the first two stages, selection and organization of actual learning activities receive direction for effective learning. Choices can no longer be made merely on a basis of what the teacher likes to do, or what curriculum or school authorities direct should be done, but also upon expert teacher judgments of which activities and experiences best promote student growth toward attainment of desired objectives. These institutional sanctions become modified in consideration of the actual characteristics of the pupils. Individual pupil differences have a very large impact at this stage of planning for instruction.

A Piagetian analysis of how the individual students differ in cognitive developmental stages may be of value in decision making at this stage. Likewise Gagné's analysis of personal learning hierarchies, especially in the cases of students who have exhibited either exceptionally strong or poor performance in past lessons, may aid in both the setting of objectives and design of instructional strategies by the teacher.

Issues which concern motivation, retention, and transfer of learning also become increasingly important in decision making at this stage of instructional planning. The following suggestions for teachers are in connection with stage three.

Suggestions Regarding Motivation

1. Seek the active participation of students in devising and organizing learning experiences.
2. Decide which course goals are most appropriate to which students in terms of prior learning experiences.
3. Provide for variations in pupil motivation and interests by selecting learning tasks at a variety of difficulty levels and interest areas.
4. Develop and identify tasks which provide for the application of the learnings in real life situations.
5. Organize activities so that each student will derive satisfaction (positive reinforcement) from the results of his/her work.

Suggestions Regarding Retention

1. Provide for *structurability, generalizability, meaningfulness, codability, familiarity,* and *imagability*. (You may wish to review the section on memory in chapter 5.) The teacher should

stimulate the student to organize material. The student should be encouraged to spend as much time and energy organizing the material as in any other learning activity. The accent must always be upon active organizing and processing. Individual peer or cross-age tutoring should aid processing when there are special problems to be overcome.

2. Anticipate the occurrence of forgetting, and decide which learning should be in relatively permanent long-term storage and which can be learned and forgotten with the view that relearning, when required, will be more efficient (savings method).
3. Provide for *overlearning* to promote long-term retention of those behaviors identified in advance as desirable in long-term memory.
4. Space practice periods and have alternative activities available for use before fatigue or "negativism" sets in.
5. Identify possible sources of *proactive* and *retroactive interference*. Try to help students learn key distinctions at a conceptual level between potentially interfering learnings. Some students will need more help than others; some will need little at all in acquiring key distinctions. Individual differences may be largely due to differences in motivation levels and in prior learnings and peer or cross-age tutoring could be used to advantage in some cases.

Suggestions Regarding Transfer

1. a) When a student is having trouble learning new material, it may be that prior learnings are responsible (negative transfer). Try to identify if there is response competition (i.e., if the desired learning competes with previously acquired responses).
   b) When a student is having trouble learning new material, it may be due to the absence of necessary prior learnings. Try to identify prerequisite and subordinate skills necessary for learning any new task and provide appropriate remedial instruction. Construct a learning hierarchy for any especially difficult task.
2. Identical elements between two tasks should provide for positive transfer. Where identical elements appear to exist, but transfer does not, it is likely that students "see" the situation differently than does their teacher. Soliciting and listening to student views can help to bridge this gap in private worlds or frames of reference.

3. Organize the learning tasks to be as much like the transfer tasks as possible; point out, and ask students to point out, possible areas of transfer for any task or class of tasks. Mere naming of transfer possibilities often is not sufficiently involving to encourage transfer and motivation (see number 4).
4. Principles, rules, and concepts provide for more transfer than does rote memorization of facts. Develop alternative ways of organizing facts. Develop alternative ways of "conceptualizing" the desired learnings. Concepts which "make sense" to teachers often are obscure to students who are operating from different frames of reference and possible different developmental levels. Clear communication with and respect for one's students helps to characterize ideas in modes meaningful to them.
5. Try to develop "advance organizers" for unfamiliar but potentially meaningful subject matter. Psychological meaningfulness (to the student) promotes acquisition, transfer, and retention. An advance organizer provides a learner with information which helps to place new experiences into personal perspectives.
6. Emphasize *process* in problem solving, not only *product* or correct solutions. Ways of generating solutions may be as or more important to transfer than are "correct" solutions. Understanding *why* a procedure *is* appropriate and the application of that procedure may be an outcome more desirable than finding the sanctioned answer to a problem.
7. Ensure meaningful learning by active student processing, organizing, and verbalizing. Proper feedback should be provided to the student on the appropriateness of his/her organizations. Highly organized meaningful material is resistant to interference effects. Note and use structures which students employ.

Stage 4: Guiding the Learning Process in the Classroom

There are several categories of comments and suggestions to teachers which are appropriate to this stage of planning for instruction, and these are listed here in outline form. These are tentative lists of points which seem to be indicated by psychological theory and research cited in previous chapters.

Suggestions Concerning Concept Formation and Problem Solving

1. Teachers should develop alternative ways of conceptualizing the ideas of the subject matter of their courses. At the very least, this amounts to having different ways to explain the same idea. Reliance upon a single set of instances or characterization of a concept may reduce the task to mere rote learning for some students. They will repeat the words that the text or teacher used in describing the concept with little understanding beyond the verbal chain of responses as given.
2. Material learned by rote is at a low level of meaningfulness for the learner. Since efficiency of learning and retention increases with meaningfulness, any time and effort expended by teachers in "conceptualizing" their subject matter should be returned in savings of subsequent work to remediate learning difficulties.
3. In line with the statement above, pupils may be expected to differ widely in their entering conceptual structures. Differences in prior learning experiences will affect the difficulty level of concept learning tasks. Levels of conceptual development (see the discussion of Piaget's work in chapter 6) may be expected to vary among students.
4. Teachers should select learning experiences at varying levels of difficulty, complexity, and abstraction in order to match the variety of student individual differences as noted above.
5. One's students may be excellent sources of ideas for the development of concepts out of the "facts" of a course since they are the ones for whom meaningfulness of content is the object. Teachers should encourage students to devise and present new combinations and applications of ideas.
6. In contrast with the rote learning of instances or names of concepts, learning a concept enhances positive transfer to new problem-solving tasks and provides increased ability to generate and apply rules out of combinations of concepts. While both outcomes may be desirable objectives, teachers should not confuse concept naming (or identification) with application.
7. Problem-solving processes may be analyzed into sequences. While it is true that the stages of a sequence are "telescoped" in most actual situations, troubles in problem solving can often be traced to one of the stages in a sequence being missed or slighted.
8. Much "important" learning takes place in the context of problem solving. The challenge presented by a problem may have positive incentive value. Too great a challenge could be

Stage 4: Guiding the Learning Process in the Classroom

perceived as threatening by the learner. Students who differ in achievement motivation respond to the "same" problem with different degrees of "challenge."
9. Transfer of learning also takes place or fails to occur in terms of problem solving, especially when "problem solving" is defined broadly so as to include personal and social problems. There seems to be a clear need for problem-oriented courses of study at all levels of education.
10. Do some students need to experience repeated failure at school tasks, as some would argue, in order to learn to accept the inevitability of some failure later in life? Or do all students need to develop a sense of personal competence and mastery over a broad range of skills thereby acquiring a positive self-image and high self-acceptance?

Suggestions to Teachers Concerning Pupil Creativity

1. Creativity frequently involves problem solving and some of the most vexing problems would seem to call for creative approaches. It has been said that while not all problem solving involves creativity, creativity invariably involves problem solving.
2. Creativity may be approached in a variety of ways (e.g., as fluency, flexibility, originality, and elaboration in problem solving) which apply in differing degrees to all educational subject areas and grade levels.
3. One way to characterize creativity is in terms of divergent thinking or problem-solving *processes*. An examination of *products*—the results of problem solving—leads to an inference that creative process has occurred.
4. Creativity on the part of a teacher may encourage pupils to perform more creatively through the social learning principles of *imitation* and *modeling*.
5. *Evaluation* is an important aspect of creativity. There are times when it is important for one to suspend judgment during creative production. Later, it is often desirable to make judgments of evaluation about products in terms of quantity, originality, usefulness, or pleasingness.
6. Respect for unusual questions or imaginative ideas of pupils may encourage creativity. Teacher unfamiliarity with a topic is by itself insufficient justification for exclusion from class consideration of that topic.
7. Individual projects, especially involving topics suggested or selected by students, can promote creativity. Such projects may depart from given specific objectives while remaining consistent with general instructional objectives.

8. Emphasis upon problems which can be solved by a variety of procedures or which can have more than one answer calls for divergent production on the part of students as does emphasis on the quality of the process of problem resolution (rather than upon a single "correct" answer).
9. School and classroom rewards systems can be set up so as to encourage originality on the part of both teachers and students. Deviance *per se* is not always undesirable. Many great achievements of human civilization are products of "deviant" behavior.
10. High creativity and high intelligence are not incompatible nor are they always strongly associated. At least some different processes or process combinations are involved in each, and these may be selectively encouraged or discouraged by school experiences.
11. Creative self-direction can be considered to be a characteristic of the highest levels of human functioning in terms of motivation and learning. Capacity for creative behavior exists in all persons and may be encouraged or stifled by school experiences.

Suggestions to Teachers Concerning Individual Differences

1. Every person—child, woman, and man—has a private world based upon his/her unique learning history and genetic inheritance. As such, everyone has a different repertoire of language, quantitative and physical skills, attitudes, values, and outlooks. There can be no two identical frames of reference.
2. Any group of students which is selected so as to be relatively homogeneous in *ability* can be expected to be more heterogeneous in terms of another characteristic, for example, *motivation*. (One may substitute any of a variety of pairs of psychological concepts in the foregoing statement—for example, intelligence and creativity, achievement and attitude, needs and values—and draw similar conclusions.)
3. An overall goal of education need not be to minimize the range of individual differences, but to promote optimum personal growth and development.
4. Many of the key differences that can be observed in school work can be stated in terms of time or speed of individual functioning. People differ widely in the amount of time taken to learn to perform a given task. Prior learnings, motivational

Stage 4: Guiding the Learning Process in the Classroom

level, task aptitude, general ability, quality of instruction, and opportunities available all affect time needed and actually spent on any task and hence task mastery.

5. One approach to individual differences which attempts to make provisions for time or speed differences is *mastery learning.* This view involves the student factors of task aptitude, ability to understand instruction, perseverance, and the "environmental" factors of quality of instruction and (time) opportunity to learn. Although this idea is controversial (most approaches to individual differences in learning seem to be subject to considerable controversy), even critics concede that it is at least appropriate at the "training" levels of education. Strategies based upon mastery learning may well prove useful to teachers to promote achievement and positive affective outcomes in a variety of subject matter areas and levels.

6. Another approach to individual differences is programmed instruction. Programmed instruction provides an opportunity for teachers to achieve new degrees of clarity concerning descriptions of student behavior patterns related to achievement both before and after (successful) completion of a course of study. Well-written programs appear to facilitate learning as well as do good books, lectures, or films.

7. Programmed instruction is neither intended nor likely to replace teachers. Rather, it represents another medium of communication of subject matter content, one which attempts to account for differences in rate of responding more than does lecture or film format media. Programmed instruction, like mastery learning, is at least appropriate at training levels of education.

8. Open education is a broad category term for approaches to pupil individual differences which involve such ideas as replacing the traditional self-contained classroom with a continuous-progress, activity-centered, flexibly scheduled and flexibly constructed arrangement. Perhaps the least researched of the three approaches to individual differences noted here, open education is no less controversial an idea. This approach appears to allow for flexible "ability groupings" which can be altered within a class area for each subject matter and student, as required. As such it may be an improvement over previous approaches of ability grouping between classrooms which may have had deleterious effects on pupils' self-concepts of ability. Needless to say, further inves-

Teacher-Influenced Learning Variables and Implications for Teaching

tigation is required to define more adequately what is meant by open education and to identify and investigate its strengths and weaknesses.
9. Teachers should consider the possible advantages to grouping students homogeneously by learning style and encouraging peer-tutoring.
10. Teacher and student personality factors may determine which approach to individual differences succeeds in a given situation.

Suggestions to Teachers Concerning Pupil Attitudes
1. Attitudes are learned—in the same ways and at the same times as are facts, skills, beliefs, concepts, and rules.
2. Simple conditioning by *contiguity* may account for much of attitude learning. Operant conditioning with mediation, concept learning, and social learning principles may also be used to describe school attitude learning phenomena, and should be considered in planning and carrying out instruction.
3. Teachers should not teach subjects that they do not themselves like or in which they do not believe themselves to be competent. Students will tend to learn the preference responses modeled for them by their teachers, their parents, and their peers.
4. Social learning theory suggests the importance of *imitation* and *modeling* of behaviors related to evaluations of subject and self in student attitude learning. Whereas formal skill learning may technically qualify a student for advanced studies, the incidental learning of positive or negative attitudes may ensure that he will actively seek or avoid advanced work with diligence.
5. Attitudes (learned covert evaluative behaviors) are not always strongly related to overt cognitive behaviors (which give rise to academic achievement). This is true because attitudes may be considered to be only one of many factors which mediate overt behavior. That is to say that two persons may (theoretically) hold identical attitudes and exhibit very diverse overt behaviors because of differences in other prior learning. Conversely, two persons may exhibit highly similar responses in a situation, but may at the same time hold markedly differing attitudes.
6. When it is the case that attitudes are strongly related to overt behaviors, attitudes may serve to facilitate or impede related learning.

Stage 4: Guiding the Learning Process in the Classroom

7. Attitudes are related to motivation in that persons who exhibit positive attitudes toward an object also tend to exhibit approach and persistence behaviors toward that object. Likewise negative attitudes tend to mediate avoidance behaviors. Such approach, persistence, or avoidance behaviors may be taken as an index of attitudes.
8. Teachers should consider evaluating their teaching by grading their work on the basis of the attitudes pupils learn in their classes.
9. Self-regarding attitudes, especially self-concept, of academic ability are learned and may be originated and changed by school experiences.
10. Most attitude learning in schools, indeed most attitude learning, takes place without the awareness of the learner or the teacher.
11. Although "attitude" is a hypothetical construct, it can be approached in terms of evaluations of belief statements made about an attitude object. It is thus possible, through careful measurement techniques, to index attitudes.

Suggestions Concerning Values

1. Values may be considered to be products of learning experiences.
2. Values can be characterized as enduring evaluations of the desirability of classes of behaviors or events. As such, values are like conceptualized attitudes.
3. Research has indicated that for major shifts in attitudes to occur, changes in one's value system may be necessary.
4. Values may be considered to function as guidelines by which to judge the behaviors of oneself and others.
5. Students can be taught to distinguish factual and value claims, and to reason more clearly about value issues.
6. A goal of public education might be that students grow toward moral maturity whereby judgments and actions are based upon "universal" principles of equality, fairness, and justice.
7. As in the case of conceptual development, students in any class are likely to exhibit a range of levels of moral development differing from one another and from their teachers.
8. As in the case of attitude learning, there can be no such thing as "value-free" curriculum or teaching. Attitudes and value assumptions exist in varying degrees of explicitness throughout education and indeed all of human experience.

9. Values can be indexed or inferred by measurement techniques such as those that involve rank ordering or choosing between competing value statements and justifications for behaviors.
10. Given the proposition: All well-educated persons are intellectually and morally mature—educators should examine their positions with regard to attitude and value learning.

Stage 5: Evaluating Pupil Outcomes

Entire courses of study have been developed to provide teachers with procedures for the measurement and evaluation of pupil outcomes. Our best suggestion is to enroll in and complete one and to read one or more of the references for chapter 9. Since measurement and evaluation deal with individual differences, they have always been controversial areas in education. But perhaps it could be said that one way to judge the importance of something is to observe how much controversy it has generated. In formal education, learning is often inferred from test scores. Attitudes, values, and social group structure can also be indexed by scores on instruments—thus the importance of careful test development and interpretation cannot be overemphasized.

Comments and Suggestions to Teachers on Measurement and Evaluation

1. Teachers should be prepared to apply measurement and evaluation techniques in all stages of instruction, wherever data may help to improve educational decision making.
2. Users of test data should bear in mind that test scores are merely *numbers* which represent samples of behavior in a certain situation. As such they are never error-free, but they frequently can be useful when taken with other information for educational decision-making purposes.
3. The difficult task of measuring and evaluating pupil learning can be facilitated by having a clear and comprehensive set of general instructional objectives which are stated in terms of classes or categories of pupil behaviors.
4. Further help in assessing student learning can be obtained through the use of a fairly large pool of specific, understandable, instructional objectives which are stated in terms of actual student behaviors.
5. A test item pool can be constructed which is based upon one or more items for each specific objective. Tests can then be constructed by sampling items from the pool for both summative and formative evaluation purposes.

Stage 5: Evaluating Pupil Outcomes

6. Test items can be improved in accordance with standard techniques of item analysis.
7. For any test a *table of specifications* can be set up which clearly shows the number and type of items in each topic category and the number of items at each level of the cognitive, affective, and psychomotor domains of behavior. This promotes *content validity* and honesty in classroom testing.
8. There are a variety of test item types which can be employed in assessing student performance. Types should be selected with a view to appropriateness of the item format to the specific objectives, and keeping measurement (and scoring) errors low.
9. The taxonomies of educational objectives were designed to assist educators in test construction. Individual items bear a one-to-one correspondence with specific instructional objectives and as such can be classified in taxonomic categories.
10. "Contract" grading may be tried as a form of summative evaluation based upon criterion-referenced assessment. In this approach, each student agrees with the teacher to complete specified work under conditions and up to standards which are mutually agreed upon in order to qualify for a certain mark. Each possible mark can be associated with a stipulated amount and quality of performance.
11. Formative (monitoring) evaluations can be performed at periodic intervals to assess student progress and teaching success. On the basis of these results, student and teacher decisions can be made as to which topics need more study or teaching time, and when to go on to the next area.
12. Summative or final evaluations can be made on the basis of a representative sample of test performance in each of the categories of the table of specifications. These may be used to establish final marks.
13. Aspects of pupil behavior other than course achievement can be indexed through the application of measurement techniques when there are sound reasons for doing so. Attitudes, values, and group social structure can be assessed for educational decision-making purposes.
14. Teachers should recognize that informal evaluation techniques are the most frequently used in education. Concern for reliability and validity of judgments in informal evaluation is no less important than is the case with more formal methods.
15. School psychologists and other specially trained personnel can be called upon to administer diagnostic tests of learning

ability and disability in special cases where such data may be needed.
16. Standardized tests, however well developed, do not yield error-free scores. Data from such tests may be useful taken together with information from other sources. Recommendations for individual students should be made with the greatest caution when test scores are the principal source of data.
17. Most school systems, colleges, and universities have measurement and evaluation specialists who can consult with practicing educators on practical problems. Often, such personnel are available for workshops and other in-service training activities.

Summary

In this chapter we have attempted to make partial and tentative comments and suggestions to teachers based upon existing knowledge and strong inference in educational psychology. Perhaps the strongest body of evidence in the psychological literature lies in an area of least concern to modern educators, factors affecting the acquisition and retention of simple unitary responses in highly controlled situations. The areas of greatest speculation and "softest" data in psychology are often those of greatest potential concern to educators—factors affecting attitudes, values, creativity, and individual differences.

It is clear to us that a high priority needs to be placed upon continued educational research, especially in the areas concerning the social context in which learning occurs. As psychologists continue to study conditions affecting learning and performance within the confines of the experimental laboratory, educational research is also required into conditions affecting learning and resistance to change in real-life situations. An important development in this area is the increased interest among teachers in research and experimentation in the schools. Even as researchers can profit from an increased orientation toward problems in teaching, so may teachers profit from an experimental outlook and research activities with their schools.

It is our hope that present and future generations of teachers will receive encouragement (and experience) in reading the growing research literature, and in contributing to it through the design and execution of "action" studies in their own schools.

Discussion Questions

1. Which of the suggestions for teachers do you find to be the most practical? Which the most idealistic?
2. In terms of research evidence, which suggestions do you take to be the most solidly supported? Which the most speculative or open to doubt?
3. Do you find any suggestions that flatly contradict your experiences or best hunches? Can you design a study to "get at" the better explanation?
4. In which stage of planning for instruction do you feel most capable right now? In which stage least capable?
5. If you were asked to help to decide on the funding of a major research project in school learning, which issue(s) do you believe should receive the highest priorities?
6. Can you provide additional suggestions to teachers for the tentative list supplied in this chapter.
7. Comment on the statement, "Many of the best teachers intuitively do the things recommended in education courses even if they haven't taken the course." What ways can "taking the course" or "reading the book" help or hinder one's teaching activities?
8. In your own words, describe the five stages of planning for instruction and some characteristics of each one.
9. In your own words describe the frame of reference concept and its importance to educators.

References and Recommended Readings

Bigge, M. L. *Learning theories for teachers.* (2nd ed.) New York: Harper & Row, 1971.

Bugelski, B. R. *The psychology of learning applied to teaching.* Indianapolis: Bobbs-Merrill, 1964 & 1971.

Clarizio, H. F. *Toward positive classroom discipline.* New York: Wiley & Sons, 1971.

Drew, C. J. Research on the psychological-behavioral effects of the physical environment. *Review of Educational Research,* 1971, *41,* 447-66.

Hilgard, E. R., & Bower, G. H. *Theories of learning.* (4th ed.) Englewood Cliffs, N. J.: Prentice-Hall, 1975.

Klausmeier, H. J., & Ripple, R. E. *Learning and human abilities.* (3rd ed.) New York: Harper & Row, 1971.

Seagoe, M. V. *The learning process and school practice.* Scranton, Pa.: Chandler, 1970.

Stone, D. R. *Are psychological principles useful?* Logan, Utah: Utah State University, 1969.

Travers, R. M. W. *Essentials of learning.* (3rd ed.) New York: Macmillan, 1972.

Wilson, J. A. R., Robeck, M., & Michael, W. B. *Psychological foundations of learning and teaching.* (2nd ed.) New York: McGraw-Hill, 1974.

Glossary

The glossary of terms given below is intended to assist the reader in using this book and in reading the educational psychological literature cited herein. It is not possible to include every term which might cause a reader difficulty nor to give complete dictionary definitions for each term. The reader is encouraged to consult standard reference works such as Drever (1966) or English and English (1958) for technical terms not given here or the *Oxford English Dictionary* or *Webster's New Collegiate Dictionary* for nontechnical words. Unfortunately, the same term is often used in the literature to mean different things. We have tried to reflect the most commonly accepted meanings which are consistent with the way in which the terms are used in this book.

Ability What an individual can do in some skill area, e.g., verbal ability, quantitative ability. Broader than **Aptitude**. (See also **Capacity**)

Ability Grouping An educational practice whereby students are separated and brought together for instruction according to similar scores on ability tests.

Ability Tests Measurement devices to determine what an individual can do within a given skill area. (See also **Aptitude Tests**)

Accountability Refers to the justification, usually to the public or to some authority, of the existence and actions of institutions or activities. In education it is often taken to be support for the proposition that funds are expended in ways which promote worthwhile student learning outcomes.

Affect Refers to feeling or emotion (as contrasted to cognition).

Affective Objectives Statements of how students' feelings, attitudes, or values should change as a consequence of instruction.

Anxiety Motivational state of arousal typified by an excited, uneasy feeling and cognitive concern. (Typically less specific than fear.)

Aptitude Capability for a task or type of skill. Usually a narrower term than **Ability**. In mastery learning terms, the time an individual requires to perform a specified task.

Aptitude by Treatment Interaction (Sometimes called *trait* or *person X treatment interaction*.) The finding that the same experience (treatment) has different effects on individuals depending upon how much of a certain characteristic (aptitude or trait) they possess.

Aptitude Tests Measurement devices used to determine how well an individual performs a set of related tasks. Results can be generalized across other tasks of the same type.

Associationism Systematic analysis of behavior from the point of view of links between events (e.g., stimulus–response associations).

Attitude Object The person, idea, event, or thing toward which one has learned positive or negative reactions.

Attitudes Learned predispositions to respond evaluatively (positively or negatively in degrees) to an object, event, person, or idea; covert evaluative behaviors; evaluative aspects or beliefs about an object.

Behavior What an individual actually does in any situation. *Overt behavior* is directly observed or measured, *covert behavior* is inferred or indexed from observations of actions but remains unobserved.

Behavior Modification Procedures of training or therapy which are based upon the principles of conditioning. *Precision teaching* is an educational form of behavior modification. (See also **Operant Conditioning**)

Behavioral Objectives Educational outcomes stated in terms of student behaviors. (See also **Instructional Objectives**)

Behaviorism A "school" of psychology in which major emphasis is placed upon external stimulation and its observable effects. Environment (including behavior) is the subject of study, and phenomena associated with *mental events* and *consciousness* are excluded from consideration.

Beliefs The ideas a person has learned concerning the existence or characteristics of another person, object, event, or idea.

Capacity The potential of an individual to develop ability. What one is potentially able to do or become.

Chaining The sequential association of two or more discrete responses such that each response becomes the stimulus for the next response.

Classical (Pavlovian or Respondent) Conditioning A learning procedure whereby a neutral event (conditioned stimulus) is paired in space and time with an unconditioned stimulus. The conditioned stimulus acquires the power to elicit a response normally only elicited by the unconditioned stimulus. In effect, a substitution of one stimulus (CS) for the usual one (UCS) in eliciting or calling out a response. The response is termed an *unconditioned response* when it occurs naturally and a *conditioned response* when it has been elicited by the CS.

Cognition Mental processes such as thinking, problem solving, and concept learning; symbolic covert events.

Cognitive Activity of knowing, believing, remembering, reasoning, etc. Whereas *cognitive* refers to reason, *affective* refers to emotion.

Cognitive Dissonance A theory of attitude change and a concept advanced by Leon Festinger whereby a discrepancy between two attitudes or beliefs held by a person arouses motivation to change so as to remove or resolve the discrepancy.

Concept Refers to a class of things or events (a class of stimuli) sharing one or more common characteristics.

Concept Learning The acquisition of knowledge about a class of stimuli usually by generalization from particular instances wherein common characteristics are observed.

Conditioning Processes of associating discrete responses with stimuli. (See also **Classical Conditioning** and **Operant Conditioning**)

Construct An idea or concept which is created for the purpose of labeling and explaining observed events or relations among events (also called *hypothetical construct*).

Construct Validity The extent to which a test is successful in actually measuring or indexing a hypothetical entity which it is supposed to assess.

Content Validity The extent to which a test contains material which is appropriate to that which the test is supposed to measure. (*Face validity* is a related construct associated with the degree to which a test *looks* as if it measures that which it is intended to measure when it is examined visually).

Contiguity The condition whereby two or more events (e.g., stimuli, responses) occur together in space and/or time. (*Spatial contiguity, temporal contiguity,* and *spatio-temporal contiguity* are terms sometimes used.)

Control Group In an experiment, a group of subjects that is as similar as possible to the experimental group (ideally both groups are drawn at random from the same population), except that the control group either receives no treatment or receives the same treatment as the experimental group excluding one critical factor. Results of experimental and control groups are then compared to determine the effects of that crucial factor. Some experiments employ more than one experimental and control group to determine the effects of more than one factor or treatment singly and in combinations. (See also **Experimental Group, Dependent Variable(s), and Independent Variable(s)**)

Correlation The degree of association between two (or more) variables.

Correlation Coefficient A statistic which indexes the degree of relationship between two sets of paired scores representing variables. The value of a correlation coefficient expressing degree of linear association (e.g., a "Pearson product-moment correlation coefficient") may vary from +1.0 through 0.0 to -1.0. Statistical correlation does not imply a cause-and-effect relationship, and coefficients cannot be interpreted as percentages unless they are first squared.

Creativity A multivariate psychological construct describing original behavior. Creativity may be characterized by a large number of responses, a variety of response types, uniqueness of responses, or elaborateness.

Criterion (pl. **Criteria**) A standard or reference value used in judging performance.

Criterion-Related Validity The extent to which a test measures what it is alleged to measure as indicated by the correlation of test scores with some standard or reference measure.

Dependent Variable(s) The outcome(s) of an experiment, that which is expected to change as a result of the experimental manipulation, or the effects created by applying the **Independent Variable(s).**

Discovery Learning Refers to instructional procedures and learning events whereby the learner produces a response, conclusion, or generalization without the teacher providing it.

Discrimination Learning The acquisition of different responses to somewhat similar stimuli.

Distributed (Spaced) Practice A series of practice trials separated by periods of rest or unrelated activity, as opposed to massed practice.

Educational Objectives (See **Affective Objectives, Behavioral Objectives, and Instructional Objectives**)

Educational Psychology The branch of applied psychology wherein the theories and findings of the behavioral sciences are studied in the context of formal education. (Other branches of applied psychology include industrial psychology and clinical psychology.)

Entering Behaviors The skills and prior learnings which are relevant to a task which the learner brings to a learning situation.

Environment Events, objects, and persons external to an individual which form the context of experience (including the stimuli impinging upon persons and the overt responses made by individuals), as distinct from internal processes and stimuli and covert responses. (Some writers assign the term *internal environment* to these latter.)

Errors of Measurement (See **Reliability** and **Validity**)

Evaluation The assignment of worth or qualitative value to an activity, event, or outcome. (See also **Summative Evaluation** and **Formative Evaluation**)

Experimental Group In a controlled study, the group(s) given the treatment or condition, the effects of which are to be evaluated. (See also **Control Group, Dependent Variable(s), Independent Variable(s)**)

Extinction The reduction in strength or occurrence of a response following nonreinforcement of that response.

Formal Mental Discipline A term given to the theoretical position that the mind and its faculties can be strengthened through appropriate "exercise" by means of learning certain subjects (e.g., Greek, Latin, or mathematics).

Formative Evaluation Evaluation of performance for the purposes of improving instruction or determining areas of strength and weakness for enrichment or remedial instruction (sometimes referred to as *diagnostic evaluation* or *monitoring evaluation*). (See also **Summative Evaluation**)

Frame of Reference A term given to the central organization of a relativistic model of behavior. The totality of a person's psychological makeup including the six states-processes of affect, concepts, interests, needs, structures, and values which interact with an individual's basic processes to produce cognition and behavior, influencing sensation, perception, reasoning, and thinking.

Generalization The application of findings or perceptions to other situations. The tendency to behave consistently in similar situations. (See also **Response Generalization** and **Stimulus Generalization**)

Genetics The study and effects of genes in inheritance. In general, the study of characteristics which are inherited rather than learned.

Gestalt Psychology A "school" of psychology in which major emphasis is placed upon organization and perception; and a de-emphasis upon simple cause-effect relations and "unnecessary fragmentation" of behavior (from the German word *Gestalt* meaning *form* or *shape*).

Habit Strength A term used to describe the likelihood or probability that a certain response will occur to a given stimulus.

Humanistic Psychology A "school" of psychology in which major emphasis is placed upon the importance and value of humanity in general and each human being in particular; tends to be transactional and wholistic rather than viewing the person as being reactive and behavior as atomistic.

Hypothesis A guess or tentative conclusion which is drawn from experience or **Theory**, often expressed in the form *if X, then Y*, and tested by means of experimentation. A *research hypothesis* states a specific prediction, whereas a **Null Hypothesis** is the contrasting prediction, typically "no difference" or "no change," or that results are the product of chance.

Imitation Behaving in the manner of another individual by copying or reproducing the other's behavior.

Incentive An external stimulus to action, a potential reinforcement for a specific behavior. (Some authors refer to *extrinsic motivation*.)

Incidental Learning Facts, concepts, or skills acquired as by-products in the process of intentional learning. Attitudes and study skills are typically incidental learnings in education.

Independent Variable(s) Factors which are manipulated in an experiment to determine the effect(s) of such manipulation. (See also **Experimental Group**)

Insight The apparently sudden perception of a relationship between elements in a problem-solving situation. In **Gestalt Psychology** a key part of learning by means of perceptual reorganization.

Instructional Objectives Statements of the desired outcomes of teaching, typically in terms of student behaviors which are acquired or changed through learning.
  General Statements concerning classes or categories of student behaviors which are intended to change as a result of teaching.
  Specific Statements of particular student behaviors which will result from successful teaching (See examples in text.)

Intelligence The abilities an individual has to cope with his/her environment and to learn from it; general level of cognitive ability; as such there are both learned and inherited aspects of intelligence.

Interests That part of an individual's frame of reference characterized by specific positive attitudes implying choice or seeking behaviors.

Intervening Variable(s) Constructs which are postulated to link or mediate between stimuli and overt responses or between **Independent** and **Dependent Variables.**

Ipsative Measurement The assessment of a profile or pattern of characteristics of an individual as contrasted to the normative (nomothetic) comparison with the characteristics of others. (Some authors use the term *ideographic*.)

Item Analysis Procedures for determining the characteristics and effectiveness of units of a test, typically including item difficulty and discrimination indices, and (in the case of recognition or selection items) effectiveness of distractors. Used to improve the **Reliability** of tests.

Learning Processes through which behavior or the capacity for behavior changes relatively permanently with experience, but excluding changes which are due exclusively to maturation, fatigue, or illness. Since the behavioral change is relatively permanent, changes in one's neurophysiology are implied.

Learning Hierarchy The pattern of intellectual and/or psychomotor skills for any task which are prerequisite to performing that task. Mastery of skills at any level implies mastery of lower skills and permits successful learning of tasks at the next higher level. (See also **Vertical Transfer**)

Learning to Learn Progressive improvement in time taken to learn new tasks as a function of having already learned related tasks. (See also **Positive Transfer**)

Level of Aspiration An individual's expectation for success for any task, or the quality of a goal which an individual desires to attain.

Massed Practice Sequence of practice trials on a task arranged in close temporal-continuity, i.e., without interpolated periods of rest or unrelated activity.

Mastery Learning An instructional approach to individual differences which emphasizes *time* in quantifying variables. Five key variables are taken in combination to predict degree of learning for any task. (See text.)

Mean The arithmetic average of a series of numbers (or scores) obtained by first summing the scores and then dividing by their number (the number of cases).

Meaningfulness The properties of stimuli which enable individuals to make sense out of them; as distinct from familiarity which is based upon mere prior acquaintance with the stimuli.

Measurement Procedures for determining (or indexing) the amount or quantity of some construct or entity; as contrasted with **Evaluation** which concerns qualitative specification.

Median The midpoint of a set of scores. That point above and below which an equal number of scores (observations) falls.

Mediation The process(es) by which individuals covertly link stimuli and overt responses. *Mediating responses* are hypothetical constructs used to explain correlation between observed stimuli and observed responses.

Memory The retention of experiences or material learned from experience.

    Long-Term Memory The relatively permanent storage of information, neurologically, in a fashion that renders it relatively accessible.

    Short-Term Memory The relatively brief (less than three seconds) storage of items which are forgotten almost immediately.

Mode The most frequently occurring score of a set of scores.

Model A representation, simplification, or simulation of events; a person who demonstrates (wittingly or not) behavior for **Imitation.**

Modeling Processes whereby a learner acquires response capability or behavioral potential by observation of a **Model** performing that behavior. (See also **No-Trial Learning**)

Motivation Internal processes which energize, direct, and sustain behavior. (Some authors use the term *intrinsic motivation*.) (See also **Incentive** and **Reinforcement**)

Motor Skills Learning (See **Psychomotor Skills Learning**)

Need(s) A motivational part of an individual's frame of reference implying a lack (or requirement) which if unfulfilled leads to frustration; if fulfilled (at least partially) leads to goal attainment and satisfaction.

    Basic Physiological requirements for survival (e.g., hunger, thirst, shelter).

    Secondary Psychological and acquired requirements for survival. (See text.)

Negative Transfer The condition where one learning makes acquisition of another learning more difficult, as contrasted with **Positive Transfer** and distinct from **Proactive Interference.**

Norm Typical performance or levels of a characteristic determined by assessment of a large representative sample of individuals.

Normal Curve The symmetrical graphic representation of a distribution of scores wherein a few cases (observations) lie at either extreme and the majority of cases cluster at the center. (Some authors refer to *bell-shaped* curve or *Gaussian* distribution.)

No-Trial Learning The acquisition of a response or behavior pattern without benefit of original practice (mental rehearsal of images may be presumed) as in learning by **Imitation** and **Modeling**. (Some authors refer to *latent learning*.)

Null Hypothesis (See **Hypothesis**)

Objectively-Scored Tests Tests composed of items (e.g., multiple-choice, true-false, matching) which are scored by means of a pre-established key; typically employing "recognition" type items. (Misleadingly referred to as *objective tests*.)

Open Education Term applied to a variety of innovative alternatives to traditional schooling; typically including student-centered and nongraded classes.

Operant Conditioning Learning a stimulus-response association by means of contiguity and reinforcement, whereby a discrete response emitted by an organism in the presence of a stimuli is reinforced and thus tends to re-occur when the same or similar stimuli are presented again.

Overlearning The experience of practicing a skill or task beyond the amount needed to learn it; associated with the long-term recall and resistance to extinction of the behavior.

Perception The processes by which sensations are received, transduced, and transmitted for impact or storage in the nervous system.

Performance The doing of a skill or task after it has been learned—as distinct from original **Learning** or skill acquisition.

Personality The dynamic organization of an individual's psychological and physiological systems serving to determine characteristic behavior and thought patterns; as such there are both learned and inherited aspects of personality.

Pleasure Principle A consistent tendency for behavior to be directed toward satisfaction of innate drives.

Positive Transfer The condition where one learning directly facilitates another; the acquisition of one response increasing the ease with which another response is acquired.

Premack Principle A given event or outcome may be used to reinforce some responses, but not others; any activity will reinforce only those activities of lower value and not those of higher value.

Proactive Interference Forgetting of a response due to the disrupting influence of something learned previously (before the forgotten response was initially learned).

Problem Solving The application of concepts, rules, or principles to the production of an answer to a question or resolution of a task, as distinct from mere recall of an answer or solution.

Programmed Instruction A manner of organizing learning materials into discrete units which require responses from each learner and provide feedback to the learner in terms of knowledge of results; typically a learner is relatively free to proceed through the units (frames) at his/her own pace.

Psychometrics The study of the development and use of statistical concepts in psychological testing and measurement.

Psychomotor Behavior Physical (muscle) movement.

Psychomotor Skills Learning Acquiring sequences of movement responses or the coordination of perceptual input with physical responses (also called *motor skills learning* and *perceptual motor learning*).

Punishment The administration of aversive stimulation.

Reinforcement The consequences of behavior which increase the likelihood of that behavior recurring under the same or similar circumstances; the production of increase in the strength or probability of a response as a result of the consequences of that response.

Negative The cessation of aversive stimulation contingent upon the performance of a given response, thereby producing an increase in the likelihood of that response recurring in similar situations.

Relativism A philosophical orientation affirming that events, objects, and characteristics are determined primarily by interactions, and transactions between events, objects, characteristics. Knowledge is determined out of interaction between the knower, the observational instruments, and the object of awareness.

Reliability The extent to which a test is consistent in measuring whatever it measures. Consistency is generally taken to be from one part of the test to another (internal consistency), or for the whole test from one time or occasion to another (stability).

Research Hypothesis (See **Hypothesis**)

Response A discrete unit of behavior.

Response Chain (See **Chaining**)

Response Generalization The likelihood that a related response will occur upon representation of a stimulus; the tendency for a stimulus to produce responses which are similar in some definable way(s) to any response which was earlier conditioned to that stimulus, especially if the initially learned response is inhibited or unavailable.

Response Latency The time lapse between presentation of the conditioned stimulus and the appearance of the conditioned response; or, more generally, an index of learning given by the time between onset of stimulus and onset of response.

Retroactive Interference Forgetting of a response due to disrupting influence of something which was learned since initial learning; (such learning occurring after the forgotten response was initially learned but before the situation where forgetting is noticed is called *interpolated learning*).

Schedules of Reinforcement Patterns for the presentation of response consequences organized according to time (interval), or rate (ratio), or both (mixed). (See text for description of major types.)

Secondary Reinforcement The process whereby an originally "neutral" stimulus acquires reinforcing properties through contiguous association with primary reinforcers (stimuli which satisfy basic needs of hunger, thirst, sex, etc.).

Self-Concept The aggregate of an individual's beliefs and attitudes about himself or herself as a person. (Related to concepts of *self-acceptance, self-esteem,* and *self-image.*)

Self-Concept of Ability Those beliefs and attitudes toward oneself in terms of one's skill or likely success at a type of task.

Set A predisposition to perceive or respond in a particular way.

Shaping (by Successive Approximations) Progressive alteration of behavior toward some desired goal (terminal behavior) by reinforcement of responses which occur in a sequence approaching that goal.

Significant Other An individual perceived as important, powerful, or of high status; someone to be emulated.

Social Learning Theory An approach to the study of behavior acquisition and performance whereby other individuals and their actions are taken as potentially important stimuli; an emphasis upon the social context of learning wherein **Imitation** and **Modeling** play key roles.

Spontaneous Recovery The re-occurrence of a response which had been extinguished or forgotten.

Stimulus (Pl. **Stimuli**) The sense impression impinging upon an organism.

Stimulus Generalization After conditioning has occurred, the tendency for stimuli which are similar to the original conditioned stimulus in definable way(s) to evoke the conditioned response. Typically, the greater the stimulus similarity, the more likely the response will be evoked, thus the greater the stimulus generalization.

Structures That part of the frame of reference consisting of organization of facts and knowledge.

Summative Evaluation Evaluation of instruction for the purposes of awarding final marks for the record. A statement of the degree to which a learner's terminal performance approximates that specified in the instructional objectives. (See **Formative Evaluation**)

Table of Specifications A means for organizing a set of specific instructional objectives or test items to assess the content validity of any test. A grid or matrix whereby each test item, specific objective, or point (out of a mark) is entered according to the topic it refers to and the type of learning it taps.

Test Reliability (See **Reliability**)

Test Validity (See **Validity**)

Theory A set of propositions which is organized according to logical rules and which serves to predict and explain observable phenomena.

Transfer of Learning The effect that one learning may have upon the acquisition of another. (See also **Negative Transfer, Positive Transfer,** and **Vertical Transfer**)

Validity The degree to which a test measures that which it is supposed to measure. (See also **Construct Validity, Content Validity,** and **Criterion-Related Validity**)

Value(s) A part of one's frame of reference comprising evaluative concepts abstracted from one's learned attitudes toward any action, event, or object of awareness. Moral values are those which relate directly to the rights of oneself or others.

Vertical Transfer The condition where learning at one level of abstraction or complexity facilitates learning at other levels (usually where simple learning, e.g., facts, aids in more complex learning, e.g., concepts).

References

Drever, J. *A dictionary of psychology.* (Rev. Ed.) Harmondsworth: Penguin, 1966.

English, H. B., & English, A. C. *A comprehensive dictionary of psychological and psychoanalytical terms: A guide to usage.* London: Longmans, Green, 1958.

Author Index

Adams, J. A., 115, 116, 120, 133, 143, 168
Ahmann, J. S., 255
Alampay, D. A., 63, 84
Alessi, S. M., 197
Allport, G. W., 9, 16, 73, 83, 202, 226
Anderson, R. C., 67, 83, 120, 121, 133, 182, 186, 188, 190, 197
Anderson, R. H., 190, 198
Anderson, T. H., 89, 142, 186, 197, 218, 229
Archer, E. J., 157, 168
Aristotle, 142
Aronfreed, J., 105, 108
Asch, S., 80, 83, 120, 133
Ashby, W. R., 118, 133
Asher, S. R., 98, 108
Ashley, W. R., 72, 83
Atkin, J. M., 244, 256
Atkinson, R. C., 117, 135
Atkinson, S. W., 74, 83, 87, 96, 108
Austin, G. A., 129, 133, 158, 168
Ausubel, D. P., 36, 38, 39, 40, 41, 49, 50, 63, 64, 84, 103, 109, 121, 132
Aylesworth, T. G., 160, 168

Backman, C. W., 225
Bagby, J. W., 62, 84
Bain, A., 142, 168
Bakan, P., 132
Baker, E. L., 50, 257
Ballachey, E. L., 203, 227
Bandura, A., 34, 50, 104, 105, 106, 108, 109, 120, 133, 204, 205, 211, 215, 216, 217, 226
Barron, F., 165, 166, 168
Bartlett, F. C., 119, 133
Barker, L. L., 198
Beadle, M., 167
Beard, R. M., 167
Becker, W. C., 108
Beier, E. G., 69, 85
Bem, D. J., 225
Bennett, E. L., 5, 16
Bereiter, C., 214, 226
Berkowitz, L., 50
Berkun, M., 100, 110
Berliner, D. C., 182, 197
Berlyne, D. E., 96, 97, 109
Bersoff, D. N., 103, 109
Bexton, W. H., 8, 16

Biddle, B. J., 46, 51
Biddle, W. B., 197
Bigge, M. S., 49, 58, 84, 277
Biggs, J. B., 49
Bijou, S. W., 99, 100, 106, 109
Billington, M. J., 131, 135
Birch, H. S., 33, 50
Blair, G. M., 75, 84
Block, J. H., 183, 196, 197, 225
Bloom, B. S., 176, 180, 182, 183, 194, 197, 222, 225, 227, 241, 246, 256
Boulding, K., 167
Bourdon, R. D., 105, 109
Bourne, L. E., 141, 143, 158, 168
Bousfield, W. A., 64, 73, 84
Bower, G. H., 21, 51, 121, 133, 261, 277
Brandt, R. M., 46, 51
Bridgman, P. W., 83
Broadbent, D. E., 125, 133
Brookover, W. B., 219, 220, 222, 225, 226, 228
Brown, F. G., 157, 168
Brittain, C. V., 14, 16
Bruner, J. S., 36, 37, 38, 45, 46, 49, 51, 63, 66, 72, 84, 87, 88, 124, 129, 133, 142, 143, 155, 158, 168, 169
Bugelski, B. R., 6, 17, 63, 70, 84, 261, 277
Butler, R. A., 9, 17, 96, 97, 100, 109
Byalick, R., 103, 109

Cahen, L. S., 182, 197
Calsyn, R., 220, 226
Calvin, A. D., 196
Campbell, D. T., 89, 229
Campbell, J. P., 164, 169
Campbell, V., 62, 84
Cantril, H., 62, 84, 86
Carlsmith, J. M., 73, 85
Carlton, L., 220, 226
Carmichael, L., 63, 85
Carnine, D., 108
Carpenter, F., 16
Carroll, J. B., 177, 178, 179, 194, 197
Carroll, J. D., 110
Cermack, L. S., 132
Chein, I., 16, 75, 87
Child, I. L., 101, 109
Clarizio, H. F., 263, 277
Cofer, C. N., 62, 63, 86, 108, 122, 134, 143, 170

Coleman, J. A., 83
Collins, M. E., 73, 85
Combs, A. W., 7, 17, 69, 85, 96, 97, 109
Cook, H., 123, 136
Cowen, E. L., 69, 85
Cram, D., 185, 197
Cremin, L. A., 190, 197
Crist, R. L., 188, 197
Cronbach, L. S., 180, 182, 198, 234, 240, 241, 256
Crutchfield, R. S., 74, 88, 203, 227
Csapo, K., 120, 135
Cunningham, D. J., 106, 109

Dalgaard, B. R., 197
Dallenbach, K. M., 115, 134
Danto, A., 83
Davidson, K. S., 88
Davis, G. A., 129, 133, 168, 171
de Charms, R., 106, 109
Deese, J., 110
Denney, D. R., 142, 169
Deno, S. L., 234, 256
Deutsch, M., 73, 85
DeVries, D. L., 105, 109
Dewey, J., 143, 144, 157, 169
Diamond, M. C., 16
Dienes, Z. P., 168
Dixon, T. R., 85
Dollard, J., 104, 105, 111
Dominowski, R. L., 168
Dorner, P., 217, 226
Drew, C. J., 277
Ducette, J., 100, 110
Dulany, D. E., 78, 79, 80, 88
Duncan, C. P., 130, 133
Duncker, K., 145, 169
Dunkin, M. J., 46, 51
Dutta, S., 70, 85
Dyk, R. B., 172

Early, C. J., 205, 226
Ebbesen, E. B., 225, 250, 257
Edgren, R. D., 86
Edwards, A. L., 72, 85
Edwards, K. J., 105, 109
Ehri, L. C., 142, 169
Eisner, E. W., 197, 256
Ekstrand, B. R., 168
Elashoff, J., 218, 226
Elkind, D., 149, 152, 169
Ellis, H. C., 132, 168
English, A. C., 58, 68, 85, 95, 109
English, H. B., 58, 68, 85, 95, 109
Engstrom, E., 190, 198
Erickson, E. L., 225, 226
Erlebacher, A. H., 124, 136
Essex, D., 142
Estes, W. K., 24, 26, 27, 28, 51
Evans, K. M., 255

Fattuson, H. F., 172
Faust, G. F., 186, 188, 197
Featherstone, J., 190, 192, 198
Feigenbaum, E. A., 145, 169
Feldman, J., 145, 169
Feldman, S., 227
Ferster, C. B., 31, 51
Festinger, L., 73, 85, 212, 226
Field, F. L., 16
Fishbein, M. F., 68, 85, 203, 204, 208, 209, 214, 226, 227
Fitzgerald, D., 64, 84
Flavell, J. H., 131, 133, 148, 149, 169
Foster, S. F., 188, 198, 209, 220, 227, 250, 253, 256
Frank, P., 83
Frankel, V. E., 96, 97, 109
Frase, L. T., 71, 85
Freeman, I. M., 57, 83, 87
Freeman, J., 62, 84
Freud, S., 8
Frick, F., 70, 86
Frick, W. B., 16
Friedlander, B. Z., 194, 198
Fulkerson, W., 69, 85
Furth, H. G., 146, 149, 169

Gagné, R. M., 21, 36, 42, 43, 44, 45, 46, 49, 50, 51, 133, 265
Galanter, E., 129, 134, 155, 170
Garrett, C. S., 106, 109
Gaydos, E. J., 62, 85
Gelfand, S., 62, 63, 86, 143, 156, 169, 170
Gentile, J. R., 110
Ginsburg, H., 168
Givner, A., 108
Glaser, R., 50, 188, 199
Glock, M. D., 255
Goldstein, S., 71, 86, 170
Goodenough, D. R., 172
Goodlad, J. I., 190, 198
Goodman, G. D., 72, 84
Goodnow, J. J., 129, 133, 158, 168
Gorman, A. H., 255
Graubard, P. S., 108
Gray, J. L., 142, 171
Green, B. I., 225
Greenwald, A. S., 27, 51
Gregory, R. L., 83
Gronlund, N. E., 16, 182, 198, 235, 236, 238, 243, 248, 252, 253, 255, 256
Gross, B., 190, 198
Gross, R., 190, 198
Guilford, J. P., 140, 161, 162, 163, 167, 169
Guthrie, E. R., 25, 26, 27, 32, 34, 42, 49, 51, 186
Guttman, L. 250

Hackett, M. G., 50

Index

Hall, E. R., 156, 170
Hall, G. S., 214, 227
Hamachek, D. E., 219, 227
Hamblin, J. A., 105, 110
Hamblin, R. L., 105, 110
Hamilton, C. E., 128, 134
Harding, S. F., 169
Harleston, B. W., 69, 85
Harlow, H. F., 9, 17, 100, 110, 128, 129, 134
Harper, R. S., 72, 83
Harris, F. R., 105, 111
Harris, M. B., 105, 109
Harvey, O. J., 88
Haselrud, G. M., 63, 85
Hastings, J. T., 197, 241, 256
Hawes, G. R., 196
Hawkins, T. D., 100, 111
Hebb, D. O., 6, 17, 59, 85
Heisenburg, W., 57
Helmstadter, G. C., 234, 256
Hernandez-Peon, R., 74, 85
Heron, W., 8, 16
Hewson, M. G., 66, 86, 153, 169
Hicks, B. L., 196
Hidde, J. L., 120, 121, 133
Hilgard, E. R., 6, 17, 21, 51, 64, 86, 261, 277
Hill, J. P., 131, 133
Hill, W. F., 21, 51
Hoffman, M. L., 215, 216, 227
Hogan, H. F., 63, 85
Holtzman, W. H., 196
Homan, L. E., 124, 134
Hood, W. R., 88
Hooper, F. H., 154, 169
Hopkins, K. D., 190, 198
Hornsby, J. R., 65, 87
Horton, D. L., 85
Hosie, T. W., 102, 110
Hovland, C. I., 130, 134, 145, 169
Hull, C., 24, 27, 28, 51, 103, 204
Hume, D., 142, 169
Hunka, S., 196
Hunnicutt, C: W., 14, 17
Hunt, D. E., 36, 41, 42, 49, 51, 182, 192, 194, 195, 196, 198
Hunt, J. McV., 5, 17
Hunter, I. M., 133

Illich, I., 176, 198
Immergluck, L., 63, 86
Inhelder, B., 65, 66, 86, 88, 129, 134, 147, 149, 152, 153, 169, 171
Irion, A. L., 70, 87
Irvine, R. P., 86
Ittelson, W. H., 62, 86
Izard, C. E., 69, 70, 89

Jacubczak, L. F., 106, 110

Jacobsen, E., 218, 228
James, W., 142, 169
Janis, V., 70, 86
Jeeves, M. A., 168
Jenkin, N., 86
Jenkins, J. G., 115, 134
Jenkins, J. J., 65, 86
Jenkins, J. R., 234, 256
Johnson, D. M., 156, 170
Johnson, D. W., 210, 227
Johnson, J., 163, 171
Johnson, R. E., 121, 134
Johnston, M. K., 105, 111
Joiner, L. M., 226
Jones, R. S., 75, 84
Jouvet, M., 85
Judd, C. H., 64, 86, 127, 134
Judson, A. J., 62, 63, 86, 143, 170

Kagan, J., 57, 86, 100, 110, 142, 170, 172
Kanfer, F. H., 99, 110
Kanungo, R. N., 70, 85
Kaplan, S., 70, 86
Karp, S. A., 172
Katona, G., 64, 65, 86
Katz, P., 62, 86
Kaufmann, H., 71, 86, 170
Kay, W., 217, 227
Keislar, E. R., 103, 111
Keller, R. S., 50
Keppel, G., 27, 52, 130, 136
Kerlinger, F. N., 197
Kibler, R. S., 182, 198
Klausmeier, H. J., 261, 278
Kleinsmith, L. J., 70, 86
Klemt, L., 197
Knapp, T. R., 255
Koffka, K., 33
Kogan, N., 162, 170
Kohl, H. R., 190, 196, 198
Kohlberg, L., 215, 216, 217, 227
Köhler, W., 33, 51, 120, 134, 144, 170
Kong, S. L., 50
Kooland, C., 62, 87
Krasner, L., 110
Krathwohl, D. R., 221, 222, 227
Krech, D., 16, 203, 227
Krumboltz, J. D., 108
Kulhavy, R. W., 102, 110, 120, 133
Kurtz, K., 62, 87

La Benne, W. D., 225
La Pere, J. M., 228
Lazarus, R. S., 101, 110
Lee, B. N., 225
Lee, J. F., 89
Lefford, A., 71, 87
Levin, J. R., 121, 135
Levine, J. M., 72, 87, 123, 134
Levine, R., 74, 87

Lewin, K., 33, 34, 41, 51, 77, 78, 195, 196
Lighthall, F. F., 88
Lilly, J. C., 8, 17, 96, 97, 110
Lindzey, G., 73, 83
Lintner, A. C., 100, 110
Lipsett, L. P., 111
Litcher, J. H., 210, 227
Logan, F. A., 108
Loree, M. R., 10, 17, 141, 155, 170, 172, 212, 227
Lott, B. E., 204, 227
Lovass, O. I. A., 105, 110
Lubker, B. J., 156, 170
Lyman, H. B., 255
Lynch, S., 121, 135
Lynn, R., 125, 134

McClelland, D. C., 74, 83, 87
McGeoch, J. A., 70, 87
McGinnies, E., 69, 72, 87, 88
McGuire, W. J., 211, 220, 227
McKie, D., 209, 227, 250, 256
MacAulay, B. A., 111
MacKinnon, D. W., 165, 170
Madaus, G., 197, 241, 256
Maehr, M. L., 96, 97, 108, 110
Mager, R. F., 16, 212, 214, 223, 227, 243, 244, 256
Maier, N. R. F., 62, 87
Malinowski, B., 5, 17
Mandler, G., 65, 87, 130, 134
March, A. M., 57, 83, 87
Markell, R. A., 98, 108
Marlett, N. J., 126, 134
Marshall, G. R., 122, 134
Masia, B. B., 222, 227
Maslow, A. H., 5, 7, 16, 17, 74, 75, 76, 82, 87, 95, 96, 97, 110
Mayer, R. E., 162, 170
Mayo, S. T., 178, 182, 198, 256
Mayzner, M. S., 73, 87
Meacham, M. L., 101, 108, 110
Meadow, A., 164, 171
Mednick, S. A., 156, 170
Meehl, P., 240, 256
Meichenbaum, D., 164, 170
Melton, A. W., 103, 110
Merrill, M. D., 64, 87, 225
Michael, W. B., 34, 52, 278
Miles, D. T., 198
Milgram, S., 80, 87
Mill, J. S., 142, 170
Miller, G. A., 64, 65, 87, 129, 134, 155, 170
Miller, N. E., 104, 105, 111
Minturn, A. L., 63, 84
Mischel, W., 216, 226
Monroe, W. S., 110
Montague, W. E., 143, 168
Montgomery, K. C., 9, 17

Moore, R. H., 220, 226
Morgenbesser, S., 83
Morrisett, L., 130, 134
Morrison, H. C., 176, 177, 198
Mouly, G., 203, 228
Moustakas, C. E., 168
Mowrer, O. H., 104, 105, 111
Munn, N. L., 145, 170
Munsat, S., 133
Murchison, G., 226
Murphy, G., 72, 74, 87, 123, 134
Murray, H. A., 63, 87, 95, 96, 97, 111
Mussen, P. H., 49, 50
Muzio, I. M., 142, 169
Myers, E. C., 177, 198

Neill, A. S., 190, 192, 199
Neimark, E. D., 129, 134
Neisser, U., 118, 120, 134
Newell, A., 146, 170
Noble, C. E., 122, 130, 134, 135
Norman, D. A., 119, 134
Nuttin, J., 27, 51
Nyquist, E. E., 196

Oldridge, O. A., 190, 191, 194, 198, 199
Olver, R. E., 65, 84, 87
Opper, S., 168
Ortony, A., 67, 83, 146, 170, 171
Osgood, C. E., 128, 135, 203, 228, 250, 257
Osler, S. F., 110
Overing, R. L. R., 64, 88, 127, 130, 135

Paden, D. W., 197
Paivio, A., 120, 121, 135
Pankone, E., 162, 170
Parnes, S. J., 163, 164, 169, 171
Paul, N. T., 130, 135
Pavlov, I. P., 21, 22, 23, 24, 25, 27, 42, 51, 92, 143, 171
Peeck, J., 124, 135
Pepper, S. C., 83
Piaget, J., 65, 66, 86, 88, 129, 134, 142, 143, 146, 147, 148, 149, 150, 151, 152, 153, 154, 155, 168, 169, 171, 215, 228, 269
Platt, J. R., 9, 17
Pliskoff, S. S., 100, 111
Poincaré, 145
Popham, W. J., 50, 244, 257
Postman, L., 64, 72, 74, 88
Potter, M. C., 66, 84, 88
Premack, D., 102, 111
Pribram, K. H., 129, 134, 155, 170
Purdom, D. M., 191, 199
Purkey, W. W., 220, 228

Rankin, H. B., 143, 171
Raynor, R., 25, 52

Index

Reagan, G. M., 160, 168
Reitman, W. R., 145, 171
Renner, K. E., 102, 111
Resnick, L. B., 50
Reynolds, J. H., 64, 88
Rhine, R. J., 204, 208, 228
Ripple, R. E., 261, 278
Risley, T., 105, 111
Robeck, M. C., 34, 52, 278
Robinson, E. S., 127, 135
Robinson, F. G., 39, 50
Robinson, J. E., 142, 171
Rock, I., 27, 51
Rogers, C., 73, 88
Rohwer, W. D., Jr., 49, 50, 121, 135
Robeach, M., 71, 72, 73, 82, 88, 222, 223, 228
Rosenbaum, M. E., 106, 109
Rosenkoetter, L. I., 217, 228
Rosenthal, 218, 228
Rosenzweig, M. R., 16, 49, 50, 133
Ross, D., 105, 109
Ross, S. A., 105, 109
Ross, W. D., 142, 171
Rothkopf, E. Z., 131, 135
Rotter, J. B., 78, 80, 88
Ruebush, B. K., 69, 88
Ruedi, J., 192, 194, 199
Runyan, D. L., 72, 83
Russell, W. A., 65, 86

Saltz, E., 163, 171
Samborski, G., 73, 84
Sapir, E., 143, 171
Saporta, S., 143, 171
Sarason, S. B., 69, 88
Saugstad, P., 63, 88
Schaefer, H. H., 188, 199
Scherrer, H., 85
Schwartz, R. D., 229
Scott, J. A., 168, 171
Scriven, M., 241, 257
Schultz, C. R., 68, 88
Schwartz, R. D., 89
Scott, T. H., 8, 16
Seagoe, M. V., 261, 278
Sechrest, L., 89, 229
Secord, P. F., 225
Segall, M., 9, 17
Shaw, M. E., 252, 257
Sherif, C. W., 88
Sherif, M., 80, 88
Shiffrin, R. M., 117, 135
Shulman, L. S., 103, 111
Shurley, J., 8, 17, 96, 97, 111
Sigel, I. E., 169
Siipola, E. M., 63, 88
Silberman, C. E., 190, 196, 199
Simon, H. A., 146, 170
Simpson, R. H., 75, 84, 223, 228

Sjogren, D. D., 97, 110
Skinner, B. F., 8, 16, 29, 30, 31, 32, 43, 51, 77, 92, 103, 107, 111, 143, 171
Sloane, H. N., Jr., 105, 111
Smith, B. O., 227
Smock, H. R., 197
Snow, R. E., 218, 226, 228
Snygg, D. L., 7, 17, 69, 85, 96, 97, 109
Sokolov, E. N., 125, 135
Spence, J. T., 87
Spence, K. W., 87
Spiker, C. C., 111, 156, 170
Sponberg, R. A., 190, 192, 199
Staats, A. W., 204, 228
Staats, C. K., 204, 228
Stake, R., 257
Stephens, J. M., 50
Stevens, B., 88
Stevens, S. S., 17
Stevenson, H. W., 227
Stiles, L. J., 50
Stolurow, L. M., 64, 88
Stone, D. R., 261, 278
Stretch, B. B., 190, 192, 199
Strike, K. A., 103, 111
Strong, E. K., 76, 89
Sturges, P. S., 99, 100, 106, 109
Suchman, J. R., 212, 228
Suchman, R. G., 156, 171
Suci, G., 228, 257
Sugarman, B., 214, 229
Sullivan, E. V., 196
Surber, J. R., 197
Suzuki, N. S., 121, 135

Taber, J. I., 188, 199
Tannenbaum, P. H., 228, 257
Taylor, C. W., 168
Terrell, G., 102, 111
Thistlewaite, D., 71, 89
Thelen, H. A., 182, 199
Thomas, D. R., 108
Thomas, S., 220, 228
Thomas, S. C., 193, 199
Thompson, G. G., 14, 17
Thorndike, E. L., 28, 29, 51, 52, 127, 135, 143, 171
Thorndike, R. L., 218, 228
Thune, L. E., 128, 135
Thurstone, L. L., 68, 89, 203, 228
Tierney, M. L., 183, 197
Tolman, E. C., 32, 34, 35, 49, 52, 233
Tomkins, S. S., 69, 70, 89
Torrance, E. P., 163, 168, 172
Trabasso, T., 133, 156, 171
Travers, R. M. W., 64, 88, 127, 130, 135, 228, 261, 278
Tresselt, M. E., 73, 87
Triandis, H. C., 225
Turiel, E., 215, 216, 228

Index

Tyler, L. E., 255

Ullman, L. P., 110
Underwood, B. J., 27, 52, 124, 130, 135, 136

Vernon, P. E., 73, 83
Vygotsky, L. S., 143, 172

Wadsworth, B. J., 149, 172
Wagner, A. R., 108
Waite, R. R., 88
Walberg, H. J., 193, 199
Walker, B. S., 131, 136
Wallach, M. A., 140, 172
Walter, A. A., 63, 85
Walters, R. H., 50, 106, 109, 110, 205, 211, 215, 226
Wardrop, J. L., 255
Watson, D., 126, 134
Watson, J. B., 25, 27, 31, 52
Webb, E. J., 57, 89, 223, 229
Weiner, B., 96, 111
Wertheimer, M., 33, 52, 144, 145, 172
West, C. K., 57, 69, 89, 155, 172, 192, 194, 199, 218, 229
Whipple, J. E., 86
White, B. J., 88

White, R. W., 7, 17, 96, 97, 111
Whiting, J. W. M., 101, 109
Wiener, D. N., 108
Wiener, N., 146, 172
Wiesen, A. E., 101, 108, 110
Wietecha, E. J., 197
Williams, N., 214, 229
Williams, T., 218, 229
Williamson, M. L., 190, 198
Wilman, C. W., 83
Wilson, J., 214, 229
Wilson, J. A. R., 34, 52, 278
Wine, J., 126, 136
Wing, J. K., 110
Witkin, H. A., 142, 172
Wittrock, M. C., 115, 123, 136
Wohlwill, J. F., 155, 172
Wolf, M., 105, 111
Wood, C., 122, 136
Worchel, P., 70, 89, 123, 136
Wright, J. E., 100, 111
Wright, J. M., 252, 257
Wright, R. J., 192, 193, 194, 199
Wyer, R., 68, 89
Wylie, R., 219, 229

Zimbardo, P., 225, 250, 257
Zubek, J. P., 8, 17

Subject Index

ability grouping, 270
academic self-concept, 220
accommodation, 147
achievement needs, 96, 97
achievement testing, 233
acquisition, 103, 115
advance organizer, 33, 267
affect
  bases for reinforcement, 68
  and cognition, 69
  and learning, 69
  and perception, 69
  and recognition, 69
  and retention, 70, 123
anxiety
  and cognitive processing, 69
  reduction of, 40, 41
artificial intelligence, 146
assimilation, 147
associationism, 142, 143
attention
  and needs, 74, 75
  selective, 59, 77, 124-125
attitudes, 200
  classical conditioning of, 205
  as concept formation, 208
  consistency theory, 211, 212
  definition of, 202
  and the frame of reference, 202
  and logic, 70, 71
  measurement of, 248
  moral, 214
  operant conditioning of, 207
  practical suggestions, 272-273
  racial, 211
  school related, 205
  self-regarding, 219
  and social learning theory, 210, 211
  teaching of 212
  theories of learning attitudes, 203

barriers, 34
behavior, samples of, 243
behavioral objectives controversy, 244
behaviorism, 25
behaviorism, purposive, 32
brainstorming, 164

categorization, functions of, 142
cause-effect relationships, 56
chaining, 31, 44

circular reactions, 150
classification, 141, 142
classroom management, 263, 264
codability, 112, 124, 265
cognition, 58
  and values, 71
cognitive style, 142
common sense and research, 260
components of the frame of reference, 61
computer simulation of thought, 145-146
concepts
  definition, 61, 62
  teaching, 160, 161, 268
concept formation, 140, 141
  practical suggestions, 160, 161, 268, 269
conditioning, classical, 4, 21
  of attitudes, 205
conditioning, operant, 29
  of attitudes, 207
contiguity, 142
contract grading, 242, 275
convergent thinking, 140
correlation, 240, 241
creativity, 138, 161
  as flexibility, 162
  as fluency, 162
  and intelligence, 162, 270
  measurement of, 162
  as originality, 162
  practical suggestions, 269-270
  teaching for, 163, 269
creative persons
  characteristics of, 165
curiosity, 8, 96, 97

decay theory of memory, 115
decentering, 147
differences, individual, 174
  instruction for, 174, 270
differentiation, in field theory, 34
discipline, 263, 264
discovery learning, 103
discrimination, 24
divergent thinking, 140
drive, curiosity, 8
drive, exploratory, 9

egocentrism, 147
entering capabilities, 12
equilibration, 147-148

Index

evaluation, 230
  formative, 98, 179, 241, 275
  of instruction, 5, 230
  practical suggestions, 274
  purposes of, 232
  summative, 180, 241, 242, 275
expectancies, 32
expectancy effects, 217
expectations
  and perception, 62
exploratory drive, 9
extinction, 24, 31

familiarity, 112, 124, 265
forgetting, 112
  interference theory, 116
  motivated forgetting, 115
  selective forgetting, 115
  theories of, 114
  trace decay theory, 115
formative evaluation, 98, 179, 241, 275
frame of reference, 54
  and affect, 68
  and cognitive behavior, 54
  and concepts, 61
  components of, 61
  educational implications, 80
  memory, 123
  motivation, 94, 95
  perception, 61
  recognition, 61
  stages of instruction, 80
  summary of model, 77
free recall task, 120

generalizability, 112, 124, 265
generalization, 24
gestalt psychology, 144, 145
grading, contract, 242, 275

habit-family hierarchy, 28
Heisenberg's uncertainty principle, 57
homogenous grouping, 174, 270

illogical devices, 160
imagability, 112, 124, 265
images, 112, 120, 124
imitation, 34, 104, 269, 272
individual differences, 174
  practical suggestions, 270
individualizing instruction, 174, 270
inserted questions, 131
insight, 33
instruction
  item analysis, 247
  item difficulty, 247
  item discrimination, 247
  and motivation, 12, 265
  stages of, 80
instructional objectives, 243, 262

interests
  and the frame of reference, 75
  and perception, 75
interference
  proactive, 116, 129, 266
  retroactive, 116, 129, 266

labels, 62
learning to learn, 128
learning, 2
  and action, 26, 35
  and affect, 68
  concreteness, 36, 37
  conditions of, 44
  contiguity, 21
  definition of, 6
  and development, 5
  by discovery, 103
  evaluation of, 230
  importance of, 4
  interpolated, 116
  latent, 32
  laws of, 28
  and neurophysiological structure, 6
  optimal environment for, 41
  predisposition toward, 36, 47
  repetition, 22
  resistance to, 9
  role of structure, 36
  theories, 21
  types of, 42
life space, 33, 34
long-term retention, 117

management, classroom, 263-264
mastery learning, 176, 271
  criticism of, 180
  mastery learning model, 177
matching instruction and students, 41
mathemagenic behavior, 131
  pros and cons, 181
  testing for, 242, 243
meaning
  logical, 38
  psychological, 39
meaningful learning, 38
meaningful learning set, 40
meaningfulness, 112, 123, 124, 265
measurement, 230
  attitudes, 248
  errors of, 237
  internal consistency, 235
  stability, 236, 237
  standard error of, 235
memory, 112
  constructive memory, 118
  forms and functions, 119
  and the frame of reference, 61, 123
  imaginal, 120, 121, 124
  reconstructive, 119

Index

memory (continued)
   as retrieval, 117
   structures, 120
   verbal, 120, 121
modeling, 34, 104
   of peers, 95
   and reinforcement, 105
modes of representation, 37
   enactive, 37
   iconic, 37
   symbolic, 37
moral development, stages of, 215, 216
motivation, 92
   achievement, 96, 97
   definition of, 92
   frame of reference, 94
   and instruction, 98, 264
   practical suggestions, 265
   specificity, 97
   transient nature of, 97
motives for change, 6

natural language mediators, 143
needs, 7, 95
   for achievement, 96, 97
   for adequacy, 7, 96, 97
   classes of, 96, 97
   for competence, 7, 96, 97
   and the frame of reference, 74
   Maslow's hierarchy, 74, 75, 97
   and perception, 74
   for stimulation, 8, 9, 96, 97
neobehaviorism, 6
no-trial learning, 34

objectives
   attitudinal, 202, 221
   behavioral, 10
   general, 243
   global, 10
   instructional, 10, 243, 261, 262
   specific, 243
   taxonomy of educational objectives, 221, 222
open education, 189, 271, 272
   arguments for and against, 193
   claimed effects, 191
   research on effects, 192
orienting reflex, 125
overlearning, 130, 266

paired associate task, 120
peer disapproval and approach, 14, 96
peer teaching, 107
perception
   and affect, 68
   and interests, 75
   and labels, 62
   and needs, 74, 75
   and structures, 63

perception (continued)
   and values, 71
pleasure principle, 8
postremity, principle of, 26
primacy-recency phenomena, 122
problem solving, 138
   guiding the problem-solver, 158
   logical analysis, 143, 144
   practical suggestions, 158, 268
   steps in problem solving, 143, 159
programmed instruction, 174, 185, 271
   active responding, 187
   arguments for and against, 187
   branched programs, 185
   frames, 185
   immediate reinforcement, 188
   linear programs, 185
projection, 70
punishment, 101, 263, 264

quantitative thinking, 152

reinforcement, 8, 24, 30, 90, 99
   extrinsic and intrinsic, 36
   issue of immediacy, 102, 188
   kinds of, 99
   negative, 30, 101
   positive, 30
   Premack principle, 102
   primary, 27
   schedules of reinforcement, 31
   secondary, 27
relativism, 56
reliability, 235
resistance to change, 9
resolution problems, 141, 142
response, conditioned, 22
response, unconditioned, 22
response analysis, 35
response generator, 112
retention
   and affect, 69, 123
   and the frame of reference, 61
   long term, 116, 122
   practical suggestions, 265, 266
   short term, 117

scales
   Likert, 252, 253
   semantic differential, 250
selectivity of attention, 125
self-actualization, 75, 96, 97
self-concept, 219
   of ability, 220
   and achievement, 219
self-regard, 219
sensory register, 117
serial tasks, 120
set, 159
   meaningful learning set, 40

set (continued)
  rote learning set, 40
shaping behavior, 30
short-term retention, 117
sign, 32
significate, 32
sociometry, 253, 254
specifications, tables of, 237
spontaneous recovery, 24, 27
stability, measurement, 236-237
stages of instruction, 2, 3, 19, 261
  and frame of reference theory, 80
  and motivation, 98
stimulation, external, 92
stimulus analysis, 35
stimulus sampling theory, 26
stimulus, conditioned, 22
stimulus, unconditioned, 22
structurability, 112, 124, 265
structures
  definition of, 63
  and the frame of reference, 63
  and learning, 63
  and memory, 63, 119
  and perception, 63
  Piagetian, 65, 66
  origins of, 65
  and recognition, 63
  and transfer, 64
subsumption theory, 38
successive approximation, 29, 30, 35
success-failure-aspirational relationships, 101

taxonomy of educational objectives, 221, 222, 275
teacher expectancy, 217
teacher praise, 96
teachers' attitudes, 217
teaching
  attitudes, 212, 272, 273
  concepts, 160, 161, 268, 269
  creativity, 163, 269, 270
  problem solving, 158, 268, 269
  for retention, 265, 266
  for transfer, 266
  values, 273
test anxiousness, 126
test items
  analysis (item), 247
  multiple choice, 247
  relationships to objective, 245
testing
  for mastery, 242, 243
  table of specifications, 237, 275
theory
  of attitude formation, 205
  classical conditioning, 21
  evaluation of, 20
  and facts, 20

theory (continued)
  field theory, 33
  functions of, 20
  gestalt theory, 33, 144
  instructional theory, 36
  of learning, 20
  of memory and forgetting, 115
  social learning theory, 34
  synopsis of instructional theory, 46
  synopsis of learning theory, 35, 46
  of transfer, 126
  and teachers' perspectives, 20, 21
thinking, 138
  centering, 151
  computer simulation, 145, 146
  concrete operation, 152, 153
  formal operation, 153, 154
  and the frame of reference, 157
  and irrelevant information, 156, 157
  and the nature of stimuli, 155
  preoperational and intuitive, 151, 152
  sensorimotor, 149, 150
transfer, 112, 126
  practical suggestions, 266

valences, 34
validity, 237
  construct, 239, 240
  content, 237
  criterion-related, 238, 239
values, 214
  and cognition, 71
  frame of reference, 71
  instrumental, 71
  and perception, 71
  political, 72
  practical suggestions, 273
  terminal, 71
vector, 34

warm-up effect, 128

zero transfer, 130

The Authors

Charles K. West, PhD, University of Alabama, is an associate professor in the Department of Educational Psychology at the University of Illinois at Urbana-Champaign, where he is currently Chairperson of the Division of Behavioral Foundations of Education. A former lieutenant in the U. S. Army Signal Corps, and a former public school teacher, Dr. West has also served as a research assistant, and visiting lecturer in the Department of Educational Psychology at the University of Alabama, and as an assistant professor of Educational Psychology at Middle Tennessee State University, Murfreesboro, Tennessee, and as visiting lecturer at Lancaster University, Bailrigg, England. He is the author and coauthor of many publications pertaining to educational psychology research and teaching areas.

Stephen F. Foster, PhD, University of Illinois, is currently an associate professor in the Department of Educational Psychology at The University of British Columbia at Vancouver where he has chaired the human learning and instruction group. He has been an instructor and visiting lecturer with the University of Illinois, Wisconsin State University, and Portland State University. Dr. Foster spent the 1975-76 academic year on leave from The University of British Columbia, is a Canada Council Fellowship Holder, and has been an honorary visiting professor in psychology at the University College—Dublin of the National University of Ireland. He has authored and coauthored numerous publications on educational and psychological research and has served as director of the Multidisciplinary Values Education Research Center at UBC.